UNHOLY TERROR

UNHOLY TERROR

The Sikhs and International Terrorism

IAN MULGREW

KEY PORTER BOOKS

TO HUGH AND JEAN MULGREW
AND WILLIAM AND AGNES HARPER

Canadian Cataloguing in Publication Data
Mulgrew, Ian, 1957 —
    Unholy terror
Bibliography: p.
Includes index.
ISBN 1-55013-052-8
1. Terrorism. 2. Sikhism — Political aspects.
3. Sikhs — Politics and government. I. Title.
HV6431.M85 1988   303.6'25'0882946   C88-093165-5

Key Porter Books Limited
70 The Esplanade
Toronto, Ontario
Canada M5E 1R2

Design: Marie Bartholomew
Typesetting: Bowne of Canada, Inc.
Printed and bound in the United States of America

88 89 90 91 6 5 4 3 2 1

CONTENTS

Preface 1

1. The Assassination 5
2. The Sikhs 23
3. Indian Politics 49
4. North America 93
5. Canada's Bhindranwale 123
6. Agents Provocateurs 143
7. Terrorism and Crime 181
8. Britain 207
9. The Front Line 225

Glossary 235
Selected Bibliography 239
Index 243

PREFACE

In the early morning of June 23, 1985, an Air India Boeing 747 jumbo jet heading to London from Toronto crashed into the North Atlantic. Three hundred and twenty-nine passengers and crew died. Less than an hour before, an explosion rocked Narita Airport, near Tokyo, Japan. The bomb, a charge of dynamite and an incendiary fluid called Liquid Fire, was disguised as a stereo tuner and hidden in a suitcase. Two baggage handlers were killed and four others were injured. The authorities immediately began an investigation of Sikhs living on Canada's west coast.

Within hours of the disaster on June 23, the expatriate Sikh separatist movement became the most tantalizing of assignments for reporters in Vancouver. As west coast bureau chief for *The Globe and Mail*, I had followed the rise of Sikh separatism in British Columbia and it intrigued me.

At first, the local Sikh community seemed to be plagued by no more than random violence. But all that changed just under four years ago, on June 5, 1984, when the Indian Army bombarded the Golden Temple in Amritsar, 400 kilometers from New Delhi, and then stormed it with machine guns and tanks. The June 23 disaster

1

was clearly a result of that assault.

Canada's domestic spy agency, the Canadian Security and Intelligence Service, and the Royal Canadian Mounted Police spent more than $60 million over the following two years trying to catch the terrorists who sent the tuner to Japan and destroyed the airliner. But the country had become a staging area for extremist Sikhs bent on sparking a revolution in India, and the Regina-trained policemen found it difficult to tell one Sikh fanatic from another.

Law enforcement officials around the world pointed accusatory fingers at Talwinder Singh Parmar, a Sikh priest who lived in Burnaby, British Columbia. Parmar's absolute commitment to his faith terrified secular authorities. If his faith was threatened, he acknowledged, he would fight back furiously, but he denied having bombed a jetliner.

The Sikh separatists do not fit the popular mold for extremists, nor do they match the general profile of a terrorist organization. They are as different from the Red Brigades as their sworn enemy, India, is from most western liberal democracies. The Sikhs proclaim the ideals of faith, family, work, and community service. As a group, they prize consensus and democratic solutions. India, on the other hand, staunchly supports Yasir Arafat and its global ally is the Soviet Union. Yet there is no denying the carnage militant Sikhs have wrought. Why do some Sikhs turn to murder and mayhem as a means of achieving political change? And why is such a strategy condoned and even encouraged by large numbers of otherwise law-abiding, expatriate Sikhs?

The dream of a Sikh homeland — dubbed Khalistan, the land of the pure — was quietly carried within the Sikh community for forty years before the assassination of Indian prime minister Indira Gandhi signaled the end of its gestation. The bloody labor that followed is a textbook example of the rise of a modern revolutionary movement and its use of terror. The struggle for Khalistan is a paradigm of the pattern that has emerged around the globe, time and time again over the last two centuries: oppression, terror, repression, revolution.

Amnesty International and experts from many nations, including Canada, have complained that the Indian government, whether by policy or lack of control, provoked the violent response through its callous and inept treatment of the Sikh minority. New Delhi allowed its law enforcement agencies to operate Latin-American-style death squads to curtail Sikh political dissent. Its anti-terrorist laws were as stringent as those used by the British colonial governors to control native opposition.

The central government's failure to act after innocent Sikhs were butchered following Mrs. Gandhi's murder was interpreted as a confirmation of the apocalyptic predictions of the extremists. So many Sikh families have lost members in the fighting that the cycle of revenge is probably unstoppable. Sikh separatism is no longer a fringe movement, but a mainstream crusade.

Those who would wrest Punjab from New Delhi dominate the Sikh community. They control many of the temples and their considerable treasuries. They provide millions of dollars to those struggling in Punjab for Sikh independence, and to those who flit about the globe advocating revolution. In the summer of 1987, a unified high command was formed to direct the extremist units. It brought together the Khalistan Commando Force, the Khalistan Liberation Force and the Bhindranwale Tiger Forces. And to coordinate the political activities of the separatist groups, it combined the World Sikh Organization, the All-India Sikh Students Federation, and the Babbar Khalsa.

After visiting Sikhs across North America, Punjab, Pakistan, and England, I have come to the conclusion that many of them feel they are an endangered species. That can mean only one thing: the violence will escalate until their concerns are addressed. The Sikh terrorists are sure that the creation of Khalistan will absolve them of their sins in the same way the birth of Israel redeemed the Zionist terrorists and the founding of India exonerated those who butchered British administrators and soldiers. Their more moderate co-religionists refuse to condemn them because they themselves have no faith in New Delhi.

Two years after three hundred and thirty-one people were murdered the Mounties who formed the Air-India Disaster Task Force were no closer to charging the culprits. For a party to mark the retirement of one task-force officer, they had circular crests created. The badges bore the RCMP insignia over the silhouette of a jumbo jet. A motto was emblazoned below: "Project Nightmare."

I can understand why the Mounties feel that way.

I set out to cover the Air-India disaster and the bombing in Japan as a reporter two years ago. This book is a product of the curiosity that has kept me interested in a global story that does not yet appear to have an end. It represents one journalist's understanding of the situation based on research, interviews, and observations made as I traveled around the world.

Along the way, I relied on the work and advice of a large number of journalists, lawyers, policemen, politicians, and ordinary people who gave freely of their time and expertise. I would like in particular to thank W.H. McLeod, Khushwant Singh, Dan Smith, Graham Rockingham, Salim Jiwa, Kim Bolan and Terry Glavin for their suggestions and help.

Aside from interviews, my appreciation of the history and contemporary political situation in northern India is culled from newspapers, magazines, and books. This is not the work of a historian or an "expert" on Sikhs. The selected bibliography identifies my main secondary sources. I would like to acknowledge my debt to the work of the journalists who covered the bloody events on the subcontinent, especially Mark Tully, Satish Jacob, Pranay Gupte, Ross H. Munro, and Patwant Singh. My family — Susan, Christopher, Deanna and Paul — are due much more than gratitude for their unflinching support of the project. I could not have completed it without their encouragement and tolerance.

Despite such support, however, I must emphasize that any errors in the text are my responsibility.

November, 1987
Vancouver

1. THE ASSASSINATION

It was shortly after nine o'clock on a sunny Wednesday morning when the murder that changed the face of Indian politics occurred. The sixty-seven-year-old, gray-haired woman stepped out of a side door into the lush garden that surrounded her sprawling white bungalow. The air was crisp, and scented by a profusion of blooming roses. One of her security guards, Narain Singh, opened a parasol over her head to block the fierce glare of the early-winter sun. The shrubbery cast mottled shadows and her bright saffron-colored sari brushed the cement walk as she strode through the garden.

At the white-and-red wicket gate in the hedge that separated the offices from Indira Gandhi's home, a twenty-eight-year-old subinspector of police stood at attention. Beant Singh had served as a guard of the prime minister for six years. Instead of saluting, he drew his .35-caliber, standard-issue revolver and fired. His partner, Constable Satwant Singh, who was stationed on the other side of the hedge, came through the gate and emptied his Thompson automatic carbine into the crumpled figure on the ground. Narain Singh dove for cover, dropping the umbrella he carried. Another guard fell, wounded in the thigh. The aging matriarch's valet and secretary, who were trailing behind in her entourage, scattered as the bullets ricocheted off the pavement.

When the machine-gun's hoarse bark stopped, the woman whose childhood ambition was to die for her country lay on the cement like a bloody rag. More than twenty bullets had ripped apart the right side of her body, shredding veins, arteries, spinal column, and major organs. The leader of the world's largest democracy had been butchered in her own backyard by the men sworn to protect her.

Satwant Singh, a $50-a-month New Delhi policeman caught selling opium only two months before, stood over the corpse with the barrel of his emptied gun smoking. There were shouts and a clatter of boots as the elite force of Indo-Tibetan border police assigned to protect the prime minister sprinted toward the sound of the gunfire. Beant Singh calmly hung his walkie-talkie on the gate, and the two killers began to pray. They had not planned an escape. They considered themselves martyrs in a holy war to dismember India. They were prepared to die so that their blood would fuel the crusade.

"We have done what we set out to do, now you can do whatever you want to do," Beant Singh said in Hindi to the policemen who formed the prime minister's outer ring of security. The hand-picked men screamed abuse as they grabbed the two pious killers. They bundled the Sikhs back to the nearby guardhouse, pushed them into a corner, and opened fire with submachine-guns. Beant Singh, a descendant of a Hindu Untouchable who had embraced Sikhism to escape the caste-prison of his own faith, died instantly. His body absorbed most of the shots and fell atop the wounded Satwant Singh.

Beyond the garden and the guardhouse the actor and film-maker, Peter Ustinov, and his film crew were on the office lawn awaiting the prime minister when they heard the report of the Sten guns. Mrs. Gandhi was being featured in a series of documentaries called *Ustinov's People* and had agreed to conduct the final interview in the affluent enclave in New Delhi where she had her home and office. The house at Number One Safdarjang Road, which had become India's equivalent to Number Ten Downing Street, had been built for British administrators at the turn of the century.

Mrs. Gandhi was heading for the interview when she was cut down. Ustinov appeared on television screens around the globe that night to describe what he heard as he stood on the lawn waiting for her.

Mrs. Gandhi's daughter-in-law, Sonia, rushed from the home in her bathrobe and began to scream when she realized that the staccato explosions were not the sound of children playing with firecrackers. "Mommy. My God! Mommy," she cried hysterically as she knelt beside the fallen prime minister. "Get a car."

A specially equipped ambulance sat nearby for just such emergencies, but the driver could not be found in the confusion. Sonia ordered the policemen to place her mother-in-law in the back seat of the family's Ambassador sedan. She crouched on the floor, crying and cradling Mrs. Gandhi's head, as the car lurched into the midst of the traffic-choked streets of New Delhi.

The man Sonia Gandhi ordered to drive to the hospital panicked and took a wrong turn. Although the All-India Institute of Medical Sciences was only four kilometers from the scene of the assassination, it took nearly forty minutes for the car to reach its gates. At the hospital, the guards refused to believe the bloody pulp on the back floor was India's prime minister and dallied before letting the car through. No one had informed them that Mrs. Gandhi had been shot.

Inside, the hospital staff was equally unprepared. There was no stretcher; orderlies had to use a makeshift gurney to carry Mrs. Gandhi into an emergency room. One doctor said the prime minister looked like "a child wrapped in a washerwoman's sheet." A young intern stared incredulously and screamed: "Madam! Madam!"

Mrs. Gandhi was clinically dead on arrival. But the doctors threaded a rubber tube down through her windpipe to fill her lungs with oxygen, inserted two intravenous lines for blood transfusions, and massaged her heart to produce the faint traces of an artificial heartbeat on a cardiac monitor. In the eighth-floor operating theater, as the heart-lung machine simulated life, surgeons plucked bullets from the corpse.

News of the shooting spread through New Delhi quickly. By lunchtime hospital doorways and corridors were choked with cabinet ministers, socialites, bureaucrats, and members of Mrs. Gandhi's staff. The doctors stopped working on the body about 2:30 P.M. and official word of her death was relayed to Rajiv Gandhi as he flew back to New Delhi from a campaign tour. He was met at the airport by his long-time friend Amitabh Bachchan. Bachchan, one of India's biggest film stars and a leading Congress Party politician, explained that senior members of the government were ready to support a quick transfer of power to Rajiv.

Mrs. Gandhi's son, a former pilot with the government-run Indian Airlines, took the news of his mother's death calmly. He had been at Hooghly Delta, just below Calcutta, trying to buttress her party's political fortunes when she was shot. The policeman who stopped his motorcade with the news knew only that terrorists had struck the Gandhi home. The soft-spoken, forty-year-old Rajiv asked if his wife and children were safe. As he waited for a helicopter to fly him to Calcutta airport, he stood in the glaring sunshine surrounded by aides and listening to a portable Sony radio. He wore his trademark aviator sunglasses, homespun white shirt, and loose trousers. A woolen Kashmir shawl was draped around his shoulders. The All-India Radio network run by the government played Hindi film music. Gandhi tuned to the British Broadcasting Corporation's world service for news.

He later took the trouble to dismiss media reports that he had been overwrought when told of the shooting. "Let me say that some newspapers or magazines reported that when I heard the news I went to the loo and had a bawl," he said. "That's all rubbish. I was fairly upset but that is not the way I give expression to my emotions."

A vast crowd stood vigil outside the hospital when Rajiv Gandhi arrived at about 4:00 P.M. Ushered inside, he spent several minutes alone in the operating room looking at the lifeless form that had been his mother. He emerged into the din of the mourners in the corridor and asked the power brokers of his mother's Congress Party to join him in a nearby boardroom. There, all agreed he should become prime minister immediately. Gandhi picked his friend Arun Nehru, a distant cousin and head of India's largest paint company, to go to the airport and inform India's president, Giani

Zail Singh, of their decision when his plane arrived.

Nehru, armed with a letter from the general secretary of the All-India Congress Committee authorized the transfer of power, and backed by a handful of senior bureaucrats and politicians, presented the president with a fait accompli. As the president's limousine sped to the hospital, the tall, burly Nehru, scion of one of India's wealthiest families, told the former Sikh preacher that Gandhi would be sworn in that evening.

By the time the motorcade reached the hospital, the crowd of a few thousand was building into a mob. The late-afternoon air was laden with diesel fumes, dust, and rumors. Word that Sikhs were responsible for killing Mrs. Gandhi was everywhere. Angry Hindus shouted vows of revenge. They stoned the passing president's car.

Witnesses said a phalanx of about thirty or forty young men then appeared, grabbed a motor scooter, and set it ablaze. The young Hindus sprinted towards crowded buses and forced them to a halt. Sikh passengers, identifiable by their turbans and beards, were pulled out onto the street and beaten. Their turbans were ripped from their heads and torched. Police wielding meter-and-a-half-long, iron-bound bamboo staves, called *lathis,* arrived about twenty minutes later to chase away the thugs.

Inside the hospital, Zail Singh embraced Rajiv Gandhi. He offered his condolences, but Gandhi responded to him curtly and headed home. Most of the crowd left in his wake. The president went into the operating room, removed the rosebud from his buttonhole and laid it on the dead prime minister.

At six o'clock, nearly nine hours after the fatal shots were fired, All-India Radio broke its silence and officially announced that Indira Gandhi had become the third Indian prime minister to die in office, the first at the hands of an assassin. Thirty minutes later, Rajiv Gandhi arrived at the presidential palace, the Rashtrapati Bhavan, to be sworn in. He had shaved and changed into a white *kurta* (or tunic), and tailored pants. Inside the imposing sandstone palace, under the glittering chandelier in Ashoka Hall, Zail Singh administered the oath that elevated Rajiv Gandhi from rookie member of parliament to the leader of eight hundred million people. He became India's seventh and youngest prime minister.

Across northern India, many Congress (Indira) Party officials were meeting and planning revenge on the people they blamed for murdering their leader: the Sikhs. In anticipation of violence between India's religious communities, the lieutenant-governor of New Delhi banned gatherings of more than five people and the bearing of arms. The edict was ignored. Near midnight, a subdued Rajiv Gandhi appeared on the government-run television network and appealed to the nation from the living room of One Safdarjang Road. A garlanded portrait of his mother hung behind him as he spoke first in English, then in Hindi. He spoke slowly and without emotion.

"She was a mother not only to me but to the whole nation," he said. "She served the Indian people to the last drop of her blood. The country knows with what tireless dedication she toiled for the development of India. You all know how dear to her heart was the dream of a united, peaceful, and prosperous India."

The dream was all that was left. Even as the new prime minister spoke, the bloodbath was beginning.

For the previous three years, Mrs. Gandhi's own instincts, her intelligence services, and her family had warned her to expect the assassins. The Sikhs were among her most-feared opponents. They were an integral part of the Indian army and civil service. If they were as disenchanted as their leaders insisted, then it was impossible to guarantee the safety of any Gandhi. Despite their minority status, the Sikhs held a disproportionate number of powerful positions and had a history of social activism.

They had been among the most vociferous opponents to her iron-fisted rule during the Emergency, which she had declared in 1975, after the courts had found her guilty of corrupt electoral practices. Mrs. Gandhi had then invoked a special provision of the Indian constitution devised for occasions of national upheaval or natural disaster. The prime minister assumed dictatorial powers. Thousands of Sikh protestors were jailed for peacefully demonstrating against the savage measures she introduced. The press was muzzled, the opposition imprisoned, the courts handcuffed, and many among the poor and illiterate were subjected to compulsory sterilization campaigns. When Mrs. Gandhi returned the country to democracy in 1977, her Congress (I) Party was crushed and she lost her own seat. "My father was a statesman; I am a political woman," said the daughter of India's first prime minister. "My father was a saint; I am not."

She was defeated in the ensuing election, but her youngest son, Sanjay, engineered her return to power in 1980, by fracturing the voting blocs that supported the coalition government that replaced her. But in victory Mrs. Gandhi refused to honor her promises and the antagonism between her and some of the vanquished politicians — particularly the Sikhs — became rancorous. In the two years before her death, she dealt with them only through intermediaries. In fact, her direct involvement in the business of cutting political deals greatly diminished, as she spent more and more time with her family following the death of Sanjay in an air accident in 1980.

Mrs. Gandhi had relied heavily on the thirty-three-year-old who was her heir apparent and main strategist. Sanjay, whose wife was a Sikh, and Giani Zail Singh, the future president, were her two key advisers throughout the 1970s. But their manipulation of the Sikh vote, coupled with her own apparent indifference to the religious minority's political demands sowed the seeds of her assassination.

Zail Singh was an opportunist from the Akali Dal, the political party formed after the First World War expressly to fight for Sikh religious rights and freedoms. He joined the Congress Party in the early 1960s when the Akali Dal's peaceful protests for political change were crushed by the government of Jawaharlal Nehru, Indira Gandhi's father. Zail Singh adopted Nehru's habit of always sporting a fresh rosebud in the third buttonhole of his *achkan*, a long, fitted jacket, and quickly rose through the ranks of the Congress Party. He became the leader of the Punjab state government and artfully exploited his religious ties by encouraging Sikh hubris, opening public functions with hymns, and organizing services, all of which wooed Sikh voters away from their own historic party, the Akali Dal.

After the victory in 1980, Mrs. Gandhi rewarded Zail Singh handsomely. She elevated him first to Home Minister, and then appointed him India's first Sikh president. But in the summer of

1980, Sanjay Gandhi was killed when a stunt plane he was piloting over New Delhi spun out of control and slammed into the ground. Mrs. Gandhi then drafted her eldest son, Rajiv, into politics to replace Sanjay. Rajiv brought with him his friends, the sons of India's corporate elite, to become the new generation of political advisers and strategists. They boasted that they would guide India into the twenty-first century. In the changes that followed, Zail Singh was one of the few close associates of Sanjay to maintain a position of influence. He continued to play a central role in the government's strategy sessions and could command Mrs. Gandhi's ear.

Her administration, however, drifted from crisis to crisis after Sanjay's death. In the years following her return to power, cabinet ministers and senior civil servants were caught spying; there was unrest over illegal immigration in the northeastern state of Assam and three thousand people were massacred; there were religious disturbances in the heartland state of Uttar Pradesh, where hundreds of Muslims were beaten to death by their Hindu neighbors; and Pakistan continued to threaten the northern Indian state of Jammu and Kashmir, where Muslim separatists were agitating. There was also strife in the Punjab, India's most affluent state and the only one in which the Sikhs maintained a slim majority. Mrs. Gandhi personally scuttled negotiations between her government and the Akali Dal in 1982, triggering a wave of sectarian violence across northern India between Sikhs and the majority Hindus.

It was a predictable result in the often coarse, violent world of Indian democracy in the 1980s. The main political parties each maintained militias. The nation's power-brokers traveled through the capital surrounded by bodyguards. At New Delhi intersections, their dark-windowed cars would stop, the doors burst open, and guards wielding machine-guns would spring onto the roadway and scan the horizon. Some of Mrs. Gandhi's principal foes among the Sikhs were Zapata look-alikes with cartridge-laden bandoliers slung across their chests, and holstered revolvers and meter-long sabres at their sides. Senior politicians rarely traveled in the Punjab or New Delhi without donning bullet-proof vests.

Hunkered down and isolated in homes surrounded by armed guards and coils of razor-edged barbed wire, the rulers of New Delhi grew paranoid and petrified. They labeled "terrorist" anyone who expressed even mild hostility to their plutocracy, which had ruled India since the British left in 1947.

The central government's grip on internal stability was considered so tenuous that draconian laws, which gagged the press, restricted travel, and fettered civil liberties, were again deemed essential by Mrs. Gandhi. Her Sikh opponents were singled out as a threat not just to her political ascendancy, but to India's national security.

The dispute between Mrs. Gandhi and the Sikh political leaders became a personal feud almost overnight in 1982. She was insulted by their chauvinism, and she considered their demands for more power, land and money the mewling of a tiny, special interest group. When they announced their opposition to the 1982 Asian Games in New Delhi — considered by many critics to be an extravagant, political coming-out party for Rajiv Gandhi — she turned on them with a vengeance. Every Sikh, regardless of political affiliation, suffered. The Sikhs were convenient scapegoats, partly because their claim to political and ethnic sovereignty seemed clearly artificial.

Mrs. Gandhi harassed her Sikh opponents with the same fervor and for the same reasons that Joe McCarthy persecuted communists: it was good politics among the Hindus who kept her in power. But by labeling them demon terrorists, Mrs. Gandhi inflated their influence and the danger they posed to secular authority in India.

The Sikh politicians were agitating for greater constitutional and religious freedom that virtually amounted to special status for the faith whose members constituted only 2 per cent of India's society. But they were also joined by several opposition state governments in their demand for a devolution of political power to state legislatures from New Delhi. They wanted a say in the development and use of state resources and finances. Nearly all of the Indian economy was controlled by the central government. The banks had been nationalized to disperse capital from affluent states such as

Punjab to the country's impoverished areas. The changes demanded by the devolutionists would have created an Indian federation similar to the United States of America. The Sikhs also wanted India's domestic borders changed, and the city of Chandigarh, which served as a shared capital for the states of Haryana and Punjab, to be proclaimed Punjab's capital.

Although she had promised similar changes when she became prime minister in 1966, Mrs. Gandhi now said that such measures were too radical and would enflame regional jealousies. The Sikhs were denied permission to establish a radio station in Amritsar for broadcasting hymns and sermons. They were ridiculed for asking New Delhi to name the train to their holy city the Harimandir Express, after the "seat of God" shrine within the Golden Temple complex. Mrs. Gandhi used the presence of a few criminals and demagogues within the Akali Dal and the Shiromani Gurdwara Prabandhak Committee, the religious bureaucracy that administers the treasuries of Sikh temples, to use the country's intelligence and law-enforcement machinery against the Sikhs.

With the approach of the Asian Games, police subjected all Sikhs to arbitrary arrest and interrogation. Even those riding in first-class railway carriages were rudely awakened in the middle of the night so that soldiers could rummage through their luggage. Their state was denied industrial licenses by the federal government, which also channeled Punjabi water and electricity to the more populous and vote-rich states of the Hindu "Cow Belt" around New Delhi.

Law-enforcement authorities admitted that scores of young Sikhs were tortured and killed over the next few years by federal and state police. This was part of their dirty war to maintain law and order in the face of a Sikh-terrorist threat. In a country inhabited by a faceless multitude, no one was prosecuted for being too zealous in the fight against India's enemies.

For many within the Sikh community, in India and abroad, the bloodshed and repression heralded an apocalypse. Before political negotiations were cut off by Mrs. Gandhi, there were only sporadic incidents of violence and they often involved internal feuds between factions within the Sikh body politic. Shut off from the prime minister, rebuffed and humiliated by her advisers, the Sikhs escalated the size and intensity of their agitations against the administration. By the spring of 1984, law and order had collapsed in northwestern India and the worst Sikh fears were confirmed.

In early June, Mrs. Gandhi ordered the army to expel reporters from the Punjab. This northwestern Indian state, the Sikhs' ancestral home, was sealed. The Indian army then launched an attack on the faith's holiest shrine, the Golden Temple in Amritsar. More than a thousand Sikh pilgrims were killed in the days that followed. The army had planned the assault on the two-hundred-year-old marble and gold-leaf shrine for more than a month using a life-sized model. The attack was code-named "Operation Bluestar". Other Sikh temples in the state were raided in a similar fashion and hundreds of Sikhs were imprisoned without charges being laid.

Mrs. Gandhi justified the carnage on the grounds that her administration was weeding out terrorists who were hiding in the Golden Temple and elsewhere in the Punjab. It was tantamount to the Canadian government ordering the military to besiege the largest churches in Montreal and justifying the civilian casualties by pointing to the corpses of suspected Quebec separatists. However, the Golden Temple was not simply a cathedral; it was the Sikh equivalent of the Vatican or Mecca and its desecration outraged Sikhs around the world.

In the aftermath of Operation Bluestar, the fundamentalists saw only one fate: perdition. And they saw only one hope: Khalistan, a land of the pure, a homeland for Sikhs in the northwestern corner of the subcontinent. When a falcon, the symbol of Gobind Rai, the greatest Sikh warrior-saint, landed on Mrs. Gandhi's home, the religious faithful among her bodyguards say they took it as a sign to begin the holy war, a *dharm yudh.*

Indira Gandhi's assassins were Sikhs, followers of one of the world's youngest major religions. Not yet five hundred years old, Sikhism has become known as a warrior faith with mores culled from the Middle Ages. A Sikh man, his mane of uncut, Samson-like hair coiled inside a turban, is called a "Lion", or Singh, and his woman is a "princess", Kaur. Theirs is a religion whose faith is simple: welcome all men to your table as brothers and always be prepared to fight your enemies. The great wars between the cross and the crescent ended centuries ago, and the Church Militant has been reduced to the tattered standard of liberation theology. But for the Sikhs, the battle between the turban and the Hindu cap truly began only five months before that Halloween morning in 1984 when Mrs. Gandhi was shot.

Sikhs within New Delhi's temples began plotting to murder the prime minister the moment Operation Bluestar ended. "The woman did not do the right thing," a shaken Beant Singh told his police colleagues after the attack on the Golden Temple. "Who knows what price she will have to pay for this?"

The policeman, who was a graduate of Punjabi University, was horrified by the destruction and the death toll. He and his brethren were incredulous at the government's excuses. Why weren't the few dozen criminals who hid within starved out? Why were hundreds of apolitical Sikhs imprisoned without charge and the entire state sealed?

Balbir Singh, another police sub-inspector attached to the prime minister's security staff, offered to kill Mrs. Gandhi for $80,000 at a June 26 meeting inside the Bangla Sahib Gurdwara, a Sikh temple in central New Delhi. There were a handful of Sikhs at the meeting who afterwards made calls to friends and family in England, Canada and the United States to arrange sanctuary for him after the killing. But the plan collapsed.

During emotional meetings at the temple and in their homes, the policemen and fellow civil servants discussed a Beirut-style suicide mission — ramming the prime minister's motorcade with a car stuffed with explosives. There was talk of planting a time bomb. The rumors of an impending assassination sparked the removal of the twelve Sikh guards in the prime minister's security cordon. Rajiv Gandhi was anxious: "I used to have meetings at Akbar Road at night and often as we were walking back to the living quarters at one o'clock or two o'clock, a couple of times I wondered at his [Beant Singh's] behavior. I used to think, you know: I have my security chaps around me, but if he presses that trigger, nobody can stop him at this range, he is already in position."

The Sikhs who killed Mrs. Gandhi had over the course of five months discussed and dismissed a variety of plots. Others in the temple knew of their intentions but did nothing to dissuade them. The two had risen on October 31 before dawn, in what the Sikhs call the ambrosial hours, to pray. They had sealed their vow to assassinate the prime minister by sharing sweetened water stirred by a double-edged dagger in an iron bowl — the traditional nectar called *amrit* that was taken by a Sikh warrior before battle.

The clean-shaven, twenty-one-year-old Satwant Singh was ineligible to serve in the prime minister's inner guard because he was raised in a village only four kilometers from the Pakistan border. His personal habits had also marked him as a security risk. He had been arrested in August 1984 for peddling opium at New Delhi's Gole Market. Nothing came of the charge and, a month or so afterwards, Beant Singh approached him for his help in killing the prime minister.

A college-educated policeman, Beant Singh was a devout Sikh who grew up on the outskirts of Chandigarh. He had married a Hindu nurse from Delhi who later converted to Sikhism. His family said that for years they had backed the Congress Party and that Beant, too, had been a stalwart supporter of Mrs. Gandhi. That changed utterly after Operation Bluestar.

"My husband told me that after learning what happened in Amritsar he was feeling hurt and wanted to become a martyr," his widow, Bimal Devi, said. "I asked him what would happen to our children, and he replied that God would look after them."

Hundreds of Sikh soldiers in the Indian army mutinied and deserted over the assault. Senior police and military officers resigned in disgust. Many became fugitives. The country's police, intelligence, and border patrols scoured the nation for them before they could rally the Sikhs to sedition. It was too late.

The assassination was discussed openly for months beforehand in Sikh temples in Vancouver, Canada, in New York, and in London, England. Thousands of expatriate Sikhs had rent the Indian flag, trashed consular offices, and attacked diplomats when they heard of the attack on the Golden Temple. Later, around countless dinner tables, husbands and wives envisioned themselves pulling the trigger and vowed to kill Mrs. Gandhi if they got the chance.

Television networks carried pictures of Sikh leaders prophesying her imminent death.

India gained independence in a large part because of the blood spilled by the minority Sikh community. Afterwards they fought valiantly in three wars with Pakistan and one with China. The Sikhs remained patient while Mrs. Gandhi broke long-standing political commitments to them. The community remained divided and politically impotent until Operation Bluestar. With the brutal military suppression of even moderate aspirations, Sikhdom was changed utterly. The attack on the Golden Temple and the wholesale and indiscriminate arrests drove the Sikh factions together.

The Sikhs form a tightly knit, clannish brotherhood because they maintain connections, networks, and a collective memory ranging over several generations and continents. The metaphorical sword of righteousness was fine in theory, but in the face of the Islamic forces of the Moguls, the Sikhs had learned the bloody lesson that steel made a more reliable weapon. The Sikhs gained a savage reputation during sporadic hit-and-run guerrilla campaigns waged against the Muslims for nearly a hundred years. As a result of the skirmishes, they were enjoined by their last spiritual leader, Guru Gobind Singh, to wear a sword, a steel bangle to protect the right wrist in combat, and soldier's breeches so that they would be forever ready to defend themselves and their faith. They maintain the traditions today.

Mrs. Gandhi defended the decision to storm the temple by claiming the murders, bombings and sabotage in India were a symptom of the great cancer of the 1980s: "international terrorism". She claimed the Sikh separatists were receiving covert support from Pakistan, North America, and Europe in a concerted campaign to politically destabilize the Indian government.

Nevertheless, a few weeks before she was murdered, Mrs. Gandhi ignored everyone's advice and demanded that Sikh guards, who had earlier been removed from her security staff, be reinstated.

Two days before the assassination, Beant Singh refused to accept her offered gift of a one-hundred-rupee note (about $8 U.S.), her traditional token to the bodyguards to mark Diwali, the Indian festival of light. Such indications that Beant Singh was no longer loyal were ignored. There were numerous other security lapses. No one reported Satwant Singh's arrest for opium trafficking and no one could explain how the clean-shaven, twenty-one-year-old with only three years' experience had insinuated himself into Mrs. Gandhi's inner guard.

With Beant's help, Satwant was given the post on the morning of the assassination after he complained that he was suffering from the most common ailment in India: diarrhea. He was stationed at the wicket gate so he could quickly reach a bathroom. The two assassins simply waited for Mrs. Gandhi to come by. Just after 9:00 A.M. they set in motion the events whose consequences exceeded the expectations of even the most sanguinary fanatic.

Satwant Singh survived the wounds he suffered after the murder and was held in solitary confinement. He said he was tortured into revealing details of the assassination plot. But the man who had always been a supporter of the Congress Party as a youth refused to appeal his death sentence after the trial.

From the moment of his ascension, Rajiv Gandhi echoed his mother's refrain of an international conspiracy. The new prime minister demanded an investigation into every aspect of the assassination and the tangled web of international connections behind it. The results of the inquiry were so volatile that he refused to make them public.

The secret report contained predictable recommendations by police and intelligence officials but went on to call for an examination of President Zail Singh's ties to the separatists. However, the investigators suggested the government wait until the president's five-year term expired in the summer of 1987 to avoid further inciting the Sikhs. There were also many embarrassing security blunders revealed in the report that no one was eager to discuss openly.

There were so many slip-ups leading to the shooting that even Rajender Kumar Dhawan, Mrs. Gandhi's special assistant who had served the aging matriarch since she entered public life twenty years before, was suspected. The forty-seven-year-old man, who wore his black hair brilliantined onto his glistening scalp, formed part of Mrs. Gandhi's ever-present entourage and escaped unscathed when she was gunned down. Afterwards, his home was watched, his friends questioned and he was relentlessly interrogated. He lost his job and became an ascetic Hindu, shaving his head and wearing a sacred mark on his forehead.

In the end, the investigators concluded that the assassins had been successful primarily because no one really believed the leader of the world's non-aligned nations would be killed. Those around her believed the myth Mrs. Gandhi had created. Security was lax because those who held the jobs considered them perquisites, a chance to rub shoulders with greatness, to travel abroad, to obtain luxury goods, and to gain foreign exchange; they fled when Beant Singh started shooting. Mrs. Gandhi had been so much larger than life. There was no politician of similar stature anywhere in India. No one expected her to be killed so casually. They anticipated a specific, sophisticated threat, or an assault. But there had only been an elderly woman's premonition.

The night before she was slain, Mrs. Gandhi's grandchildren were in a car crash. She had been campaigning in the eastern Indian state of Orissa at the time. She hastened home fearing they had been attacked by terrorists. Fortunately, the teenaged children of Rajiv and his wife Sonia, were unhurt. Indira Gandhi's response underscored her dread. Death threats came daily.

Mrs. Gandhi claimed foreign agents were trying to destabilize her government. They came from Pakistan mainly, but also she said the terrorists were receiving support from the United States, Canada, and Britain. Indeed, after Operation Bluestar, there was no shortage of Sikhs around the globe who would rejoice at her death. Her intelligence services and Zail Singh's private network of informants kept her apprised of their sentiments and agitation.

In a book-lined study at the rear of Mrs. Gandhi's colonial-style house, she had begun working on her will. Her childhood heroine was Joan of Arc, and the hand-written draft that lay unfinished on her desk revealed her preoccupation with the idea of martyrdom. "If I die a violent death as some fear and a few are plotting," she wrote, "I know the violence will be in the thought and the action of the assassin, not in my dying — for no hate is dark enough to overshadow the extent of my love for my people and my country; no force is strong enough to divert me from my purpose and my endeavor to take this country forward."

Mrs. Gandhi claimed to have a vision of what India should be: a humane, democratic, and secular state. Like those of her father's generation, she thought of herself as a revolutionary. As a child she was forced to survive on her own when the ruling British imprisoned her parents, her grandfather, and her aunt. Schooled in Switzerland, she returned to India when she was almost twelve to help organize a twelve-thousand-strong army of child guerrillas called the Monkey Brigade. "I liked dolls," the woman who was jailed for subversion during the Second World War once confided. "I had many dolls. And you know how I played with them? By performing insurrections, assemblies, scenes of arrest. My dolls were never babies to be nursed but men and women who attacked barracks and ended up in prison."

In power, Mrs. Gandhi envisioned herself dragging into the twentieth century an immense land that remained mired in the Middle Ages. The mass of nameless humanity who inhabited it was so diverse that it was virtually impossible to avoid violently altering someone's world, or trampling on some community's rights. It was a country in which there were regular battles between civilization and primitive nomads who still inhabited its jungles and hills.

"A poet has written of his 'love' — 'How can I feel humble with the wealth of you beside me?' — I can say the same of India," Mrs. Gandhi wrote. In a country in which children go blind every day from malnutrition and thousands can be left homeless by a flash flood, she continued: "I cannot understand how anyone can be an Indian and not be proud — the richness and infinite variety of our composite heritage, the magnificence of the people's spirit, equal to any disaster or burden, firm in their faith, gay spontaneity even in poverty and hardship."

2. THE SIKHS

The man who founded Sikhism did not intend to create a warrior religion. For one hundred years his descendants and disciples lived quietly and peacefully. They were part of an egalitarian society that lived cooperatively, sang hymns, and worshiped in the contemplative mystic tradition known as *bhakti,* or religion of the heart. Within four generations, however, those who called themselves Sikhs strapped on the sword. The Sikhs embraced martial traditions and their religious gatherings became forums for an incipient nationalism.

From the evidence that remains, the founder of Sikhism, Nanak Das Bedi, was born in 1469 in a tiny farming village known as Talwandi Rai Bhoe, about sixty kilometers from the city of Lahore, in what is now Pakistan. He was born into an affluent merchant family of Hindus and his relatives had connections with the governing Mogul administrators. His father, Mehta Kalian Das Bedi was an accountant but not much else is known about the family.

The first stories about Nanak weren't written down until several decades after his death. By then the details of his life were obscure and the legend, enormous. The first Sikh scriptures were poems and hymns ascribed to Nanak and the holy men who assumed his mantle. Later, canonical works, hagiographies, and other poems and hymns were added to the body of Sikh literature. But the history of the founding and development of the religion that they portray is sketchy and often ambiguous.

Before Operation Bluestar the Sikhs maintained a library in the Golden Temple, housing thousands of centuries-old manuscripts, many covered in elaborate filigree. The collection, which included documents signed and written by the original Sikh gurus, survived the armed assault, but three days into the army's occupation a fire destroyed everything. Some Sikhs claim that Russian military advisers to the Indian government ordered the books burned to erase their culture as part of an official program of genocide. Mrs. Gandhi said the fire broke out when soldiers tried to flush out a Sikh sniper who had escaped their initial sweep through the dank, arched cloisters of the temple complex.

It is written that Nanak began his public ministry at about the age of thirty after a profound visionary experience. He is supposed to have gone swimming late one evening and to have vanished. A servant who accompanied him is said to have heard a voice in the darkness saying, "Do not lose patience." While the river was being dredged, according to Sikh tradition, Nanak ascended to God. Three days later he emerged from the river a changed man.

Nanak abandoned the traditions of Hinduism and founded a commune whose most significant features were that its members shared their food and sang hymns. Their prayers stressed that God was unique, omnipotent, and immortal, and that knowledge of him could only be obtained through a guru. Everything was simple. Nanak and his followers rejected the external images of God and the richness typical of Hindu temple sects. They worshiped God by concentrating on his name, a symbol of the ultimate truth in their eyes. So powerful were Nanak's verses and charisma that his message spread across the Punjab and his followers declared themselves his disciples, or Sikhs.

The Punjab in the fifteenth century was a province of cosmopolitan tolerance. It was the northwestern gateway to India where numerous wanderers and conquerors had settled after falling in love with the fertile plain. The Mongols conquered it in the thirteenth century and established the overland highway between China and the West through India.

There were two important cities: Lahore, which was the seat of most governments, and Multan, a caravan-choked trading center in the south. The north was still a jungle then, populated by rhinoceroses and cloaked by huge forests. There was an abundance of markets, traveling tradesmen, and merchants. Farmers grew sugarcane, rice, cotton, wheat, millet, and, one of the most important cash crops, the opium poppy. In this respect, not much has changed over the last five centuries.

The society reflected the heritage of the Aryans, tall, fair nomads who had arrived two millennia earlier from arid Rajasthan in the south. They were drawn by the prosperity promised by the water from five rivers — the Jhelum, Chenab, Ravi, Beas, and the Sutlej — that dissected the region and gave it its name: *pan,* meaning "five"; *jab,* meaning "waters". Even today the state's motto is: "Strength from the Waters".

The Jats were a tribe who migrated into the Punjab from the south. Like the highlanders of Scotland, extended Jat families lived together in villages, the most prominent of which continue to exist: Sidhu, Sandhu, Gill, Dhillon, Dhariwal, Bains. They paid taxes to the regional government and were considered just another part of the Indian mosaic in which everyone knew his or her place. The Muslims formed the government and dominated the plains. In the cities they shared the businesses with the Hindu trading castes: the Banias, Mahajans, Suds, Khatris, and Aroras. The Hindu Brahmans and the Kshatrya princes ruled in the Himalayan foothills.

From most accounts, Nanak was a precocious child who learned Arabic and Persian as well as the local Punjabi dialect. He was married by his parents at the age of twelve and his wife came to live with him when she reached the age of nineteen. The couple had two sons, Sri Chand in 1494 and Lakhmi Das three years later.

Nanak's brother-in-law got him an administrative job through a relative of the reigning Sultan of Delhi. He began to attract attention when he and a Muslim minstrel defied the dictates of caste by inviting people over for supper and hymns. It was during such an all-night chanting session in 1499 that Nanak is said to have disappeared. On his return, he is reported to have given away his possessions, told his family and his friends that "there is no Hindu, there is no Mussalman [Muslim]", and abandoned the rituals he was expected to perform daily.

Nanak became an itinerant preacher in the style of Jesus. He captivated people with his message of other-worldly quietism and brotherly love. Many of the rural Jat farming families, who respected Nanak as a teacher, considered themselves his followers. He started a community kitchen, or *langar,* as a symbol of equality and he and his disciples ate together. In a country of endemic poverty, he attacked the Brahmans for demanding donations and insisting that even the shadow of a lower-caste man in a kitchen made its food unclean. He preached across northern India and there is evidence that he traveled as far east as Baghdad.

His sermons appealed particularly to the illiterate peasants because he spoke in their language. Unlike the Brahmans or the mullahs, Nanak spoke in Punjabi, a local tongue that was a variant of Hindi and an offshoot of Sanskrit. His speeches were simple, direct, and filled with rural similes. Like the Buddhists and Jains before him, he pleaded with the downtrodden to throw off the shackles of caste. He saw the good as a path, not a goal. He loved hymns and advised his followers to rise before dawn so they could listen to music under the stars during the "ambrosial hours".

Nanak's message was perceived as a new religious ethic that emphasized what people shared rather than what set them apart. As he lay dying in 1539, Nanak designated a man named Lehna to carry on his work and called him Guru Angad, "of my own limb".

Over the next century, middle-class merchants, farmers, and the agricultural poor adopted Nanak's beliefs. They established parishes and chose from among themselves people to act as officials, called *mosands,* to collect offerings. The money was used to acquire land. Dedicated scribes began recording the hymns of Nanak and the teachings of successive gurus.

They wrote in Punjabi, using a little-known indigenous alphabet of thirty-five letters they called *gurmukhi,* "from the mouth of the guru". It was a sharp departure from the practices of Hinduism or

Islam, whose sacred texts required the interpretation of the Brahman or the mullah. In emphasizing the language of the people, Nanak drew on the common bond among his followers but he also wedded the faith's future to the survival of Punjabi and *gurmukhi*. Without knowledge of the language and script, one had no access to the teachings of the gurus.

The Sikhs' holy book, the Adi Granth, or "first book", was completed in 1604, about the time Shakespeare was publishing his great comedies. The completion of the text consummated Nanak's union of faith and language. The Sikhs became a people of the book and with it grew need for scribes, copyists, teachers, exegetes, and a bureaucracy to coordinate such activity. The Mogul emperor Akbar was so impressed by the text — which contained roughly six thousand hymns by the gurus and selections from four centuries of Indian religious thought, including compositions by Hindus and Muslims — that he presented the Sikhs with gifts of gold and cloth.

By the beginning of the seventeenth century, the number of Punjabis who called themselves Sikhs was considerable and the faith was developing from a loosely organized community into an institutionalized religion. Families who could trace their roots to the original disciples were venerated. The Sikhs adopted a belief that bloodlines conferred virtue; guruship was consequently inherited, not earned. Leadership was passed from father to son and a priestly class emerged among those who advised the spiritual leader of the faithful.

Akbar's patronage and the growing wealth of the Sikhs spurred their fifth guru, Arjun Mal, to build a shrine in the middle of a man-made pond about sixty kilometers east of Lahore. He introduced a 10 per cent tax on the faithful, and the tithe was the beginning of the Sikh treasury.

Arjun invited a Muslim mystic to lay the foundation stone for the temple he called the Harimandir, or "shrine of God", in the middle of the pool. The temple was lower than the surrounding land so worshipers would be forced to step down, a reminder that they were below God. Unlike the Hindu temples, Arjun also left the Harimandir open on four sides to indicate it was open to all four castes of Indian society. The water-filled tank in which it sat was called Amritsar, or "pool of nectar". With the Harimandir in the center, the pool and its surrounding buildings became the hub of what was considered the Sikh's city, their equivalent of the Muslim's Mecca or the Hindu's Benares. The complex of shrines is their Vatican.

But the faith's prominence and growth grated on Akbar's more devout successor, Jehangir, who decided that the Sikhs "should be brought into the fold of Islam". When Arjun refused to pay the levies Jehangir imposed to cripple the Sikh treasury, he was imprisoned and tortured to death. It was the first taste of oppression for the still loosely organized brotherhood of the Sikhs. After a century of holding non-confrontational, pacifist beliefs, the Sikhs responded by taking up the sword to defend their right to live as they wanted. After Arjun's death at the hands of the Moguls, his eleven-year-old son, Hargobind, assumed his place as guru with two swords strapped to his waist: one a symbol of spiritual supremacy, the other a symbol of temporal power. The act ended what had been for a hundred years the religion's tacit acceptance of the separation of temple and state. It began the militarization of the faith which led ultimately to the conception of a Sikh theocracy that would grow into the modern demand for Khalistan.

Manipulated by his father's friends and relatives, the child-guru defied the emperor, too. His supporters built a fortress at Amritsar called Lohgarh, or "castle of steel". Across from the Harimandir, on the edge of the sacred pool, they constructed another temple called the Akal Takht, the "shrine of the timeless God", to serve as their secular house of parliament. The Harimandir reverberated with the chanting of the Sikhs at prayer, while the Akal Takht echoed with the din of the Sikhs forging their military and political strategy. Inside, Hargobind sat on a throne higher than the emperor's in a game of seventeenth-century one-upmanship. But despite the Sikh bravado, there was little chance of them ever seriously challenging the Mogul's dominance.

The guru was intermittently imprisoned. When a squad of bailiffs sent to arrest him again in 1627 was murdered, however, the ensuing manhunt forced Hargobind's family and the others to flee

into the Himalayan foothills near Tibet. The Sikhs were no match
for the Mogul army in open battle. For the rest of the seventeenth
century, they contented themselves with living in mountain
hideouts, occasionally venturing from their strongholds to skirmish
with opposing hill chiefs and the Mogul army.

Still, across Punjab their temples were destroyed and captured
Sikhs were forcibly converted to Islam. Many Sikhs refused to
renounce Nanak even under threat of execution. The ninth Sikh
guru, Tegh Bahadur, was beheaded for refusing to embrace Islam,
and the sanguinary spectacle strengthened the resolve of the Sikhs
to resist what they interpreted as religious oppression. Martyrdom
became a cornerstone of the religion, a sign of its authenticity and a
measure of its members.

Tegh Bahadur's son, Gobind Rai, was nine in 1675 when his
father's head was brought home to the Sikh city of Anandpur, the
guru's "haven of bliss". Nevertheless, he had an ample treasury to
support him and his family and he grew into a Sikh Renaissance
man, able to ride, shoot, and fence. He composed poems in Sanskrit,
Persian, Hindi, and Punjabi about moonlit nights heavy with the
scent of wild jasmine and the heat of lovers trysting by a river that
appears as a ribbon of quicksilver flashing through black mountains.
When he assumed the role of guru, his court had as many as fifty
poets and balladeers in residence in addition to warriors.

Gobind Rai wrote that his God was present in the "ambrosial
hours" of the morning and was *sarab-loh,* or "all steel" — the
sword. "I came into the world charged with the duty to uphold the
right in every place, to destroy sin and evil. O ye holy men, know it
well in your hearts that the only reason I took birth was to see that
righteousness may flourish: that the good may live and tyrants be
torn out by their roots."

Gobind Rai asked the Sikhs to give horses and arms in lieu of
money; he recruited volunteers and hired mercenaries. His moral
imperative for challenging the authority of the Moguls who
executed his father has been quoted by Sikhs ever since to justify
their use of violence: "When all avenues have been explored, all
means tried, it is rightful to draw the sword out of the scabbard and
wield it with your hand."

The tenth guru led his army to several victories and has become a mythic figure. His fame spread with the legends that were attached to his name. It was said that he could fire a shaft as far as the eye could see and that his arrowtips were made of gold to provide for the family of those he killed. He was pictured leading his troops into battle mounted on a roan stallion. They called him "rider of the blue horse", "lord of the white hawks", "the wearer of plumes".

But Gobind Rai could see that while rural Punjabis welcomed him, embraced Sikhism, and paid him homage when he was victorious, most denounced him when the Moguls returned. He saw that if the way of life Sikhs believed in was to survive, then those who believed in it must be ready to fight to the death. Gobind resolved to make it more difficult for Sikhs to flee or deny their faith. Aside from their rejection of the rituals of caste, there was nothing to differentiate a Sikh from a Hindu in the Punjab. Gobind Rai completed the transformation of the pacifist, egalitarian faith of Nanak into a militant, religious body distinct from both Hinduism and Islam.

In 1699, he asked everyone who called himself a Sikh to come to the mountain city for the harvest festival of Baisakh. At morning service on the first day of the spring holiday, the guru appeared before the crowd, brandished his sword, and demanded five martyrs. One man rose and was led inside a tent by Gobind. There was a scream, blood seeped under the tent flap, and the guru emerged calling for another. The performance continued until five of his followers had volunteered, entered the tent, screamed, and apparently died.

After the fifth martyr, the guru came out and so did the men. Inside the tent were five butchered goats. Gobind told the crowd that it was the men's willingness to die that saved them. He called them his beloved and announced that they would form the backbone of the new militant order he was founding: the Khalsa, "the pure". It was the climax of the militarization of the Sikh faith begun under his grandfather, Hargobind.

With a double-edged dagger, Gobind Rai stirred an iron bowl filled with sugared water he called *amrit,* or nectar. As he chanted, he baptised the men whose names are still repeated at the end of the faithful's every prayer: Daya Ram, Dharam Das, Mohkam Chand, Sahib Chand, and Himmat Rai. One was a Brahman, one a Kshatrya, and the rest commoners. All drank from the bowl, emphasizing the elimination of caste. Gobind told them that they had been reborn and would call themselves Singh, or lion. Their women would be called Kaur, a word meaning lioness or princess. He was their father: Gobind Singh. Their mother was his barren third wife, Sahib Devan. They were to be one family, a brotherhood of the pure.

He gave them signs called "the Five Ks" so they would recognize each other: they should let their hair (*kesh*) grow uncut as God intended; they should carry a comb (*kangha*); they should wear soldier's breeches (*kachha*) at all times so they are ready to defend themselves; they should wear a steel bracelet (*kara*) on their right wrist; and they should wear a sword (*kirpan*). The signs would also make it difficult for them to pretend to be Hindus in times of crisis.

Gobind hailed the brotherhood as God's elect and told them to similarly baptise all Sikhs. It was a turning point in the faith's history and the root of its modern-day crisis. The tenth guru had established two classes of Sikhs: the *keshadhari,* or initiated, those who wore their hair uncut, and the *sahajdharis,* or slow adopters. But schisms among the followers of Nanak were nothing new. For several generations, there were Punjabis who considered themselves Sikhs, but who had rejected the leadership of the guru. There had been disputes about the selection of some gurus, and various pretenders led small communities of followers.

Without formal strictures, initiation rites, or ceremonies, Sikhism had developed in a haphazard fashion. Guru Hargobind had modified Nanak's message by grafting onto it the martial requirements dictated by the politics of the day. It had remained a religion whose distinguishing features were its social policies and belief in communal dining and meditation. Gobind Singh, however, not only established a military paradigm for Sikhs but proclaimed it as a definition: a true Sikh was a *keshadhari* Sikh. The *sahajdharis* were looked upon as Sikhs who hadn't yet made a full commitment to the faith, but one day would.

"When the guru had thus addressed the crowd, several Brahmans and Khatris stood up and said they accepted the religion of Nanak and the other gurus," reported the Mogul spies who watched the ceremony. "Thus, though several refused to accept the guru's religion, about twenty thousand men stood up and promised to obey him, as they had the fullest faith in his divine mission."

Gobind began military training and formed squads of warriors known as "Nihangs", a Persian word meaning "crocodile" that was used to describe the advance guards of the Mogul army. The Sikh Nihangs wore the same bright blue *kurta* and conducted mock battles in Anandpur to prepare for their holy war. The bulk of Gobind's new troops called themselves "Akalis", or servants of the timeless God. But the Sikhs never really bothered the Moguls enough to warrant the emperor's full attention.

Gobind Singh was stabbed in 1707 and, since he had no heir, on his deathbed he told his followers they should worship no one after him. Instead, he instructed them to consider the Adi Granth as their guide and only guru. It was an edict as controversial as his militarization of the faith. By making the holy book the supreme authority, Gobind also invested power in the strongest families within Sikhdom's body politic, the *keshadharis*. Popular support, not piety or blood, would be the measure of would-be Sikh leaders. The *keshadharis* represented a majority among the religion's establishment and they would make their decisions collectively at assemblies usually held at the Akal Takht in Amritsar.

By 1776, the Muslim empire was collapsing. The English and French were insinuating themselves into the subcontinent's economy and the Mogul emperor was more than amenable to making his peace with the Sikhs. He agreed to accept the estates their leaders had created and acknowledged their right to collect tithes from landowners in their district.

The struggle for political control of the Punjab, however, would continue. The success and affluence of the Sikh leaders and their support among the rural families nurtured the nascent nationalism of the dominant Jats. The home-grown faith, the emphasis on the language of the people, the democratic structures and the implicit idea of the rule of the righteous fostered a belief that the Punjab should be ruled by the people who lived there. The man who fulfilled those longings for self-government was born on November 13, 1780.

Ranjit Singh Sukerchakia was said to be a descendant of Budh Singh, a man said to have been baptised by Guru Gobind Singh. His father died when he was twelve and bequeathed to Ranjit a large district in the heart of the Punjab. Ranjit, a wiry man of swarthy complexion, was blinded in his left eye by smallpox, and his face was deeply pitted. He learned to hunt and ride, fight and drink. Through marriage, he gained control of a huge swath of the Punjab and dreamed of carving an empire for himself. His ambition had little to do with piety; it was the passion of a man who would be king.

He achieved his dream at eighteen when he led a united Sikh army against the invading Afghan Chief Shah Zaman who hoped to exploit India's political unrest. "The Khalsa [the pure] shall rule," chanted the Sikh crusaders. "Their enemies will be scattered. Only they that seek refuge will be saved."

Ranjit's forces defeated the Afghan and captured Lahore in 1799. His first public act was to pay homage at the city's mosques. On the first day of the spring harvest festival Baisakh in 1801, the anniversary of the founding of the militant *keshadhari* community that now called itself the Khalsa, Ranjit Singh's forehead was daubed with saffron paste and he was proclaimed Maharajah of the Punjab. A royal salute was fired, Ranjit Singh mounted an elephant and moved through the city showering people with gold and silver coins bearing the image of Nanak, the first Sikh guru.

Ranjit consolidated his power by regularly holding court. He recruited new administrators and revised the revenue and judicial systems of the Moguls. He repaired the city, posted pickets at strategic points to curb crime, and divided the region into wards, each under a head man who reported to him. Since most of his subjects in Lahore were Muslim, he established separate courts for them. He opened dispensaries where medicine was available free. While Ranjit considered himself a Sikh, and the backbone of his army was culled from Jat peasant stock, he emphasized that his was not a Sikh kingdom but a Punjabi state.

The first Sikh maharaja made it clear that there was a complete separation of temple and state by engaging in a variety of activities expressly forbidden by the ten Sikh gurus. He paid homage to Hindu gods and Muslim divines. "God wanted me to look upon all religions with one eye; that is why he took away the light from the other," he explained.

He surrounded himself with soothsayers, astrologers, and charlatans, liked a glass of Scotch whisky, and had his own brandy distilled, it is said, using crushed pearls. But he also listened to the poetry of the Adi Granth for an hour a day, bathed in the sacred pool at Amritsar, and reconstructed the Harimandir in marble and gold leaf to create a golden temple.

In later years, Ranjit Singh was a laudanum addict who looked "exactly like an old mouse, with gray whiskers". But he established a kingdom from the Kashmir and the borders of China to the Khyber Pass and the deserts of Sindh. Only the British who propped up the Mogul emperor in Delhi kept him from expanding south.

The British recognized Ranjit's military might early in his reign and opened diplomatic relations with him by sending Lord William Godolphin Osborne to his court. "The coup d'oeil was most striking," he reported. "Every walk in the garden was lined with troops, and the whole space behind the throne was crowded with Runjeet's chiefs, mingled with natives from Candahar, Caubul and Afghanistan, blazing with gold and jewels, and dressed and armed in every conceivable variety of color and fashion. Cross-legged in a golden chair, dressed in simple white, wearing no ornaments but a single string of pearls around the waist, and the celebrated Koh-y-Nur [diamond], or mountain of light, on his arm — the jewel rivalled, if not surpassed, in brilliancy by the glance of fire which every now and then shot from his single eye as it wandered restlessly round the circle — sat the lion of Lahore."

On June 27, 1839, forty years after he entered Lahore as a conquering hero, Ranjit Singh died.

While Ranjit Singh's secular accomplishments were enormous, the Sikh faith had continued to fracture. Gobind Singh had created two classes of Sikhs and his refusal to appoint a successor made it possible for Ranjit Singh to cleave the union of temple and state that guruship had represented after Hargobind. Now, there were Khalsa Sikhs who aspired to secular political leadership and others more concerned about religious affairs, such as maintaining the temples and studying and copying the Adi Granth. There were also large numbers of *sahajdharis* and others who called themselves Sikhs but venerated their own leaders. In the political upheaval that followed Ranjit's death, there were predictions that the schisms would become so serious that the religion would soon be absorbed back into Hinduism. The British saved the Khalsa Sikhs.

The English merchants of the British East India Company recognized the rifts in the Sikh community and skillfully exploited them to undermine the kingdom established by Ranjit Singh. By the end of 1846 the British had assumed full control of the Punjab and its administration.

There were insurrections over the following three years, and at Chillianwala a Sikh force handed the British one of their worst defeats on the subcontinent. But on March 29, 1849, Sikh rule in the Punjab ended. Ranjit's ten-year-old son, Dalip Singh, handed over the Koh-i-noor diamond and abdicated. The Union Jack fluttered over Lahore, Sikh currencies were withdrawn, and the East India Company's rupee became the coin of the realm. Punjabis were ordered to surrender their weapons, and a board of civilian and army officers ruled.

The British introduced a new criminal code, demolished the forts, and redistributed land. New varieties of crops were introduced: New Orleans cotton, flax, and tobacco. Italian rams were imported, as were silkworms. The tax system was refined, and the British assumed control of the lucrative salt mines.

The British alienated the local chieftains by decreeing that on their deaths their estates would lapse to the East India Company. Even the Mogul royal family was forced to hand over its palace and the massive Red Fort at New Delhi. The demand for written title in illiterate India caused even greater anxiety and unrest. At the same time, Christian missionaries were swarming across the continent and winning large numbers of converts. The Khalsa Sikhs, with their still swollen pride, were stunned when Ranjit Singh's son Dalip converted to Christianity in 1853 and left for England where he was given an estate in Suffolk and became a favorite of Queen Victoria.

Leaderless, stripped of their weapons, the Khalsa were dejected. But when the Hindus and Muslims, enraged at what they considered an attempt by the British to eradicate their faiths, mutinied in 1857, the Sikhs rallied behind the Raj.

In the Punjab, the Sikhs were reluctant to return to war, especially to restore either Mogul or Hindu rule. The Khalsa had been fighting the Moguls for centuries and they weren't about to join in common cause with the Hindus who only eight years before had helped to destroy their kingdom and who insisted on treating them as men of low caste. Most of the Sikhs remained loyal to the British. Sikh gunners were recruited and laborers who had been working on roads and canals were conscripted.

The uprising was quelled and the Sikhs were rewarded for their loyalty with grants of territory, confiscated palaces, titles, and new jobs. In reordering the British army afterwards, the English designated *keshadhari* Sikhs a "martial race" and declared many of the Hindus, who had won most of the battles for the East India Company, unfit for military service and "non-martial". The government reserved administrative posts for *keshadhari* Sikhs and began recruiting them for the army. Regulations were enacted stipulating that their separate identity must be maintained: "The paol, or religious pledges of Sikh fraternity, should on no account be interfered with. . . . Any invasion, however slight, of these obligations would be construed as a desire to subvert his faith, lead to evil consequences, and naturally inspire general distrust and alarm. Even those who have assumed the outward conventional characteristics of Sikhs should not be permitted after entering the British Army to drop them."

Officers scoured Punjabi villages and distributed land to the *keshadhari* Sikhs they considered the best farmers to colonize the stretches of barren wasteland to be serviced by new canals. Selected Sikh peasants, mainly Jats, were given free parcels of up to 6.5 hectares, and more affluent Sikhs were sold larger tracts of scrubland for nominal sums.

By 1861 there was a rail link between Lahore and Amritsar and over the next thirty years a network of tracks was laid down connecting the canal colonies with the cities. As a result, land prices soared and the Khalsa Sikhs joined the most prosperous of the Punjabis.

The British had inadvertently resuscitated the Sikh community by endorsing Gobind Singh's vision as a definition of a Sikh: in the eyes of the government a true Sikh was a *keshadhari*, a member of the Khalsa. The British made it profitable to be a baptised Sikh and the rest of India's poverty-stricken people took note. The Jats who joined Gobind's crusade had risen to become the land-owning aristocracy under Ranjit Singh, and had cemented their position under the British. They rose above even the Brahmans. Other Sikh families were able to abandon their hereditary callings as scavengers and laborers to become soldiers and farmers. Their fellow Untouchables who remained Hindus and the Muslims received no similar benefits.

As a result of the British initiatives, the ranks of the Sikhs swelled with new converts. The Muslims largely shunned the Sikhs with whom they had been battling for the better part of two centuries. But many Hindu families began raising one of their sons as a Sikh so he would benefit from the economic measures specially introduced to reward the Khalsa.

It was easy for the Hindus to embrace Sikhism for several reasons not the least of which was that many believed that it was only a branch of their own multi-faceted faith. The distinction between the two religions in theory always had been blurred in practice.

Sikhism had few special rites that set it apart — although to Gobind Singh's commandments, the faith had added prohibitions against tobacco, alcohol, meat, and sex with Muslim women. Many of the Sikh temples, or *gurdwaras*, were used by both faiths and controlled by Hindus whose families were given the job during the Muslim persecutions when a *gurdwara* manager would have been killed had he been a Sikh.

But if the new converts helped resurrect Sikh pride they also exacerbated the fragmentation of the faith and heightened concern among the Khalsa leaders that the schisms would ultimately destroy the religion.

Dyal Das, a bullion merchant in Peshawar, was an example of what they feared. The son of a Hindu, Das was raised a Sikh and became a respected religious leader by condemning idol worship, obeisance to holy men, pilgrimages, and Brahmanic rituals. He argued that the most important aspect of Nanak's message was his conception of God as formless, or *nirankar*, and not the martial traditions added later. He called himself a Nirankari.

His followers, the Nirankaris, fell somewhere between orthodox Hinduism, with its castes and rituals, and the Sikhism of the Khalsa, with its central tenets of Gobind Singh's martial imperatives. The Nirankaris built their own temples, the largest outside of Rawalpindi in what is today northern Pakistan.

The Nirankaris, who continued to use the Granth as their holy book, also developed a series of standardized services for births, marriages and deaths. They claimed to have developed the Anand Marriage, a ceremony adopted by Khalsa Sikhs in which the bride and groom walk around the Granth. Such marriages were given legal status in 1909.

There really was little difference between the Khalsa and the Nirankaris other than the latter's refusal to accept the primacy of the militarist elements of Sikhism and insistence on recognizing a living guru. At the end of their prayers, they closed with the word *nirankar*, or "formless", instead of the word used by Khalsa Sikhs, *bhagwati*, or "sword". The Nirankari disliked the image of God as the "all-steel" crucifix of Gobind Singh and argued that the word was also the name of a Hindu goddess. The Nirankaris called Das and his descendants "the true guru" and "his holy eminence", which was a blasphemy to the Khalsa. They were the most hated of the heretics and would spark the Khalsa's bloody crusade against the Indian government nearly a century later.

The concerns of the Khalsa leadership over the fracturing of the faith were heightened, however, by the rise of Hindu chauvinism led by a Brahman named Swami Dayanand Sarswati. He was an iconoclast whose powerful sermons, monotheism, and egalitarian message appealed to Sikhs while his motto "back to the Vedas" and emphasis on early Aryan traditions appealed to the Hindus. He gained many converts, established a paramilitary group too, and published a book that was banned by the government because of its virulent attack on the Sikh, Christian, and Muslim traditions.

In response to such threats, the affluent Sikh leadership — the families of those rewarded by the British for undermining Ranjit Singh's kingdom as well as those who had prospered since the Mutiny — founded a society called the Singh Sabha to shore up the faith of the Khalsa. Encouraged by the English because they preached undying loyalty to the Raj, the group opened schools, published religious literature, and campaigned against illiteracy.

The political climate deteriorated rapidly in the Punjab at the turn of the century when famines, pestilence, punitive land laws, and tax hikes ravaged the state. Those who could afford to, began to emigrate; those who remained began demonstrating and killing Englishmen. The unrest forced the British administration to examine Punjab society and devise political institutions to defuse the problem. The electoral process was amended in 1909 but the changes began what has become a frustrating pattern of rejections for the Khalsa Sikh leadership's desire for secular power.

The Muslims demanded and received a separate system that allowed them to vote for their own candidates. The Sikhs, who numbered about three million out of a total Punjab population of about twenty-four million, made claims for similar treatment saying they were a "distinct and important people." They were rebuffed.

The Sikhs failed where the two dominant Indian religions succeeded partly because they lacked an effective leadership — their leading families owed too much to British patronage to offer serious opposition. They also were too indistinct a community as the existence of the various sects attested. Their disenchantment manifested itself in a fiery rekindling of the pride that had lain dormant since the days of Ranjit Singh. They began to clear their temples of Hindu idols and non-Sikh managers, many of whom had registered the *gurdwaras* and attached grounds in their own names with the introduction of written land title.

Many of the Sikhs who had migrated to North America returned complaining about discrimination and fomenting revolt. The activists among them argued that if Sikhs wanted real freedom and equality they would have to fight for it, as they had under Gobind Singh and under Ranjit Singh. The returning immigrants brought news of a network of revolutionaries operating within Indian communities along the west coast of Canada and the United States. They distributed copies of the fiery San Francisco newspaper published by the radicals called *Ghadr*, or "Revolution". They received help from the German government and claimed that if only those in the Punjab rose up, help would pour in from around the globe.

With money and guns supplied from North America, a wave of violence was unleashed in northern India. British offices were dynamited, train tracks sabotaged, and crowded stations and markets bombed. The British clamped down with repressive measures and staged a series of infamous conspiracy trials that ended in nearly five thousand Sikhs being convicted on flimsy or fabricated evidence. They were hanged, deported, or interned. In the temples, they were hailed as martyrs and elevated to the faith's pantheon of heroes.

The outbreak of the First World War gave U.S. authorities an excuse to arrest a leader of the *Ghadr* and an editor of the paper, Har Dayal, an Oxford-educated Indian, on charges of being an undesirable alien. Har Dayal skipped bail and fled to Germany where he joined a growing number of disenchanted Indians. He later returned to the United States to become a professor of Sanskrit and philosophy at the University of California at Berkeley.

The war sapped what little enthusiasm there was for protest among the Sikhs. Many of them had enlisted in the army, some because they wanted to support the British effort and others because of the economic opportunity it offered as a stepping-stone to prosperity. The Sikhs fought on all fronts and of the twenty-two military crosses awarded for conspicuous gallantry to Indians the Sikhs won fourteen. They returned home, however, not to be rewarded and respected for their sacrifices but to find local officials and police still treating them like peasants.

The Punjab at the time was also seething after bad harvests, enormous tax increases, and the restrictive measures introduced to suppress the nascent nationalist movement. Calls for self-government were dismissed by the British lieutenant-governor of the Punjab, Sir Michael O'Dwyer.

The pugnacious Irishman hated educated Indians and insulted them regularly with couplets culled from Alexander Pope. O'Dwyer was born in 1864, near Tipperary, one of fourteen children of an Irish farmer, and educated by the Jesuits. He went to India believing he had a divine right to rule. At fifty-four, in 1913, he was named lieutenant-governor of the Punjab and was described by his superiors as "determined to maintain his position as the idol of the reactionary forces, and to try and govern by the iron hand". He crushed the *Ghadr* movement, and when the Sikhs joined Mahatma Gandhi in opposing his repressive regime he vowed to crush them too.

O'Dwyer banned nationalist leaders from Punjab. There were riots. Police opened fire on crowds. In Amritsar when a group complained about arbitrary arrests, police killed two dozen and wounded thirty more while dispersing the crowd. A mob of thousands began to assault whites. At the English-owned Alliance Bank, the mob clubbed the manager to death, hurled his body from the balcony, and cremated it on a pile of bank furniture soaked in kerosene. The safe was robbed. In all, five Englishmen were killed and a woman missionary was badly beaten.

The British military commander, Brigadier General Reginald (Rex) Dyer declared a state of emergency. The fifty-five-year-old was the scion of a well-known family of northern Indian brewers, Dyer Meakin and Co. He was schooled at Simla, the summer residence of the British perched high in the Himalayas, and later at Sandhurst. He lived the life of a boy scout and grew up firmly believing whites were a superior race and chain-smoking cigarettes. Dyer was commissioned in 1885 and served in Ireland keeping apart the Orangemen and Republicans. He won a medal in Burma before returning to India in 1887 to establish his name as a swashbuckling soldier. "There should be an Eleventh Commandment in India," in his view: "Thou shalt not agitate."

Three days after the riots, on April 13, inside a dusty, walled square known as Jallianwala Bagh, in Amritsar, people were preparing to celebrate the spring harvest festival of Baisakh. They had begun to arrive in the square about a block from the Golden Temple before dawn. At dusk that evening, Dyer arrived with a platoon of infantry and blocked the only entrance. Without warning, the troops opened fire on the crowd. His fifty riflemen killed 379 people and wounded more than 1,000. They fired 1,650 rounds, and when they turned and marched out, the square was covered with the dead and wounded. The massacre shocked the world. As happened throughout the struggle for Indian independence, the blood of the Sikhs helped produce the change.

Whatever remained of the civilized rule of law collapsed. Dyer cut off the Sikh holy city's water and electricity. On the street where the English missionary woman was assaulted, he forced Indians at bayonet point to crawl on their bellies. Dozens of people lived in the multistoried buildings that flank the narrow, squalid lane. All who wanted to return to their homes were forced to crawl even though they had had nothing to do with the riots or the killings. Indians were flogged without trial and their vehicles confiscated.

Specially constituted courts summarily ordered fifty-one executions and the imprisonment of hundreds of men. There were reports of torture. It was illegal for more than two Indians to walk abreast. Electrical appliances such as fans were confiscated and distributed to British soldiers. Students were required to report to police four times a day. An Indian who failed to greet a white properly was forced to rub his nose on the ground and grovel. A local poet was ordered to write paeans to martial law and Dyer. Newspapers that dared to carry reports were banned and their editors imprisoned. In seven weeks, some 1,200 people were killed and at least 3,600 wounded.

A later British government enquiry unanimously recommended General Dyer's dismissal. But in India the British rallied around Dyer and a fund set up by the *Morning Post* in London raised an enormous sum for the soldier's retirement — Rudyard Kipling, W. B. Gladstone and other celebrities contributed money for "The Man Who Saved India". Dyer returned to England from India and died a broken man eight years after the massacre. He insisted to the last that he had only done his duty. His boss, O'Dwyer, was unscathed by the controversy. But twenty years later, at a meeting in London on March 13, 1940, he was assassinated by a Sikh orphan who had survived the slaughter.

Udham Singh, a nineteen-year-old carpenter distributing water to the crowd at the time, was shot in the arm. Later, as he bathed at the Golden Temple, he vowed to kill the bigoted lieutenant-governor. He left for America soon afterwards where he met with the survivors of the *Ghadr* movement. He smuggled guns into the Punjab with the help of a German woman and spent five years in prison after he was caught. On his release, he moved to Germany where there was a flourishing community of Indian radicals. Today there are a large number of Sikhs who still live there, maintaining their revolutionary politics and support for Khalistan.

Udham Singh entered Britain with a phony passport in 1933 and forged ties with Irish Republican Army gun-runners on the Isle of Wight. He was a clean-shaven Sikh who liked well-cut suits, spoke good English, and was soon a well-known figure in London's Sikh community. After he gunned down the seventy-five-year-old O'Dwyer, he was hailed by Germany as a freedom fighter and the Sikhs raised money for his defense.

The government carefully censored news from the trial. The jury deliberated only an hour and forty minutes before convicting him. As the Battle of Britain raged overhead, Udham Singh was hanged on June 13, 1940, and buried in an unmarked grave. The government refused the request of a Sikh temple for the return of his corpse. But thirty-four years later, at dawn on June 10, 1974, his body was exhumed and an Air India jet bore his remains back to India to be received by Punjab's chief minister Zail Singh with a martyr's welcome. In the Golden Temple his picture was hung as an inspiration to Sikhs over a sign that read: "A great revolutionary".

The British government sealed many of the documents concerning the Amritsar massacre for fifty years and documents concerning O'Dwyer's assassination remain sealed for a hundred years.

After the massacre at Jallianwala Bagh, the Sikhs became strident in their demand for control of their temples. The government made token gestures to appease them. It exempted the Sikhs from weapons restrictions to allow them to carry their swords, and it permitted jailed Sikhs to wear their religious emblems. But on November 15, 1920, the Sikhs convened at the Akal Takht and demanded the right to manage all of their shrines and administer their considerable treasuries. They announced that a committee of Khalsa Sikhs had been formed to carry this out. It was called the Shiromani Gurdwara Prabandhak Committee — the Central Shrine Management Committee.

They also formed a paramilitary organization called the Akali Dal, or "Army of Immortals", to peacefully recover the *gurdwaras* still in the hands of recalcitrant, British-backed managers known as *mahants*. The Akali Dal would become the Sikh political party. Extremist Sikhs formed a group called the Babbar Akalis, or the "Immortal Tigers". They launched a campaign of terror to support the Akali's peaceful protests.

Many of the *mahants* handed over the properties to elected committees and became paid *granthis*, or priests. At some temples, however, the battle became bloody. As a result of the violence and demonstrations, several districts were again placed under martial law and the Khalsa leaders jailed. The Sikhs donned black turbans in honor of those who were killed in the struggle. They boycotted British goods, and the government responded with another clampdown, this time jailing 1,200 people. *Jathas*, or squads, of one hundred Akalis were formed to protest the arrests.

Protestors gathered at the Golden Temple. They swore to remain non-violent and would march out of the temple to protest. The police would meet them on the road and order them to disperse. When the Akalis refused, they were beaten to the ground with *lathis*. The news dispatches horrified the world.

Nearly two thousand Sikhs required hospital treatment before the police were ordered to stop the beatings. Thousands of people were restricted to their villages and the property of Akali supporters was confiscated. State police fired on groups of unarmed demonstrators and the government accused the Akalis of trying to restore Sikh rule in the Punjab. The charge only brought more support to the party.

More than 10,000 were arrested by October when the government finally capitulated by passing the Sikh Gurdwaras Act of 1925, which met all the Akali demands. Elected management committees replaced the *mahants*. They reported to the 151 members of the SGPC, the Central Shrine Management Committee, which would form the religious parliament of the Sikhs.

The SGPC was given control over two hundred shrines and their revenue in the Punjab. Today it controls several hundred shrines and their annual revenue of about $12 million (U.S.). It is the main Sikh political institution. There was patronage in the appointment of hundreds of *granthis*, temple servants, teachers, and professors for Sikh schools and colleges. There were arrangements for the training of *granthis* and for missionaries outside of the Punjab. Its control became the focal point of Sikh politics and it ended the debate over who a Sikh was: He was a member of the Khalsa, a follower of Gobind Singh, and only baptised Sikhs would be eligible to vote and to participate in the SGPC.

More than 30,000 Sikhs had been arrested, 400 killed and 2,000 wounded. Retired soldiers had forfeited their pensions and a ban had been placed on civil and military recruitment of Sikhs. The number of Sikhs in the army was reduced from 20 per cent in 1914 to 13 per cent in 1930.

With their political base and treasuries returned and the feeling that India would soon be free, the Sikhs turned their attention to achieving secular power. The burning issue became whether they or the Muslims would rule the Punjab after India gained independence. The killings and violence were no longer directed at the British but at the rival religious community. The Second World War heightened the tension and differences between the two faiths that had warred for centuries. The Hindus, who were assured of power in an independent India because of their numbers, were above the fight.

In 1940 the Muslim League passed a resolution demanding a sovereign state incorporating the Islamic communities of India and most of the Punjab. The Sikhs, who had fought Muslim domination from the time of their sixth guru, realized that they were trapped: they could join with the India National Congress and fight the Muslims, or call for their own state. The outbreak of the war in the Pacific split the Sikhs.

When the Hindu-dominated Congress Party asked for non-cooperation with the government, the Sikhs were caught in an economic and political bind. The Akali party couldn't decide where it stood. Many of them served in the armed forces and civil service and few wanted to jeopardize their jobs. In the end, the Akalis agreed to back the government in exchange for more Sikh recruitment. Master Tara Singh, a leading Sikh Akali since the 1920s, broke with Congress over the issue and earned the enmity of its leaders who would later dominate Indian politics.

Born a Hindu, Tara Singh had converted to Sikhism at school and became a schoolmaster after earning his B.A., then deserted the classroom for politics. He was photographed promoting recruitment with a steel helmet over his turban. Still, many Sikhs with him disagreed and many actively fought the British through sabotage in India or by joining the Japanese.

A squadron of the Central India Horse refused orders to head overseas. More than a hundred soldiers were court-martialed, there were several executions, and Sikh leaders were deported to the Andaman Islands. Some Sikhs deserted and there was a ban on Sikh recruitment.

After Pearl Harbor, the Japanese began meeting with rebel Indian leaders. There were two million Indians, many of them Sikhs, scattered across southern Asia: in Thailand, Cambodia, the Philippines, Burma, Malaya, and Singapore. Sikh agents for the Japanese had infiltrated into Malaya and were caught and sentenced to ten years in jail before they were freed by the Japanese. Three of the men who formed the Provincial Government of Azad Hind (Free India), an aspiring Asian Vichy recognized by the Axis powers, were Sikhs. It declared war on Britain and the United States.

As they moved across Asia, the Japanese recruited Indian prisoners of war from captured British units to form the Indian National Army. Half of the twenty thousand men who joined were Sikhs, and the first brigade was at the vanguard of the Japanese assault that captured Singapore. But its record in battle was dismal. Of the six thousand soldiers who set out to capture Imphal, more than fifteen hundred deserted or surrendered; only four hundred died in battle. Disease killed nearly two thousand. After the war, the British were reluctant to prosecute the INA soldiers as they were seen as fighting for Indian independence, a prospect now imminent.

After the war, the Sikhs were faced with two rival freedom movements. The Congress Party wanted an independent India but was unwilling to concede to the Sikhs the economic privileges they enjoyed under the Raj; the Muslim League wanted to divide the Punjab. Many Sikhs originally pinned their hopes on the Congress, but broke with the Hindu-dominated party when it agreed to Partition. They opposed the division of India and said that if the Muslims were to get a nation, they wanted one too. On March 22, 1946, the Akali Dal passed a resolution calling for the creation of "Sikhistan". It was the beginning of the modern Sikh separatist movement.

The Sikhs argued that they owned the richest farms and were the pioneers who colonized most of the Punjab. They claimed the Muslims were using faulty census figures to buttress the call for Pakistan. The British ignored the Sikh pleas. Sir Stafford Cripps told the British Parliament: "The difficulty arises, not from anyone's underestimation of the importance of the Sikh community, but from the inescapable geographical facts of the situation. What the Sikhs demand is some special treatment analogous to that given to the Muslims. The Sikhs, however, are a much smaller community, five-and-a-half million against ninety million, and are not geographically situated so that any area as yet desired . . . can be carved out in which they would find themselves in a majority."

His argument has been the bane of those who would create Sikhistan, or Khalistan, ever since.

The British gave thirteen of the twenty-nine districts of the Punjab to India. The rest, about 62 per cent of the province, was awarded to Pakistan. The richest Sikh lands, half the Sikh population, and more than 150 of the religion's shrines, including Guru Nanak's birthplace and Ranjit Singh's capital, were inside the new Muslim state.

India received mainly scrubland and little of the irrigation system built by the British. Two million Sikhs caught on the wrong side of the line were terrified of being trapped in a Muslim theocracy.

There were riots and massacres across the state as the two communities turned on each other ferociously. Faced with Muslim domination, the easily identifiable Sikhs began fleeing into the central and eastern Punjab. They were murdered, their women raped and abducted, and many were forced to convert to Islam. They fled along with an estimated two million Hindus. An equal number of Muslims inside India started moving in the opposite direction.

Nearly 10 million people were marching across Punjab, and the violence was savage. Roads were littered with corpses. Trains arrived in stations bearing grisly cargoes of slaughtered passengers. The sick, the aged, the infirm, and the young were butchered. It was a holocaust of unimaginable proportions. One estimate put the number of dead at 500,000.

In refugee camps operated by the Indian government more than 700,000 sought shelter. The property abandoned by the Muslims was distributed to the refugees where possible. The official figures indicated about 4.3 million people fled Pakistan and a similar number of Muslims left India. The land the Muslims abandoned amounted to almost 5 million acres of relatively poor soil, while the Sikhs and Hindus had abandoned nearly 7 million acres of rich wheat-bearing land.

In the newly created country of India, laws were passed restricting the size of land holdings to 12 hectares. Consequently, Sikh farmers could not hope to acquire land such as they had owned before. The urban Sikhs were also hurt. The Muslims had left almost no city property compared with what the Sikhs had relinquished in Pakistan. Sikh merchants found themselves having to set up shop again and compete not only with Hindu refugees but also with the established traders. The trucking and transportation industry, in which Sikhs maintained a veritable monopoly, was nationalized. Their control of taxi and bus services in Calcutta was ended. The privileged access they had enjoyed to the armed forces and the civil service was reduced. Sikh political aspirations had been frustrated and remained unfulfilled. The glowing embers of the ambition Gobind Singh instilled in the Khalsa would be ignited rather than doused in the new nation.

3. INDIAN POLITICS

India's first prime minister, Jawaharlal Nehru, assumed office at midnight on August 15, 1947. He presided over a nation of 300 million peasants who earned an average wage of a nickel a day. All but one in ten were illiterate. One in four residents of India's two largest cities lived, procreated, and died on the sidewalks. But for the first time in a millennium their plight couldn't be blamed on foreigners — they were a free and independent nation. Overhead fluttered a tricolored sash of homespun cotton. At the center of the horizontal bands of saffron, white, and green was a wheel framed by two rampant lions. It was the wheel of the cosmic order, a symbol of the Hindu empire founded three centuries before the birth of Christ.

Nehru's government was faced with the monumental task of redrawing the country's internal map. British India had a dual personality: one was a collection of provinces administered from Delhi and the other was composed of 562 princely states, some the remnants of the Sikh empire. The princes had maintained their rights and powers by signing treaties with the British recognizing their military superiority and the supremacy of the Viceroy in New

Delhi. Some held sway over kingdoms little bigger than a cow pasture, but all were sovereign and some maintained armies equipped with tanks.

India's religions further complicated Nehru's task. With their warlords, private militias, and fanatics, the holy men were as much of a threat to the new country's stability as the principalities. The communal riots and the bloodbath of Partition had proven that. Less than six months later, the point was emphasized when a Hindu extremist pumped three bullets out of a black Beretta pistol into the chest of the nation's spiritual leader Mahatma Gandhi. Nehru's new government was to build a nation from a country that appeared always on the verge of a religious apocalypse. The Sikhs were only one fuse to the powder keg.

In the initial reorganization of the country, the Punjab was split into two administrative units. The Sikh princely states were merged into an area known as the Patiala and the East Punjab States Union. Roughly half of the people in the new province were Sikh and the other half were Hindu. The Sikhs, bloodied and angered by Partition, expected at the very least to have their own state within the new federation. For them, independence was a tragedy. Many had lost everything and their beloved province had been mutilated. "You will err in attempting to extinguish, in the name of nationalism, the distinctive entity of the Sikhs," the Akali Dal leader Master Tara Singh told the new government. "We value our honor. If we have no separate existence, we shall have nothing to be proud of."

But Nehru dismissed the request. He also refused to name Amritsar the capital of the Indian Punjab saying it was too close to the border with Pakistan. Instead, Nehru commissioned the Swiss architect Le Corbusier to build a new city called Chandigarh on the banks of a man-made lake. (Le Corbusier laid down a grid and threw up massive administrative buildings that are considered among his finest pieces of work.) And Nehru tried to appease the Sikhs by pouring millions of dollars into the Punjab for canals and dams. It was not enough. The Sikhs wanted a state they could call their own, where their language would be spoken and their faith protected.

The government, however, declared the Punjab bilingual. The Akalis attacked the move saying that the only spoken language in the state was Punjabi and that the local literature, except for the works of the Muslim Sufis, was in the *gurmukhi* script. Haryana, a dry, sandy region attached to the Punjab after the Mutiny in 1857, was the only Hindi-speaking region and the Akalis argued that it should be severed.

There were three languages in the Punjab: Urdu, Hindi and Punjabi, which was the most widely spoken. The languages had become synonymous with the three religions: Urdu with Islam, Hindi with Hinduism and Punjabi with Sikhism. The Akalis wanted Punjabi written in *gurmukhi* script — the alphabet of the gurus — to be the official language. It was a demand motivated as much by religious chauvinism as linguistic fealty: Punjabi and Sikhism are integral. Where Punjabi fluency falls off, the rate of apostasy soars. The faithful cannot read the Granth, or observe Sikh ritual or Khalsa tradition without the language. Modern Punjabi bears much the same relation to the language of the gurus as modern English bears to the language of Chaucer.

The state government created three areas in which the students were taught in the predominant language. The Akalis responded by agitating for a Punjabi state, a "Punjabi Suba". It was a demand for a separate Sikh state although the politicians pretended it was a language dispute. "This cover," Tara Singh admitted later, "of a Punjabi-speaking-state slogan serves my purpose well since it does not offend against nationalism. The government should accept our demand under the slogan of a Punjabi-speaking state without a probe — what we want is Azadi [independence]. We will revolt to win our Azadi."

Revolt they did. The first riots between the Hindus and the Sikhs over the issue occurred in 1951. To defuse the situation and similar tensions elsewhere, Nehru established the States Reorganization Commission with a view to creating linguistic states. It raised Sikh hopes that they would one day rule again and they began demonstrating to increase their chances. Their hopes were dashed when the commission issued its report. It recommended thirteen of India's fifteen major languages receive formal homes but rejected the Sikh claim because Punjabi wasn't sufficiently distinct from Hindi and lacked "the general support of the people."

Tara Singh labeled the ruling a "decree of annihilation" and began another agitation. He rode through the warren-like lanes of Amritsar on an elephant. Behind him marched a huge procession of Sikhs brandishing swords and axes. New Delhi agreed to talks but, throughout, Nehru and the Congress Party stonewalled while siphoning support from the Akalis by exploiting the internal rifts of the Sikh community. Many of the faith's best politicians defected or were lured into joining the Congress with the promise of top jobs.

Sikh businessmen and merchants, who were a minority within the faith but who had dominated its leadership since the days of the gurus, feared the increasing militancy of the peasants who constituted a majority within the religion. The middle class backed the Congress because they believed it would better protect their interests and because they believed the Akalis had little chance of forming a government because of their narrow religious platform. In breaking with their brethren they turned their fear into a self-fulfilling prophesy.

After a decade of frustration, Tara Singh asked the Central Shrine Management Committee, or SGPC, for a mandate to launch peaceful agitations against New Delhi. He was assured of finding support as only those who maintained Khalsa traditions were eligible to vote for what is considered the Sikh Parliament. He and his supporters won nearly all the seats in the 1960 SGPC elections, and the victory emboldened them. Posters appeared across the province warning Sikhs that the Hindus were readying to destroy the Sikhs and calling for a crusade, a *dharm yudh*.

Tara Singh and more than twenty thousand of his supporters were arrested in the ensuing nonviolent protests. With the rural Sikhs continuing to demonstrate and the jails bursting, the government capitulated. The Sikh leader was released and the holy war called off in January 1961 when the Congress administration promised to look into Sikh grievances. When little progress was made, Tara Singh began a fast unto death. But he abandoned it six weeks later amid rumors that he was actually gaining weight. It was a political suicide. He was arraigned at the Akal Takht, and sentenced to clean the shoes of pilgrims for five days. He was quickly ousted from both the Akali Dal party and the SGPC, and died in ignominy.

Sant Fateh Singh, a Jat Sikh priest-cum-social-worker, replaced Tara Singh. It was a fundamental change in the Sikh leadership as the dominant caste, the Jats, had finally gained control. The ten gurus and almost every Sikh leader after them, including Tara Singh, were members of the Khatri caste, the urban merchants who numbered about 20 per cent of the faithful. The China-Indian War kept the Sikhs from protesting and both the state and national governments used the time to forestall future outbreaks.

When Nehru died in 1964 and Shri Lal Bahadur Shastri was appointed prime minister, Fateh Singh used the political turmoil to launch another campaign for a Punjabi state. But his fast unto death was postponed by the Pakistani invasion of India.

Shastri died in the Soviet city of Tashkent only hours after he signed the treaty formally ending the 1965 war. The Congress Party bosses were divided over the succession but elected Nehru's daughter, Indira Gandhi, partly because they believed her inexperience would make it easy to manipulate her. They were wrong.

After she became prime minister, Mrs. Gandhi immediately sought allies to help her break the grip of the men known as the Syndicate who had engineered her victory. In March 1966, she agreed to create a Punjabi-speaking state after assurances from Sikh leader Fateh Singh that his demand was linguistic and not secessionist. The valor of the Sikhs in the border areas during the war with Pakistan provided ample proof of their nationalism and, under a reorganization bill, the Punjab was split into three states. The Hindi-speaking plains became the new state of Haryana with a border running up to Delhi. The foothills of the Himalayas became the new state of Himachal Pradesh. The rest remained Punjab, a state of about twelve million people, roughly half of whom were Sikhs.

It was an auspicious beginning for Mrs. Gandhi's relationship with the influential minority. But by failing to live up to many of the promises she made she also sowed the seeds of anger that led finally to her assassination.

The Sikhs had their state but it was only nine of the original thirteen British districts awarded to India. They were also forced to share the capital city of Chandigarh with neighboring Haryana until that state built its own capital. In the meantime, the city would be administered by the central government and house both state assemblies.

Even in a greatly shrunken Punjab, however, the Sikhs lacked the numbers to govern in a democracy. The urban poor and the businessmen who were Sikhs had competing economic interests and balked at supporting the Akali Dal politically with its socialist policies aimed primarily at aiding the peasants and the farmers. The Congress Party was able to hold the Akali Dal to a constituency of only about 30 per cent of the total vote in the newly created state of Punjab. In the first election in 1967, Congress elected more Sikhs than the Akali Dal.

The Sikhs' political aspirations were suppressed, but the Punjab was prospering. Using new strains of wheat and heavy doses of fertilizers, the Sikh farmers increased their output enormously thanks largely to the investments of the central government. The state's industrial growth was more than 8 per cent a year — double the national average. The state was also changing from a land of villages to a modern urban society.

There are few mud huts in the Punjab unlike other Indian states and the young are relatively educated. More than twelve thousand primary schools were constructed, more than two thousand high schools, nearly two hundred colleges, and nine medical schools. The state's civil service was among the largest in India. The money allowed Sikhs to emigrate in record numbers to North America, particularly Canada, Europe, and the Gulf states. Sikhs who moved overseas sent home an estimated billion dollars a year. Television aerials cluttered the sky; furniture, refrigerators, stoves, fancy foodstuffs, and textiles filled the shops. The affluence dulled enthusiasm for political upheaval.

Still, the cities were dominated by non-Sikhs and the incoming industries were owned by Hindus who utilized cheap laborers from elsewhere. The Akalis had little political clout, and the Sikhs were losing their state. But the winds of the recession that began to blow across the industrialized world in the late 1970s began to take their toll on the faithful.

Overseas employment dried up as one foreign country after another demanded work permits and visas. There was no major industry in the Punjab to absorb the idle. The fabric of Sikh society began unraveling as men with waist-length hair sporting swords found it easier to change their ways than to maintain the outward manifestations of the Khalsa. The safety razor became the symbol of their heresy.

The central government further angered Sikhs by using its control of industrial licenses to steer investment to the poorer, more populous and vote-rich states of the "Cow Belt", the five Hindu states encircling New Delhi. About 70 per cent of the cotton and 60 per cent of the molasses were transported outside of the Punjab for processing because New Delhi wouldn't grant licences to local refineries. Farmers lined up for days at Punjabi sugar mills while identical mills in Haryana stood idle. The nationalization of the banks had dispersed capital, hindering private development in the state. Unemployment rose and land holdings shrank. The Sikhs demanded that the annual influx of two hundred thousand migrant Hindu farmhands from the states of Uttar Pradesh and Bihar be banned.

Mrs. Gandhi quieted the growing clamor for political change by announcing that the Punjab could have Chandigarh if it surrendered to Haryana two areas — Abohar and Fazilka — in which the Hindus were in a majority. Once again, she seemed to have appeased the Sikhs. When she crushed the Muslim army and amputated East Pakistan in 1971, her ascendancy was assured. She swept state elections and won a massive majority nationally. But she ignored her promise to the Sikhs and they began to realize that political realities condemned them forever to minority status.

The Akalis responded by rekindling the militant fundamentalism of Gobind Singh. In 1973, on the anniversary of the founding of the Khalsa, the Akali Dal met at Anandpur, the guru's "haven of bliss". The Sikhs hoped the site would help spark the old crusading fire and they emerged from the meeting armed with a radical set of demands known as the Anandpur Sahib Resolution. It proposed limiting New Delhi's constitutional powers to defense, foreign affairs, banking, and communications.

The resolution emphasized the priorities of the agricultural Sikhs, the descendants of the Jats. It demanded land reforms, fixed crop prices, cheap loans for farmers and the "perceptible improvement in the standard of living of all rural classes, more particularly of the poor and middle class farmers". The Akalis also wanted to nationalize all key industries.

The Akalis wanted Chandigarh declared solely the Punjab's capital, the state's borders shifted to include several "Sikh-populated, Punjabi-speaking areas", and the interests of Sikhism specifically protected. The Sikhs also wanted the scope of the central *gurdwara* management committee, the SGPC, extended to cover all Sikh temples in India, not just those in the Punjab. Such a move would have vastly increased the SGPC's revenue, to close to $20 million annually, and enlarged its network of patronage.

The resolution's most important recommendations concerned the life-blood of the Punjab — water. Under treaties signed with Pakistan, India was entitled to the rivers Sutlej, Ravi, and Beas. Although the Sikh farmers considered the water their property, the central government was intent on using much of it to fuel development in other less-prosperous states through irrigation and electrification. There was no shortage and, in fact, India's water was flowing into Pakistan because the irrigation schemes to channel it remained incomplete. The Sikhs wanted to insure they continued to receive the lion's share.

Mrs. Gandhi turned to her Sikh specialist, Giani Zail Singh, who was chief minister of the Punjab. He devoted his energies to loosening the Akali stranglehold on the temples and their treasuries by making the Congress Party appear a more strident and effective defender of the faith than the Akali Dal.

The former preacher organized religious services and opened public functions with Sikh hymns to assuage Sikh fears of Hindu dominance. The ex-Akali Dal politician linked the places where the last guru preached by a road he named after Gobind Singh. A string of horses alleged to be descendants of Guru Gobind Singh's stallion was led down the road and villagers were encouraged to collect the manure. Behind them followed Zail Singh and a cavalcade of tractors, trailers, trucks, buses, and cars. The motley parade stopped at every *gurdwara* and Zail Singh preached a sermon. It took four days for the procession to cover the 640 kilometers from Anandpur in the east to the western borders of the Punjab. A new town was named after one of the guru's sons. Zail Singh arranged and received the remains of Udham Singh, O'Dwyer's assassin, from Britain and orchestrated the extraordinary state funeral.

Mrs. Gandhi brushed off concerns that such religious politicking risked the Congress Party's reputation for secularism and threatened to ignite the religious chauvinism many feared would destroy India. She refused to argue with Zail Singh's success.

On June 26, 1975, however, she gave the Akalis the issue they needed to galvanize and unite Sikh opposition. Convicted of corruption, Mrs. Gandhi refused to resign. Instead, she declared a state of emergency and assumed dictatorial powers. More than six hundred opposition politicians were imprisoned and journalists censored. "There is nothing to panic about," she calmly told the nation in an 8:00 A.M. broadcast on the All-India Radio. "I am sure you are conscious of the deep and widespread conspiracy which has been brewing ever since I began to introduce certain progressive measures of benefit to the common man and woman of India."

She blamed "widespread conspiracies" whenever her decisions were questioned. In the days that followed, more than 100,000 people were arrested and detained without trial. India's bill of rights was nullified. Newspapers were barred from publishing the names of those arrested and police were not required to tell people why they were arrested or to inform the judicial authorities. People simply disappeared. Mrs. Gandhi invoked the name of Joan of Arc and said she was struggling to save the country, insisting that "what has been done is not an abrogation of democracy but an effort to safeguard it."

India's constitution contained a clause that, in times of an emergency, allowed the federal government to suspend a state's elected administration and impose what was called "president's rule". Under prime ministers Nehru and Shastri, from 1950 to 1966, it was used only eight times. During Mrs. Gandhi's initial two terms in office it was imposed forty-two times, usually with clearly partisan motivation.

The Akali Dal was at the vanguard of the opposition. Thousands of Sikhs were jailed, and the three leaders who would dominate Punjabi politics for the next decade emerged from the struggle: Prakash Singh Badal, a rich farmer who was first elected to the Punjab legislature in 1957, Harchand Singh Longowal, and Gurcharan Singh Tohra, the often coarse communist politician who headed the SGPC. Later, Badal and Tohra would be branded "terrorists" by Mrs. Gandhi and her son Rajiv.

Longowal stepped into the leadership vacuum left when Mrs. Gandhi imprisoned the other two politicians. The Sikh preacher with leftist sentiments had been elected on the Akali slate in the 1969 elections. Short, soft-spoken, pot-bellied, with a straggly beard, Longowal was a backbencher until the Emergency. Every day Longowal's squads of protesters marched out of the Golden Temple as their forefathers had, shouting: "Raj Karega Khalsa", the Khalsa shall rule.

After eighteen months, Mrs. Gandhi ended emergency rule and she and her party were trounced in the election that followed. Mrs. Gandhi lost her own seat and her party was rent by recriminations. In Punjab, the Akali Dal made its best showing ever, but still couldn't form a government on its own and was forced to join with a group of other parties in a coalition called the Janata Party. Badal became chief minister for the state, but he and the other Akalis did little to implement the policies outlined in the Anandpur Resolution.

Out of power, Mrs. Gandhi was briefly jailed after she and her son were convicted of corruption. Sanjay, who called himself an automobile designer, although he failed to complete an apprenticeship with Rolls-Royce, was the most powerful man in India during the Emergency. He terrified civil servants, used draconian powers that were unprecedented in their scope and severity, and established a police state. The twenty-nine-year-old was sentenced to two years in jail. He remained free while his appeal made its way through the clogged Indian courts.

Mrs. Gandhi and Sanjay began to rebuild their party and political careers by looking for ways to split the coalition. Zail Singh — the defeated Congress chief minister of Punjab who was also convicted of misusing power — recommended that they weaken the trinity of Akali leaders to bring down the coalition government. He and Sanjay compiled a list of priests from which they planned to select one who could be promoted and built up as a rival leader to undermine the Akalis. They used a similar strategy elsewhere in India, particularly in Assam. The man they chose in the Punjab was Jarnail Singh Bhindranwale.

The tall young priest had just become head of the historic Dam Dami Taksal, a school founded by one of the great heroes of Sikhism, Baba Deep Singh, who was decapitated defending the Golden Temple from the Muslim army in the eighteenth century. The school, built like a fortress, had been at the forefront of the fight against Sikh apostasy for two hundred years.

The young holy man, or Sant, was born Jarnail Singh Brar in 1947 at a village about 135 kilometers from Amritsar. His name, Jarnail, was a Punjabi transliteration of the English "general", and his father, Joginder Singh Brar, was a poor Jat farmer. The Brar family were mentioned by Guru Gobind Singh in a letter, and the Sant later claimed to be a descendant of Mohan Singh, grandson of one of the guru's top generals. Local soothsayers and the head of the nearby Sikh school prophesied great things for the frail child and his father said that as a boy he "could fell a tree in a single blow and at the same time memorize whole chapters of the scriptures and recite them a hundred times a day".

At the age of five, his family took him to the nearby *taksal* — literally a mint where counterfeit thoughts are purified. Inside, Sant Gurbachan Singh blessed him and urged the parents to send him for religious training. By the age of seven, Jarnail Singh was studying full time at the school where the Gobind Singh is reputed to have taught his disciples the correct way of chanting the hymns in the Granth Sahib. The Dam Dami Taksal remains one of the few institutions devoted to the correct enunciation and intonation in reading the text.

Jarnail Singh married Pritam Kaur in 1966 and she bore him two sons. But his life revolved around his vocation. Gurbachan Singh's own spiritualism was so renowned that when he died in 1971, he received a state funeral. After Gurbachan Singh's death, a maverick separatist Sikh theologian named Kartar Singh took over the school and moved it to Chowk Mehta, about thirty-five kilometers from Amritsar. During the emergency, Kartar Singh led protest marches. But in August 1977, Kartar Singh suffered a serious head injury in a car crash. He died rather than allow doctors to cut his hair. Before he died, however, he named Jarnail Singh his successor. Kartar Singh's son Amrik Singh, who was studying Punjabi literature and organizing students at the Khalsa College, would become the new Sant's main political adviser.

At six feet tall, Jarnail Singh had become the dominant figure at the school. He looked the part of a prophet, with his angular face, strong nose, and dark, deeply set eyes. There was a sinister quality about him that those who met him remembered — a fatalism. People waited for him to smile first. He wore a blue or saffron-colored turban tied in towering tiers and the traditional Nihang knee-length tunic, or *kurta*. Across his chest hung his sword, pistol, and a bandolier loaded with ammunition.

Like the leaders of the order before him, the new Sant added the appellation "Bhindranwale" ("of the village Bhindran") to his name and continued his teacher's crusade to "cleanse the Sikhs of the impurities which had entered their hearts and was manifest in their actions". He toured villages urging Sikhs to return to the Spartan traditions of the Khalsa: not to clip their beards, to abstain from smoking, drinking liquor, and taking drugs. He baptised hundreds of young men as he went. He advocated that they bear arms as their warrior leader Gobind Singh had done. He also virulently attacked the Nirankaris, the nineteenth-century heretical Sikh sect whose members had prospered along with the mainstream of the faith. In 1973, with the rise of Sikh fundamentalism, the priests who ran the Golden Temple and who were considered the faith's ecclesiastical governors formally excommunicated the Nirankaris.

The Sant's attack on the sect was a devious move in that the governing Akalis could not agree to his demand that the Nirankaris be banned. It highlighted the problem of a religious party holding secular power that has dogged every government of which the Akali Dal has been part. The country not only was a democracy with constitutional guarantees of religious freedom, but many Nirankaris were powerful, affluent businessmen who supported the Akali's partners, the Janata Party, in the coalition government.

The Congress Party, through one of Zail Singh's proteges, provided Bhindranwale with money and gun licenses for his followers. Bhindranwale traveled about the state attacking the Akali Dal party and the SGPC for not living up to the Anandpur Resolution or following the decree of the priests. In April 1978, with the help of his Congress backers he formed a new political party called the Dal Khalsa, the name of the old Sikh army. Several Congress supporters attended the inaugural meeting in Chandigarh and some were elected directors. Aides to Zail Singh paid the Aroma Hotel bill for the meeting and hoped the new party would embarrass the Akali Dal.

A week later, Bhindranwale led his first militant march against the Nirankari sect. He was outraged that they were allowed to hold a convention in Amritsar, a city of about one million people, 60 per cent of whom are Hindus. "We will not allow this Nirankari convention to take place," shouted the Sikh priest to a crowd inside the Golden Temple. "We are going to march there and cut them to pieces."

The fundamentalist Sikhs stormed through the dusty streets but when they arrived at the convention they found the Nirankaris armed and waiting. The meter-long *kirpans* the Sikhs wielded were little match for the automatic pistols the Nirankaris drew. In the melee that followed, twelve Sikhs and three Nirankaris were killed. The government claimed "armed Akalis raided a peaceful Nirankari meeting". Amarjit Kaur, the principal of an Amritsar girls' school renowned for her singing, called it a massacre. Her husband, Fauja Singh, a state agricultural inspector, was fatally shot reportedly after he took a swipe at the Nirankari's guru, Baba Gurbachan Singh.

Amarjit Kaur vowed revenge and moved into one of the hostels among the sprawling collection of dank, multi-storied buildings that constituted the Golden Temple. Inside, she led a group called the Akhand Kirtani Jatha which practiced singing the hypnotic Sikh hymns for days at a time. Branches of the group reached around the globe, especially in Canada and England, and were renowned for their fundamentalist views. They would soon be blamed for numerous murders.

Demonstrations were organized in New Delhi by Congress workers who proclaimed Bhindranwale a hero and the dead Sikhs martyrs. The Akali leadership began to panic as they saw their religious constituency slipping into the hands of the fundamentalists and their Congress allies.

Chief minister Badal and SGPC president Tohra, both of whom represented the affluent farmers of the Punjab, urged the Sikhs to remain moderate and work with the other parties. They stressed that without compromise the Akalis could never win power in the state. They wanted to build bridges to other national opposition parties and transform the Akali Dal into a genuine regional party. But Bhindranwale demanded Sikh rule. "I would like Sikhs to rule; rule Delhi, rule the world," he said. "In the next ten years, the Sikhs will get their liberation. That will definitely happen . . . . after all, Pakistan was created."

He drew his support from crowds of students, unemployed workers, and peasants. Half of Punjab's farmers worked on less than five acres and in total held only 13 per cent of the arable land. Almost 40 per cent of the state's farmland was controlled by only 10 per cent of the people. The Sikhs found little work in the cities where the Hindus controlled the trading houses, factories, and businesses. New Delhi controlled roughly 95 per cent of the country's industrial production and across the Punjab less than 5 per cent of big factories were in the hands of Sikhs. There were only 50,000 unemployed in 1966, and nearly half a million by the end of the 1970s.

Although Bhindranwale and his Dal Khalsa candidates won only 4 of the 140 seats during the elections to the SGPC, he was gaining an enormous following. Surrounded by heavily armed young Sikhs dressed in similar seventeenth-century skirts and bandoliers, he moved about the countryside preaching and uttering bloody aphorisms.

Women came to Bhindranwale pleading for his help against abusive husbands in the still-feudal society and received it. Villagers would complain of police brutality or thievery and he provided rough-and-ready justice. His growing stature also proved useful whenever the Congress Party needed a crowd.

Bhindranwale was on the dais when Mrs. Gandhi made a political swing through the state. His name appeared on the posters of candidates during the election: "Bhindranwale supports me". The Sant's followers acted as polling agents for Zail Singh and the wife of P.S. Bhinder, a police officer who had earned a controversial reputation during the Emergency. Two years later Bhinder was appointed Punjab police commissioner, and indiscriminate killings in the countryside became commonplace. The Sant was also supported by Gurdev Singh, the deputy commissioner of Amritsar, and a respected policeman named Simranjit Singh Mann.

Mann was a senior officer who was instrumental in suppressing the Maoist-inspired Naxalite uprising in Faridkot district, the Punjab's sandy cotton belt that was Bhindranwale's home. He was accused in 1980 of ordering mounted police to trample cotton crops around villages sympathetic to the communists. Mann was related to the local Congress member of parliament and his was a key posting in a sensitive political district. Badal and Zail Singh were both from Faridkot. It was also Mann who decided police shouldn't search trucks carrying grain into the temples for the *langar,* or community kitchen, each *gurdwara* operated. When the government decided Bhindranwale was really a "terrorist", it claimed the Golden Temple and other *gurdwaras* were fortified by arms smuggled past police checkpoints hidden in the grain.

Mann courted the young priest who appeared to have similar political connections to the Congress Party, and he encouraged his men to be baptised by Bhindranwale. Many of them later deserted to join the priest's crusade and Mann would remain a central figure in the Punjab police until only a few months before Mrs. Gandhi ordered the attack on the Golden Temple.

But that was still in the future during the campaign that led to the 1980 election. On January 14, only thirty-three months after she had been hounded from office and into a jail cell, Mrs. Gandhi won a landslide victory, capturing two-thirds of the seats. Zail Singh was named home minister, and would later become president. Mrs. Gandhi immediately dismissed the Akali state government.

With the two religious communities inflamed, the Congress (I) Party returned to power in the state election and its leader, Darbara Singh, Zail Singh's Sikh rival for the prime minister's ear, became chief minister. Unlike other Sikh politicians within Mrs. Gandhi's Congress, Darbara Singh had not been an Akali. The Akali Dal leaders interpreted their defeat as an indication that they would lose their power base unless they followed Bhindranwale's fundamentalist tack.

In the midst of the developing political maelstrom, Nirankari guru Gurbachan Singh was assassinated. The police report pointed to Bhindranwale and he fled inside the sanctuary of the Golden Temple. He said that the killer deserved to be honored by the priests of the Akal Takht and promised to weigh the assassin in gold if he came to him. Zail Singh defended Bhindranwale in parliament. But India's Central Bureau of Investigation blamed seven of his disciples for the murder.

It was the first indication Congress and Mrs. Gandhi had miscalculated in choosing Bhindranwale as a means of weakening the Sikhs' political strength. The priest was, if nothing else, sincere in his fundamentalism. The newspapers and the politicians called him a "Mad Monk" and a "deranged Indian Rasputin", but his charisma and his insistence on resurrecting the ideals of the Khalsa provided him with a massive and loyal following. He could produce a crowd of a hundred thousand supporters overnight. When Mrs. Gandhi showed as little enthusiasm for his program as the Akalis when they were in power, he turned on her. The terror his followers unleashed triggered an armed clamp-down by the Gandhi government of a nature normally only seen in dictatorships or totalitarian states. It drove the Khalsa Sikhs together and alienated them from the central government.

Darbara Singh and Home Minister Zail Singh disagreed on how to deal with the growing strife in the Punjab between Hindus and Sikhs. Darbara Singh believed in Nehru's policy of orthodox secularism. While Zail Singh preached the politics of accommodation, Darbara Singh championed confrontation. He complained that Zail Singh's policies of appeasement encouraged the violence.

There was a spate of killings in the Punjab after ripped and burned copies of the Sikh holy book were found in several villages, and Bhindranwale stepped up his fundamentalist crusade over the next year with the support of the Akali Dal. Party leader Harchand Singh Longowal joined Bhindranwale's agitations against the government to win back the Sikh constituency. The fifty-one-year-old Longowal had worked for Sant Fateh Singh at the age of sixteen and by the time he was thirty-two was a power-broker within the religious party. At the All-World Sikh Convention, the Sikh leaders joined Bhindranwale in calling for a holy war against New Delhi.

The Akalis submitted a list of grievances to the central government that included the demands of the Anandpur Sahib Resolution and a number of secondary, seemingly trivial issues. The Sikhs wanted Mrs. Gandhi to make good on her promise to give them Chandigarh as their capital and they wanted the recruitment quota for Sikhs in the armed forces restored. Although Sikhs counted for 10 per cent of the armed forces, recruitment was being trimmed until that number matched the percentage of Sikhs in the national population, about 2 per cent. Economic issues were the crux of their complaints. There had been increases in bus fares and power rates, and the Sikhs saw the need for more water and irrigation as a matter of future survival.

Hindu revivalists, led by Lala Jagat Narain, owner of the most powerful chain of newspapers in the Punjab, scoffed at the Sikhs' grievances and said the religious minority had been pampered since the days when they betrayed India and stood with the British during the Mutiny. Narain created a new paper called the *Punjab Kesari* to espouse the Hindu cause and challenge the *Ajit*, a pro-Akali paper.

Narain, who witnessed the Sikh-Nirankari riot in 1978, wrote strident editorials against proposals for Khalistan and equated Sikh autonomy with treason. He complained that minorities within Punjab were living in fear of Bhindranwale and that the police actively supported the radical Sant. The day after the Sikhs presented their list of demands to New Delhi, Narain was gunned down on the Punjab's main highway.

One of the assassins who was captured claimed that Bhindranwale had ordered the killing and Punjab chief minister Darbara Singh called for his arrest. Police surrounded a *gurdwara* in Haryana that the Sant was reportedly visiting. As they went to enter the Chando Kalan temple, police say someone shot at them. When the shooting stopped, twenty Sikhs were dead. The Hindu police ransacked the buildings and torched the library, destroying valuable manuscripts. They also incinerated a van containing Bhindranwale's collected works, which had been recorded over the years by an amanuensis. The destruction outraged Bhindranwale who had left long before the police arrived after a warning from Zail Singh.

Home minister Zail Singh fearing the arrest might spark widespread rioting had telephoned Haryana chief minister Bhajan Lal and engineered the Sant's escape. Lal was a close political ally of Mrs. Gandhi and had immediately switched his state government's allegiance on her re-election. One police officer said an official car picked up Bhindranwale at the temple and took him to his school at Chowk Mehta. Behind the high walls, he was protected by an estimated 150 Sikhs sporting automatic weapons. Bhindranwale plotted his strategy with Amrik Singh, the son of his mentor at the Dam Dami Taksal and the unsophisticated priest's political strategist. Amrik Singh was also the leader of the militant All-India Sikh Students Federation.

Bhindranwale received a senior police delegation, which included many of the officers who supported him, the state's director general of police and newly appointed senior superintendent of police. They agreed that he could surrender to a Khalsa policeman on September 20 after he had visited the Akal Takht and that only Khalsa Sikhs with full, flowing beards would be his jailers.

When the day of the arrest came, more than one hundred

thousand Sikhs surrounded the *gurdwara*. Bhindranwale appeared in a saffron-colored turban and a blue *kurta*, the skirt-like uniform of Maharaja Ranjit Singh's Nihang warriors. The fierce-looking priest preached a fiery sermon against the government but urged the crowd to remain peaceful.

After he left, police said there was gunfire and they were forced to kill more than twenty-five people in the shoot-out that followed. The next day a telegraph office was bombed, railway tracks were sabotaged, and three turbaned men on motorcycles sprayed a crowded market with machine-gun fire killing four Hindus and wounding twelve others. There were huge rallies across the state calling for Bhindranwale's release. "What I could not achieve in a year," the Sant told reporters from captivity, "they have done for me in a week."

Opposition parties campaigned for Bhindranwale's release and Akali leader Longowal appealed to Sikhs to pray for his freedom. Although Darbara Singh demanded the central government ban two of the fundamentalist organizations backing Bhindranwale, the Dal Khalsa and the National Council of Khalistan, New Delhi refused. Zail Singh rose in Parliament and said the police had no evidence against Bhindranwale and that the priest who had not yet appeared in a court would be freed.

The Sant and his followers rode through the streets of New Delhi sitting atop buses, waving their rifles and swords. Santokh Singh, head of the Delhi temples management committee and a friend of Mrs. Gandhi's, roused support for the freed holy man. He had attended the talks preceding the Sant's surrender and paid his legal fees. "If the government arrests Bhindranwale," he explained, "they catch at the hearts of Sikhs. If he is arrested under any false charges the Sikh people will blow up like a volcano and the molten lava will drown this country."

Mrs. Gandhi invited Longowal for talks and offered to hold a judicial inquiry into the police killings at the two Sikh temples. Longowal submitted a revised set of demands. He emphasized that the Sikhs should enjoy special rights as a nation and that Punjabi should have recognized second-language status in the handful of nearby predominantly Hindu states.

The talks collapsed when Haryana chief minister and Hindu revivalist leader Bhajan Lal along with other Congress (I) Party heavyweights told the prime minister to maintain her intransigence or risk political defeat. Lal threatened to turn the Haryana River red with blood if the Akalis continued their agitations. She never talked to them face to face again, and the violence escalated.

On December 22, 1981, Mrs. Gandhi's Sikh ally Santokh Singh was gunned down. During the memorial services, Zail Singh and Rajiv Gandhi chatted with Bhindranwale. Zail Singh and Buta Singh, Union Minister for Sports and Parliamentary Affairs, touched Bhindranwale's feet in a show of respect. But it was a chilly meeting punctuated by the Sant's jibes about Zail Singh's dyed beard.

Bhindranwale's strategist, Amrik Singh, was arrested and accused of trying to murder the Nirankari's publicity chief, and Darbara Singh's village home was bombed. "I have been telling you to stop buying television sets and refrigerators and to buy guns," Bhindranwale said. "Now if these Hindus start coming with Sten guns, what are you going to do? Hit them with your television wires?"

Akali Dal leader Longowal demanded Amrik Singh be freed and crowds of unemployed students again streamed from the Golden Temple to be arrested. Former chief minister Badal led the first group of three hundred Khalsa Sikh demonstrators on August 4, 1982. They were jailed under a law that banned more than five people from gathering within the Punjab. Within weeks, the prisons were bursting with more than 30,000 Akali volunteers. Some were under house arrest, others were in specially constructed camps. Bhindranwale and his armed followers led demonstrations through the streets of New Delhi.

When a bus carrying thirty-eight arrested Akalis was hit by a train at an unmanned crossing in September 1982, Bhindranwale and Longowal both accused the government of deliberately murdering the protestors. Sikhs carried the ashes of the people killed in the crash through the streets of New Delhi. A group of protestors rushed the parliament buildings and police opened fire, killing four. In the following days across New Delhi there were clashes between riot forces firing tear gas and rock-hurling Sikhs who set buses ablaze and toppled light standards.

The government finally agreed to discuss outstanding issues with the Akalis, and on October 13 it freed those imprisoned and issued a blanket pardon. Mrs. Gandhi continued to follow Zail Singh's advice and said she would accept some of their religious demands, such as allowing Sikhs to carry daggers less than 15 cm in length onto domestic airline flights. Meat, liquor, and tobacco sales and consumption were restricted in Amritsar and Mrs. Gandhi also appointed a retired Supreme Court judge to examine the constitutional arrangements between the central government and the states.

But she balked at the main demands and on November 4 the Akalis announced they would disrupt the upcoming Asian Games. Rajiv Gandhi, who had taken over from his dead brother, Sanjay, was in charge of staging the billion-dollar extravaganza for which the government built seven new stadiums, a handful of luxury hotels, and an Olympic-style village.

Haryana chief Bhajan Lal assured Mrs. Gandhi that he would prevent Sikh demonstrators getting to New Delhi. Every Sikh approaching Delhi was roughly searched by the Hindu paramilitary police. Retired Indian Air chief marshal Arjun Singh was questioned as was Lieutenant-General Jagjit Singh Aurora, the man who accepted the surrender of the Pakistani army after the 1972 war. Congress member of parliament Amarjit Kaur was in tears when she complained to the House about being coarsely searched by the Haryana police.

Hundreds of mid-level Akali Dal party workers were arrested, the Haryana and Punjab border and routes to Delhi were sealed, and Sikhs entering the capital were questioned. Most were refused entry to prevent the demonstrations. Trains carrying protesters were unhitched and truck owners were threatened with having their vehicles confiscated if they carried anyone who planned to demonstrate. Sikhs were pulled out of first-class, air-conditioned train coaches at wayside stations at midnight to be interrogated and have their luggage checked. Newspapers reported almost nothing of the outrages. The Sikhs were stunned at the treatment. "You want to know what are the signs that the Sikhs are slaves of the Hindus?" asked Bhindranwale. "The first is that Sikhs were prevented from attending the Asian Games in Delhi."

He now had a sizable entourage that included a growing number of Sikh civil servants and former soldiers. Retired major-general Jaswant Singh Bhullar sat at his feet as did ex-major-general Shahbeg Singh.

Shahbeg Singh was an expert in guerrilla and psychological warfare who had infiltrated East Pakistan before the war of 1971 to train insurgents. In the army the slight man in wire-rimmed glasses had worn his hair cropped and his beard trimmed. But days before he was to retire, he was dismissed on unsubstantiated corruption charges. Without his pension and shattered by the unfounded accusations, he was baptised and spent hours praying. He believed he was being persecuted because he was a Sikh and that the only way Sikhs could survive the state-sponsored oppression was to have their own state.

Support was spreading for the Akali leaders and Bhindranwale's holy war to protect Sikh civil rights. From the sanctuary of the temple, Bhindranwale and his military aides — Shahbeg Singh and Jaswant Singh Bhullar, who would later flee to the United States — counselled armed insurrection. In the countryside and in the cities, political and religious killings were occurring with sickening regularity, and the trail of responsibility led into a labyrinth that connected New Delhi's politicians to the dank, warren-like passageways of the Golden Temple and its precincts.

Harsimran Singh, chief of Bhindranwale's political party the Dal Khalsa, was arrested and police said he confessed to several murders and named Congress leaders including Zail Singh and other top administrators as people who supported and aided him. When charges against the accused killer were not prepared in time, Harsimran Singh was detained under the National Security Act, India's broad anti-terrorist law that stripped citizens of even basic rights in the name of the national security. In front of the High Court, Harsimran Singh said police hung him upside down and tortured him into signing the confession before he was released.

At the same time, chief minister Darbara Singh sent New Delhi a list of twenty-two senior government officials, including police officers, judges, and supervisors, who were involved with the extremists. Mann's name appeared on the list. It was ignored even though the violence seemed to be centered in the Faridkot district, home constituency for Zail Singh.

From 1981 to 1984, Indian intelligence agents drew up a list of the connections they believed existed between four thousand policemen, about one hundred of them officers and a half dozen commanders, who were linked by family or politics to the militant Sikh leaders. The state government claimed it was losing the power to implement policies that would crush the separatist movement because sympathizers within the administration and police force believed they had the tacit support of federal politicians who wanted to keep the state legislators' power circumscribed.

Darbara Singh had ordered those policemen he could trust to suppress what he called "extremism". But there were calls on the floor of the state legislature for an inquiry into police brutality in border villages where Sikh youths had been tortured and killed. Official figures gave the number of dead, in what were euphemistically called "police encounters", as seventy, but unofficially the number was believed to be five times as high. Darbara Singh acknowledged his policemen committed "excesses" but that they were accidents that were necessary if the violence was to be stopped.

Embittered at his federal counterparts, Darbara Singh blamed Zail Singh for the state's slide into lawlessness. One of his aides accused the president of being in daily contact with Bhindranwale. The soon-to-be deposed chief minister was unrepentant. "Encounters did take place and Sikhs were killed," Darbara Singh said. "I told my senior police officers, 'You kill the killers and I will take the responsibility.' "

Every week, police interrogated an average of fifty Sikh youths and killed another half-dozen during "encounters". There were nearly 800 Sikhs in jail under the draconian security laws as suspected terrorists and several extra battalions of police were stationed in Amritsar.

From inside the now-sandbagged Golden Temple, Longowal

threatened to begin fighting in the streets if the government didn't meet the Sikh demands. Darbara Singh, his education minister, and another prominent Congress member were attacked. Bhindranwale went to Delhi in a convoy of armed men and met with Congress leaders but days later the talks between the government and the Sikhs collapsed. The terror campaign waged by the Akalis and Bhindranwale's supporters had triggered an iron-fisted response from the administration and driven Sikhs to embrace the fundamentalists who seemed to be more able to protect them from Hindu reprisals.

Senior policemen were gunned down, bodies disfigured by torture were discovered clogging sewers leading from the Golden Temple, and there were daily body counts in the state. *The Times* of India demanded Bhindranwale's arrest. Darbara Singh said he wanted to send police into the Golden Temple but he was stopped by New Delhi.

President Zail Singh and Congress Party officials were discussing a possible coalition with the Akalis behind Darbara Singh's back. They proposed installing ex-chief-minister Badal as the head of the new government to end the bloodshed. The deal was not consummated but in June 1983, the central government named P.S. Bhinder inspector general of police. His wife was one of the Congress candidates helped by Bhindranwale during the election campaign. Bhinder transferred four senior superintendents, ten superintendents, and several assistant superintendents — most with a reputation for having been brutal to Akali Dal supporters. Despite its rhetoric, Mrs. Gandhi's government acted as if what was happening in the Punjab was simply a squabble for the spoils between the Congress state government and the Sikhs who lost the election.

There was widespread violence across the Punjab. Demonstrations were tear-gassed and *lathi*-charged. Police opened fire on one crowd, killing twenty-one people. Two magistrates and 175 policemen were injured in a single day. Hindu shops were looted across the Punjab and decomposing bodies were regularly discovered in the fields. Still, seven other states were supporting the Sikh demands for more autonomy and decentralization of government power.

Retired Indian generals gave lectures to the "new Khalsa" on military tactics, secret communications networks were established, Sikh farmers vowed to produce only enough grain to feed the Punjab. When Mrs. Gandhi toured the Punjab from behind a heavy screen of security, two Sikh women were arrested for hurling homemade bombs at her.

In the first week of June 1983, Bhindranwale said he had slipped into Pakistan on a pilgrimage to the guru's shrine at Nankana Sahib. There he had a vision in which he was ordered to purify the Sikhs. Afterwards he declared that he was the descendent of a long line of prophets and began to carry a metal arrow that was the hallmark of Guru Gobind Singh. Bhindranwale also formed a praetorian guard.

The courts had acquitted all those arrested in five murders for lack of evidence. In eleven cases against members of the Dal Khalsa or the National Council of Khalistan, two were discharged, eight acquitted, and only one convicted. Four of the five arrested for attacks on Nirankaris were also acquitted.

Few wanted to testify against the militants for fear of reprisals. Bhindranwale urged Sikh youth to "give up all worldly pleasures and buy one motorcycle and a revolver". He held court every afternoon, surrounded by his gun-toting followers. They would often arrive in shops and demand goods, saying they were for the Sant. No one complained. Law and order had completely collapsed in the state.

On September 28, a group of turbaned men machine-gunned a party of Hindus. A week later, on October 5, a bus traveling on the national highway from Amritsar to New Delhi was hijacked. The turbaned killers separated the six Hindu passengers from the rest and executed them.

Late in the afternoon the following day, President's rule was imposed on Punjab, and Darbara Singh ousted. Paramilitary police under the central government's command immediately appeared on the streets of Amritsar, and a new ordinance declared the Punjab, a "disturbed area". Police had almost total freedom from the courts. Throughout the state there were military trucks, jeeps, and anti-personnel vehicles sprouting machine-guns. Four senior bureaucrats were appointed to run the Punjab government.

By the government's own figures as many as 2,500 people were suspected "terrorists", but most of those on the list were little more than petty criminals and bootleggers. The new government solved little. A train was derailed, killing 19 and injuring 129. On November 18, another bus was hijacked and four Hindus shot dead. In December New Delhi blamed most of the extremist violence on Bhindranwale and claimed the Punjab government had been loath to arrest him for the previous ten months. The Sant protested his innocence. "I can prove to you that it was the Indira Congress people in the Punjab who killed Atwal," he claimed. "Why does the government accuse me of being a murderer? In my whole life I haven't killed even a sparrow."

Bhindranwale lived in a dark, low-ceilinged room at the top of a narrow staircase built into the wall on the third floor of one of the buildings surrounding the Golden Temple. He would sit on a mattress in one corner with his legs stretched in front of him. His soldiers lounged around the room and guarded the entrance. During the day, Bhindranwale would sit on the roof of the building that housed the huge kitchen and discuss the Granth or make tapes of his sermons with the latest Sony recorders.

"My responsibility is to see that your beards remain intact, your hair is uncut, and that you do not go after the evil things," he said.

If any of our leaders accepts anything less than all the Anandpur Sahib demands, I will expose him in front of the *sangat* [congregation].... For every village you should keep one motorcycle, three young baptised Sikhs and three revolvers. These are not meant for killing innocent people. For a Sikh to have arms and kill an innocent person is a serious sin. But, Khalsaji [members of the Khalsa], to have arms and not to get your legitimate rights is an even bigger sin. It is for you to decide how to use those arms. If you want to remove the shackles of your slavery you must have a plan. I once again, with my hands folded at your feet, appeal to you — if you have not entered the Anandpur Sahib House, if you do not have the Five Ks, if you are not armed with a rifle and a spear, you will be given the beating of your lives by the Hindus. The Khalsa belongs to the Lord — all victory is his!

The temple bristled with long-barreled machine-gun emplacements. Elsewhere within its walls, other militant groups spat out similar gobbets of hate and jockeyed for interviews with journalists from around the globe. A crew arrived from the television program *60 Minutes* to cover the worsening disturbances. "It will start in Punjab, then it will end up in the whole world," said Sukhdev Singh, who called himself the military commander of the Babbar Khalsa.

They were a small group of Sikhs who had adopted the name used by Sikh terrorists in the 1920s. The Babbar Akalis were militants involved in the *gurdwara* reform movement and were responsible for killing police informers, among others. "The Khalsa will rule," the twenty-eight-year-old militant Sukhdev Singh vowed, "all over the world.... We do not keep a count of who we kill anymore. When we go to kill, we leave our pamphlets. It is the government's duty to see who has done it."

As he sat inside another building guarded by gun emplacements on its balconies, Sukhdev Singh claimed his Babbars had killed forty-five Nirankaris. He also said that they acted as bodyguards for Longowal and that their leader was a Canadian citizen named Talwinder Singh Parmar, who had moved back to Burnaby, British Columbia.

In January 1984, the Akali Dal leaders launched yet another attack on the government. They flew the saffron-colored flag of Khalistan above the temple complex and there were marches through the city as the Akalis brandished their sabers and intimidated shopkeepers and government offices into closing. Badal and other leading Akalis burned copies of the constitution and were arrested. In February, the Akalis disrupted the state with a general strike and in the first three days of the month thirty-five people were murdered.

By April, the militants were so well organized they simultaneously attacked thirty-seven local railway stations in twelve districts. The situation was clearly out of hand. Respected newspapers dubbed Bhindranwale "the prophet of terror" and reported bizarre initiation rites in which prospective disciples were told to commit murder. Those who failed were publicly whipped. "They are killing Sikhs," Bhindranwale said. "There are sixteen or seventeen people drinking the blood of Sikhs . . . . I want to bring an end to the slavery around the neck of the Sikhs . . . . I have never attacked anyone. I have only answered back. I have not ever praised the killing of a good man. But I have praised the killing of a cruel man."

What analysts read in the beginning as a Machiavellian plan to manipulate a voting bloc degenerated into a medieval blood bath. The Indian government began plotting an attack on the Golden Temple.

It justified the plan by claiming it had learned of two letters smuggled into the temple from Pakistan. One was sent to ex-major general Shahbeg Singh, and the other to Amrik Singh, president of the All-India Sikh Students Federation. The Indian intelligence agency RAW (the Research and Analysis Wing of the Prime Minister's office) maintained that Pakistan was sending a military adviser to India and that a Sikh uprising would coincide with a Pakistani invasion in June or July. The Chinese were also being approached, according to the government. There was support pouring into the temple from Canada, England, and the United States. Mrs. Gandhi cut short a six-day trip to Africa on hearing that an attack was imminent and returned to India determined to eliminate the Sikh threat.

The Punjab government banned the All-India Sikh Students Federation and other separatist organizations and Rajiv Gandhi began to publicly advocate the right of police to enter the Golden Temple. Anti-guerrilla squads from the army were posted to Amritsar. The city was filled with troops and armed men. The olive-uniformed paramilitary Central Reserve Police wanted to search every vehicle going past the Golden Temple but the brown-shirted Punjab police disagreed. Police chief Bhinder asked Mrs. Gandhi to tell the federal police not to interfere with traffic as it could cause an uprising among the peasantry. His request was denied.

When police tried to search a young Sikh outside the temple, a fire-fight erupted and police marksmen on nearby rooftops returned a fusillade from the temple. A shaken Longowal called Bhinder, demanding the police withdraw but it wasn't ended until Zail Singh, who had no constitutional authority to issue the order, called the commanders and demanded that the firing stop.

In the aftermath, the local police became even more hostile to the federal forces. Longowal refused afterwards to meet with government ministers and accused them of ordering the execution of Sikhs. He claimed the government was planning to arrest and murder Bhindranwale. The Akalis announced a new campaign of mass non-cooperation with the government to begin June 3. They would not get the chance to launch it.

For weeks the army practiced storming the assault on a full-size model of the temple complex at a camp of the Special Frontier Force in the foothills of the Himalayas. Lieutenant-General Ranjit Singh Dayal, a Sikh war hero in the 1965 and 1971 wars with Pakistan, planned Operation Bluestar. The countdown began on May 15. Two days later, the selected army regiments were deployed in the Punjab. On May 27 and 28, Mrs. Gandhi's officials met Tohra and Badal to talk them out of their planned demonstration but made no mention of the impending military action. After the meeting, the government ordered the soldiers to lay siege to the state's major Sikh temples.

On May 31, Bhindranwale and Longowal both issued ultimatums threatening demonstrations if the siege of the thirty-seven temples wasn't lifted. As Bhindranwale sat on the roof the next day, police snipers opened fire on him. They missed and the Sant's followers fired back, killing ten policemen. One seven-hour skirmish during the night left eleven dead and twenty-five injured.

As army units replaced the Central Reserve police in Amritsar, Mrs. Gandhi scheduled a nationally televised speech to the nation for Saturday, June 2, at 8: 30 P.M. It began forty-five minutes late. She told the country she had done everything possible to prevent the bloodshed. "Even at this late hour," she said, "I appeal to the Akali leaders to call off their threatened agitation and accept the framework of the peaceful settlement which we have offered. Let us join together to heal wounds. The best memorial to those who have lost their lives is to restore normalcy and harmony in the Punjab which they loved and served. To all sections of Punjabis I appeal: Don't shed blood, shed hatred.''

But even if they wanted to, the Akali leaders could not respond. A blanket curfew was placed on the Punjab's major cities of Amritsar, Patiala and Ludhiana. Hundreds of pilgrims were trapped inside the Golden Temple, where they had planned to celebrate the martyrdom of Guru Arjun Dev, whose execution triggered the faith's transformation.

On Sunday morning, a five-hour gun battle erupted outside the temple. Inside, Bhindranwale and his followers loaded rifles and strengthened the fortifications. All communications to and from the Punjab were cut, road blocks prevented anyone from entering the state, and airline service was halted. Indian and foreign reporters who were in Amritsar in anticipation of the showdown were escorted out of the state. About fifty meters from the Golden Temple, the army established a command post.

Some but not all the residents from adjoining buildings were evacuated. The attack began just before dawn on Monday, June 4, with the whoosh of mortars and rattle of machine-gun fire. The army and the Sikhs exchanged light-arms fire for almost five hours. The next day, the army began an artillery bombardment to destroy the pill boxes atop the big eighteenth-century towers called the Ramgaria Bungas. Scores of buildings in and around the temple were blazing, and one shell had landed more than five kilometers away. Others destroyed the bejeweled canopy donated to the temple by Maharaja Ranjit Singh.

Between volleys, the army would call to the terrified pilgrims to come out. They huddled inside sure they would be murdered in the crossfire between Bhindranwale's men and the army if they emerged.

At dusk, the soldiers managed to fight their way into the temple through opposite gates but the specially trained commandos told to capture the Akali leaders were cut down by withering machine-gun fire when they tried to cross the courtyard.

Six Vijayanta, or "Victory", tanks were ordered up and they battered down the temple gate and crushed the marble steps leading into the shrine. High-intensity searchlights blinded the Sikhs inside the temple and a helicopter hovered overhead directing the artillery fire. The Akali leaders were captured along with about 400 pilgrims at about 1:00 A.M. Already some 250 troops and more than 30 women and children had died. More than 70 corpses were strewn around the sacred pool on the 10-meter-wide marble-tiled promenade, called the *parikrama*. The *sarowar,* or holy pool, was filled with bloated bodies. More than a thousand troops were fighting throughout the temple complex.

On June 7 the fighting was sporadic until evening when more personnel carriers, more tanks, and more soldiers were thrown into the fray. The army's heavy guns demolished the marble inlay, gold filigree, and the gilded dome of the Akal Takht. In the basement, Bhindranwale and his aides were found dead. Rumors spread that the bullet-ridden but still breathing Bhindranwale had raised his head and spat out his last words: "Tell Indira Gandhi that she is a son of a bitch."

Many of the adjoining buildings were also destroyed. Residents who were moved out before the assault returned to find their homes ransacked and looted of stoves, television sets, and radios. Temple funds also vanished. Several hundred soldiers and civilians were killed. Municipal sweepers refused to enter the shrine to remove the bodies.

Soldiers walked about the temple in their shoes — a sacrilege — and ignored Sikh prohibitions against drinking alcohol or smoking within its precincts. During the mopping-up operations, the archives and library which housed priceless manuscripts signed by the gurus caught fire.

President Zail Singh arrived on June 8 to survey the destruction in an immaculate, white achkan jacket with a fresh rosebud stuck in the buttonhole. There were three corpses still floating in the sacred pool, bloodstains on the marble, and an acrid smell of gunpowder and rotting flesh hung like a pall over the smoldering shrine.

The Sikhs called the attack "Ghallughara," a reference to the holocaust of murder and destruction in 1762 by Afghan Ahmed Shah Abdali, the last ruler to destroy the Golden Temple. The army refused to let the Red Cross enter the temple during the fighting and afterwards cremated most of the dead before they could be identified or claimed by their families. Hindus distributed candy and liquor to the soldiers and congratulated them on a job well done.

Sikhs in India were horrified. Elsewhere in the world they lashed out at the Indian government. In Vancouver and Toronto, consulates were stormed and wrecked by Sikhs brandishing swords and screaming obscenities. An angry mob of more than two hundred marched on the Indian Embassy in Washington, and in London similarly impassioned Sikhs protested the assault. Mrs. Gandhi was burned in effigy and Indian flags were torched in nearly every city with a substantial Sikh community.

Within days, the Indian government's propaganda machine produced a white paper on the attack and dozens of press releases minimizing the carnage and damage. Indian spokesmen abroad calmly dismissed Sikh concerns and portrayed the assault as little more than a well-run policing operation. No independent reporters were allowed near the temple to present an impartial view.

Mrs. Gandhi's administration claimed the soldiers hadn't fired on the Harimandir although it was pock-marked with bullet holes. The government said the army used only light machine guns and no tanks. Official records said only four officers had died and gave a vastly understated body count. The government said only 83 soldiers were killed and 249 wounded, while 493 "civilian/terrorists" were dead and 86 wounded. There were 592 "terrorist/civilians" under arrest, it said. The Sikh militants were described not as men, but as monsters who strapped sticks of dynamite to children and hurled them from second-storey windows.

"The Indian security forces did not storm the temple," India's ambassador to the United States, K. Shankar Bajpai, told network television interviewers. "We have tried as a government to find a solution through negotiations. . . . Those negotiations were always sabotaged by the extremists. . . . There was no alternative [but] to flush them out."

Within days, however, the Sikhs were distributing videotapes and photographs of the destruction proving their contention that women and children were among the dead.

Brahma Chellaney, of the Associated Press, was the only reporter to have escaped expulsion from Amritsar. He reported that more than one thousand Sikhs had been killed during Operation Bluestar. A policeman and a doctor told him the army summarily executed Sikh men after binding their hands. Indian papers were censored but the report was published in *The Times* of London. Four months later the Indian government charged Chellaney with sedition for the story and he would be subjected to months of police and judicial harassment before being cleared.

Hundreds of Sikh soldiers mutinied and thousands of young Sikh men fled to Pakistan after the assault. There were complaints across the Punjab of police and army atrocities while the state was sealed.

Simranjit Singh Mann, who had been recently promoted from the Punjab to group commandant of the Industrial Security Force in Bombay, was overwhelmed by what his Congress bosses had done. He resigned in a letter to Zail Singh which, in its highly-charged and emotional language, reflected the feelings of many Sikhs:

You will recall that in 1919, Sir Michael O'Dwyer, the Lt. Governor of Punjab, while defending Gen. Dyer's action had put up a similar defence for slaying two thousand persons at Jallianwala Bagh by stating that the military action was inevitable because the population was rising as it had done in 1857 and thus tried to justify his actions. Since you are Supreme Commander of the armed forces it is my duty to inform you that Sikhs with a few weapons, which only a platoon in an infantry battalion has, cannot wage a war against the Government of India, and attacking them with such ferocity has only made our worse fears come true that the Government of India is bent upon committing the genocide of the Sikhs.... The government of India is far too strong and only the paranoid, the mentally sick and the jingoistic Hindus will believe that the Sikhs were about to wage a war against the Government of India.... The army has already killed well over twenty thousand of our youth and the whereabouts of fifty thousand are not known. Your Prime Minister and her Generals are pursuing a policy that has already made Gen. Dyer look mild in comparison.

A warrant for Mann's arrest was issued under the country's sweeping anti-terrorist National Security Act. His picture was distributed to security officers and pasted to walls at immigration posts. But he vanished. On July 2, he sent another emotional missive to President Zail Singh:

Other Sikhs captured inside the shrine were herded together in another batch. Indian army *jawans* [soldiers], under the supervision of their officers, took off their turbans within the Golden Temple and tied their hands behind their backs. Their hair tied in a knot were untied, they were blindfolded and their flowing beards stuffed into their mouths. They were all put to death with a machine-gun. On accomplishing this gruesome task which has not been witnessed since Auschwitz, the dead in their thousands including women, children and pilgrims were taken in truck-loads to the Gobind Garh Fort and laid out in the *maidan* [parade ground] facing it. Kerosene was sprinkled on large dumps made up of masses of dead Sikhs. . . . Terror is being spread on a wide scale in Punjab and villagers are herded out as suspects by the Indian army. We are being subjected to wide-scale searches and thus being humiliated as a race. . . . Amongst the government's allies only Yasir Arafat, a factional leader of the Palestine Liberation Organization, has supported the barbaric action of the government.

President Zail Singh was excommunicated by the priests of the Golden Temple and returned to beg for "sincere forgiveness from the gurus for the unfortunate incidents". His penance was to clean the shoes of pilgrims at the temple. The Indian government spent forty million dollars restoring the Akal Takht. But it wasn't enough. Militant Sikhs would later demolish it and erect their own.

Mrs. Gandhi's inability to deal firmly with extremist violence in the beginning and her party's initial support of Bhindranwale lent credence to the Akali claim that there was an official conspiracy against the Sikhs. The attack on the temple was seen as a deliberate humiliation of their community, and the damage to their sacred property became a powerful symbol of official repression.

The detention and interrogation of thousands of Sikhs without due process escalated the Sikh feelings of victimization. In October the temple complex was handed back to the Sikhs but hundreds of them remained jailed and everywhere the faithful nursed thoughts of revenge.

Mrs. Gandhi had restored her political fortunes in the Hindu heartland of India but the cost had been enormous. She grew melancholic and meditated on death. "I have lived with danger all my life and I think I've led a very full life," she said bravely. "It makes no difference whether you die in bed or die standing up."

A few days later, she was assassinated walking through her garden by her Sikh bodyguards. As he stood outside the operating theater in the All-India Institute of Medical Sciences, Rajiv Gandhi had little to say to Zail Singh. Once installed as prime minister, Rajiv prevented the president of India from traveling abroad because of the concerns about his loyalty.

Zail Singh not only knew most of the Sikh leaders personally, he had lunched and stayed with the most important members of the expatriate community who Gandhi believed were instrumental in the plot against his mother. Gandhi stopped briefing the constitutional head of state on important issues, such as security and the Punjab. And he made no attempt to have Zail Singh serve a second term as president.

But on the evening of the day that changed the complexion of Indian politics, such concerns were about to become irrelevant — a vicious backlash against the Sikhs was about to begin.

For ten days across northern India following Mrs. Gandhi's death, Sikhs were butchered, their possessions looted or incinerated, and their homes destroyed. Much of the frenzy of violence that erupted was organized and directed by Mrs. Gandhi's followers within the Congress Party and police forces.

Led by local leaders of the Congress (I) Party and Delhi administrative officials, Hindu mobs ran amuck. Houses were torched, women raped, Sikh shops looted, Sikh men mutilated and murdered. The slaughter was ignored or encouraged by many of the city's police. Although one in five members of the thirty-thousand-man Delhi force was Sikh, they could do little to help their religious brethren. Some were jailed by their superiors who claimed it was for their own protection.

"There was a police vehicle with four policemen parked near Bhogal market," a shaken Ashwini Ray, head of the political science department at Delhi's Jawaharlal Nehru University, said later. "I came out of my house and saw smoke billowing out. I heard the sound of a tire bursting. Policemen were reading newspapers and drinking tea inside their car while arson was going on all around. I went to the police car to ask why they were not stopping the arson and I was told to mind my own business. I then saw several looters carrying off radio and television sets from stores right in front of the parked police vehicles. Some of the policemen asked the people to hurry with the loot."

In the Sultanpuri district of Delhi, the police arrived and found that Sikhs armed with swords had beaten back a mob. Witnesses said the police quickly disarmed the Sikhs, shot a number who refused to hand over their weapons and ordered the rest to return to their homes. The mob quickly returned, dragged the unarmed Sikhs from their homes, sprinkled them with kerosene, and burned them alive.

Hundreds of policemen were ordered to protect politicians and the famous from around the globe who were arriving for Mrs. Gandhi's cremation. Other policemen flocked to Teen Murti house to pay their respects to the dead prime minister. The house was designed for the commander-in-chief of Britian's Indian Army and had been the residence of India's first prime minister Pandit Nehru, Mrs. Gandhi's father. She and her two children lived there after she left her husband in 1947. Now, the leader of the world's non-aligned movement lay in state amid clouds of cloyingly sweet incense from joss sticks; a blanket of flowers was tucked under her chin and a pink shawl covered her head.

In many parts of the city, the Hindu thugs arrived in Delhi Transport Corporation buses and in Congress Party workers' vans and buses. They were incited by stories of Sikhs celebrating Mrs. Gandhi's death by dancing in the streets of New York, London, Vancouver, and fabricated reports that Sikhs had poisoned Delhi's water supply.

In the Trilokpuri housing project, charred bodies littered every verandah of Block 32. Beside each was a small pile of hair. Some bodies were impaled on iron bars. The homes were ransacked. Dazed women and children milled around or sat in the dusty road. "Hordes of people," one woman told reporters. "Hordes. Mobs in their hundreds invaded this block. They killed and burned all Sikh men they could find. There was no way of escaping. They were like wild beasts, not humans. We had done them no harm."

Witnesses described a blood bath. Plumes of acrid smoke spiraled upwards from burning flesh. The drains were choked with dismembered limbs and masses of hair. Naked bodies, brutally hacked beyond recognition, were strewn in the streets. Lifeless arms were draped over balconies; bodies were piled three deep on the doorsteps of many houses. The butchery lasted for hours. Photographers snapped pictures of dogs gnawing on the blackened remains.

Gurdip Kaur, a forty-five-year-old woman who survived the massacre at Trilokpuri, said the mob arrived about noon as her family sat watching the televised coverage of Indira Gandhi's body lying in state. Her husband and two eldest sons ran outside to fend them off but were beaten unconscious, doused with kerosene, and immolated. The teenage thugs stormed into the house and stripped her and raped her in front of her youngest son. Later they returned for him. "They took him to the street corner, hit him with lathis, sprinkled kerosene over him, and burnt him alive," she says. "I tried to save him but they struck me with knives and broke my arm."

Voters' lists and ration-shop records were used by the organizers to point out the homes and shops owned by Sikhs. Affidavits from hundreds of refugees paint a picture of organized gangs being directed by local ruling party leaders. They named more than two hundred people including sixteen Congress MPs, metropolitan councillors, Congress youth workers, thirteen policemen, and residents. None was charged with a murder.

H.K.L. Bhagat, minister of state for information and broadcasting, was accused of trying to boost his political fortunes in the new government by fomenting the violence. The government-run television service, Doordarshan, broadcast the cries of Hindu mourners: "Blood will be revenged with blood." Sajjan Kumar, a Congress MP, reportedly promised one hundred rupees (about $8 U.S.) and a bottle of liquor to every man involved in the killing. Lalit Maken, a Congress trade-union leader and Delhi councilman, was spotted at the head of one mob. Jagdish Tytler, another

Congress MP, was seen distributing voters' lists so the mobs could identify Sikhs. Other Congress officials were named by witnesses as playing similar roles. Hundreds of people who were neighbors of the Sikhs watched silently from their roofs and courtyards. While some helped shelter and hide Sikhs, most in the poorer neighborhoods did not intervene.

Over the first four days after the assassination, more than two thousand Sikh men were butchered. In Uttar Pradesh, more than a thousand Sikhs were killed. In Haryana, hundreds died. It was the same in Bihar. There were massacres in Madhya Pradesh, Himachal Pradesh, and Maharashtra, all states governed by the Congress (I) Party. Most of the women survived, but many were raped and beaten.

Estimates of property loss topped $250 million (U.S.), only a quarter of Delhi's 450 Sikh temples were not damaged and hundreds of vehicles were burned. The rampaging mobs were well armed and well informed about where Sikhs lived, not only in poor neighborhoods but also in the more affluent enclaves. Three hundred factories and several hundred vehicles were destroyed. Trains arriving in Delhi bore a gruesome cargo: scores of Sikh bodies. Many more were burnt to death on railway sidings in Haryana and Rajasthan.

In the *gurdwara* in Dugapuri, on the Delhi-Uttar Pradesh border, 2,000 refugees huddled. There were refugee camps across New Delhi. The Gandhi Model School, the largest, housed an estimated 18,000 Sikhs. As many as 50,000 Sikhs began an exodus back to their ancestral home in Punjab.

It took two days for the army to restore order. Gandhi toured the riot areas only hours before his mother's cremation. He ordered drastic measures. By midday, tracked armored personnel carriers were stationed throughout New Delhi and soldiers patrolled the streets with orders to shoot to kill. The capital was nearly deserted as the gun carriage bearing Indira Gandhi's body rumbled its way slowly to the bank of the Yamuna River. The grim procession was a marked contrast to the funerals of India's spiritual founder Mahatma Gandhi and the other two prime ministers who had died in office, Nehru and Shastri. Their pyres were reflected in the faces of tens of thousands of mourners; Mrs. Gandhi's shone mainly on the faces of her soldiers.

Within days, her son's administration was pushing the Sikh refugees out of the government-run camps where they huddled in tents and hovels. The government announced compensation for those who had family members killed or property damaged. But compensation for next-of-kin was set at about $800 (U.S.) for those killed or whose homes were destroyed; about $400 (U.S.) for those seriously injured or whose homes were substantially damaged and about $180 (U.S.) for the slightly injured or those whose homes suffered only light damage. But the refugees were then forced to battle a Hindu-dominated bureaucracy that failed to distribute sufficient numbers of compensation forms while demanding certificates, verifications, and affidavits to authenticate claims from the largely illiterate victims.

The government acknowledged the deaths of 2,717 — 2,150 in Delhi — but the unofficial toll estimated by social workers working in the refugee camps was three times higher.

In the face of the government's refusal to mount an official inquiry, groups of prominent citizens investigated the pogrom. A former chief justice of India, a former home secretary, a former secretary of the commonwealth, and a former secretary of external affairs conducted hearings and concluded: "The remarkable uniformity in the pattern of crimes committed with some local variations, strongly suggests that at least at some state the objective became to teach the Sikhs a lesson."

Two other groups with similarly impeccable credentials, the People's Union for Democratic Rights and the People's Union for Civil Liberties, issued a joint report: "In the areas which were most affected, such as Trilokpuri, Mangolpuri and Sultanpuri, the mobs were led by local Congress (Indira) politicians and hoodlums from that locality. . . ."

The investigators concluded:

The social and political consequences of the government's stance during the carnage, its deliberate inaction and its callousness towards relief and rehabilitation are far reaching . . . . The riots were well organized and were of unprecedented brutality. Several very disturbing questions arise that must be answered: What were the government and the Delhi administration doing for several hours between the time of the assassination and the announcement of Mrs. Gandhi's death? Why did the government refuse to take cognizance of the reports of the looting and murders and call in troops even after the military had been "alerted"? Who was responsible for the planned and deliberate police inaction and often active role in inciting the murders and the looting? Why has the Congress Party not set up an inquiry into the role of its members in the arson and looting?

The government's response was to ban the reports, jail the authors under national-security legislation, and stonewall calls for a public inquiry. Rajiv Gandhi and his advisers planned to call a snap election to capitalize on the wave of sympathy generated by his mother's murder. Mrs. Gandhi was readying for an election when she was gunned down. With roughly a year left in her constitutional mandate, many believed her suppression of Sikh political aspirations in the Punjab during the previous months was designed to win votes among India's Hindus, the religious majority of 650 million people who dominated the country. Her son called an election and reaped tremendous benefit from similarly attacking Sikh subversives, especially since the minority's prosperity ignited such sanguinary envy.

In a nation where nearly 500 million people can't read or write, a slick, $300-million advertising campaign was created by a Bombay firm known as Rediffusion. Gandhi was extolled across the nation as "Mr. Clean", an uncorrupted political leader who would lead India into the twenty-first century. In the "Cow Belt", the ring of Hindi-speaking states — Uttar Pradesh, Haryana, Bihar, Madhya Pradesh, and Rajasthan — around New Delhi, billboards depicted Gandhi cradling his mother's bleeding corpse while two Sikhs crouched in the background with smoking guns.

Gandhi toured the country clad in a bullet-proof vest, reminiscing about his murdered mother. He warned that nations such as China and Pakistan were trying to dismember India. He railed against Canada, the United States, and Britain for harboring terrorists who would destroy India. In his analysis, many of India's fourteen million

Sikhs had embraced terrorism and were being manipulated by foreign powers. His mother was the victim of a worldwide conspiracy and India's intelligence agencies had proof, he said.

In September and early October, while underground and on the run, the former Punjab policeman, S. S. Mann, met with Beant Singh. Statements from his fellow assassin, Satwant Singh, and his widow indicated the disciple of Bhindranwale and the prime minister's bodyguard discussed killing Mrs. Gandhi.

Although Mann could not substantiate most of the charges contained in his letters to Zail Singh, the government had sealed the state to disinterested observers and done nothing to dispel the fears and rumors raging through the Sikh community. The misleading and factually incorrect propaganda it distributed after the assault on the temple only further incited distraught Sikhs like Mann.

Satwant Singh, who recovered from his wounds sufficiently to walk with a slight limp, told his interrogators that Mann had instigated the assassination. He also implicated Kehar Singh, a relative of Beant Singh's and a clerk at the Directorate-General of Supply and Disposal. Kehar Singh, an elderly gray-bearded man, was quickly arrested after the shooting. He was a fundamentalist whose colleagues had nicknamed "our Bhindranwale".

The two killers had gone to Kehar Singh's house before the assassination to drink *amrit*, the sugared water traditionally taken by a Sikh warrior before battle. But there appeared to be no evidence against Mann except Satwant's confession which had been wrung from him.

The bushy-bearded Balbir Singh, who was involved in the discussions about the slaying, was arrested in December and security forces grabbed Mann near the India-Nepal border. The rugged boundary country is a favorite of smugglers and anyone trying to flee India. He was with four wealthy Sikh contractors from Calcutta.

Indian intelligence officers insisted Mann was a central cog in a global terrorist machine and that he had been operating as a fugitive from Calcutta with the help of prominent Sikh merchants. When the court found the evidence against Mann to be nonexistent, he was jailed by the government under its sweeping anti-terrorist laws "for his own protection". The other three devout Sikhs were sentenced to death for their roles in the assassination.

The Indian administration said militant Sikhs were operating in England, the United States, and Canada, planning more bloodshed in an attempt to overthrow Gandhi and wrest the most prosperous province away from India. They painted a picture of secular India under siege from religious fanatics who would stop at nothing to create a separate Sikh state in the Punjab.

Outside of India, revenge was being plotted by those who sympathized with the assassins, their fellow conspirators, S.S. Mann, and the hundreds of Sikhs who had remained jailed without charge since Operation Bluestar. In Canada, unleashing a wave of attacks in India was discussed. In the United States and in England, Sikhs considered murdering Rajiv Gandhi and other top government officials.

Tejinder S. Kahlon, a lawyer who was president of the Sikh Council of North America, an umbrella group that claims to represent a quarter of a million American Sikhs, blamed Mrs. Gandhi for her own murder.

"The reaction, I would say is relief," said the bespectacled man in a three-piece gray suit and a saffron-colored turban. "It was expected. . . . It had to happen. As a matter of fact, we congratulate the brave people who did it. They redeemed the humiliation of the Sikh religion. As a matter of fact, the whole Sikh nation is indebted to those people who paid the extreme sacrifice and simply redeemed the humiliation the Sikhs suffered at her hands."

During the election campaign, Rajiv Gandhi hammered at the need for Indians to rally behind him and defeat the international conspiracy that he said threatened the country's unity. His wife, Sonia, had lost weight since the assassination and was paranoid about security. Whenever she heard the sound of firecrackers, she told her closest friends, she was overwhelmed with terrifying memories of her mother-in-law's killing. The family lived and moved behind cordons of heavily armed soldiers.

The Punjab electorate was denied the vote because of the unrest. Meanwhile Congress (I) Party posters in Delhi cast aspersions on

Sikh taxi drivers: "Would you trust a taxi driver from another state? For better security, vote Congress."

Congress won a landslide victory and Rajiv Gandhi became the most powerful and the most paranoid prime minister in India's history. The Congress (I) Party gained 49 per cent of the vote and captured 80 per cent of the seats — its greatest victory ever. Only one Sikh ran for office — Buta Singh, a Congress heavyweight from Rajasthan. Zail Singh became only a figurehead who was locked out of any policy- or decision-making role.

Even in victory, Gandhi refused to order an inquiry into the riots that followed his mother's assassination. Instead, he called on Britain, Canada, and the United States to help him stamp out Sikh terrorism. Gandhi labelled twenty-seven North American Sikh organizations "terrorist" and warned that Canada, the United States and Britain risked losing India's friendship.

The academics and politicians supporting Khalistan were mainly based in London. The fund-raising and global politicking was being handled in Washington, where the Khalsa had moved fully armed into the boardrooms. Canada had attracted thousands of Sikh laborers, most of them the descendants of the Jats, who were ready not only to contribute money but also to become soldiers for Khalistan. There was also a holy man in Burnaby, B.C., named Talwinder Singh Parmar. He would become as committed and as respected as Bhindranwale.

Gandhi blamed Pakistan for inciting, arming, and supporting the Sikhs. What had been a domestic political problem in the northwestern corner of India created in part by his mother's ambition was suddenly a global terrorist threat.

In the Punjab, Bhindranwale's eighty-five-year-old father picked up the torch, and around the globe Sikh expatriates vowed vengeance. On the streets of New Delhi, Sikh cab drivers stood around a sidewalk vendor roasting the mildly narcotic betel nuts over a tiny fire and laughed at a macabre joke: "Mrs. Gandhi had two sons. One was a politician who died trying to be a pilot. The other was a pilot who will die trying to be a politician."

4. NORTH AMERICA

All but perhaps two million of the roughly fourteen million Sikhs in the world still live in India, the vast majority in the Punjab. The rest live mainly in North America and Britain. They began coming to Canada in 1903 fleeing the high taxes, bubonic plague, and poverty of their homeland. Some say they were drawn by stories about its westernmost province, British Columbia, from a Hong-Kong-based Sikh army regiment that passed through en route to the coronation of Edward VII in London. Others attributed the influx to the advertisements of steamship companies and the Canadian Pacific Railway. The immigrants disembarked with few possessions, their monotheistic faith, and the expectation that the lumberyards and sawmills of the province would make them rich. They lived in crowded houses, bought land together, and sent back to the Punjab money or an invitation to come to a nation where the forest and mining industries, the fruit growers, and the railway needed cheap labor.

Still, Canada proved less than receptive to the Sikhs, perhaps because they were a little too flamboyant with their towering turbans, steel bracelets, and daggers. Although many prospered and conformed, the federal government prohibited them from voting, buying public land, or practising law. It also tightly controlled the number of Indian immigrants — an estimated nine out of ten were Punjabi Sikhs — it would let in with quotas. All but 1 per cent would settle in British Columbia.

By 1906 there were 1,500 Sikhs in Vancouver and over the next few years another 5,000 arrived. An economic recession, however, kept lumber prices low and pushed more and more men out of work, causing the predominantly British residents to blame the Asians and the trade unions to demand that the federal government stop immigration. The Sikhs faced the same discriminatory British policies they had tried to escape by fleeing India.

A ship bringing Indians to Canada in October 1906 was diverted to Victoria from Vancouver because the city's mayor refused to let it dock. The city council was cheered for demanding a stop to Indian immigration. In July of the following year, there were race riots in the city. A front-page headline in *The Vancouver Daily Province* claimed "Hindus cover dead bodies with butter", and the popular song "White Canada For Ever" captured the mood.

The B. C. Legislature passed several laws excluding Indians from certain jobs and restricting immigration. But the Indians were British subjects and posed a legal quandary for the dominion government. The laws were subsequently overturned and Canada asked the British governors of India to stop the immigration. In 1909 only six Indians were allowed into Canada. The Sikhs were asked politely by the Canadians to move to British Honduras and even taken on an official government mission to the Central American country. But they didn't like the weather, and wages were low because slavery was rampant.

Liberal prime minister Sir Wilfrid Laurier exhorted the Sikhs to leave, saying they were "unsuited to live in the climatic conditions of British Columbia and were a serious disturbance to industrial and economic conditions in portions of the Dominions". He confided in a letter to the Indian viceroy Lord Minto: "Strange to say the Hindus . . . are looked upon by our people in British Columbia with still more disfavor than the Chinese. They seem to be less adaptable to our ways and manners than all the other Oriental races that come to us."

William Lyon MacKenzie King, a senior civil servant and future Liberal prime minister of Canada, went to London and Calcutta to lobby against Indian immigration. He demanded a ban on overseas-travel advertisements and want-ads enticing people from India. At the same time, the Canadian government passed two orders-in-council: one required that each Indian immigrant arrive with two hundred dollars (the previous requirement had been twenty-five dollars) and the other prohibited immigrants who did not arrive from their country of citizenship by a continuous journey. No ship at the time sailed from India to North America without stopping, and the Chinese and Japanese were exempted.

The discrimination convinced hundreds of Sikhs to return home or to move south into the United States, where most settled in California. The Indian population in British Columbia was cut in half between 1908 and 1911, when only 2,342 Hindus — the government's generic term for Indians — were counted in Canada, all but 27 in British Columbia. Wives and children were prevented by law from joining their husbands and fathers.

About six hundred Sikhs moved south into the United States between 1904 and 1906, and the numbers increased in the following years. They found similar jobs in Washington, Oregon, and California, and established communities in the San Joaquin, Sacramento and Imperial valleys where the weather is similar to that in northern India. Immigration directly from India to the United States also increased, but soon the racism the Sikhs had faced in Canada surfaced in America, too. In California, the Asiatic Exclusion League was formed, its members regularly attacking non-whites and inciting race riots. By the end of 1910 there were about six thousand Indians in California and the newspapers were filled with stories about the "turban tide" and "ragheads".

Those Sikhs who stayed in Canada were determined to flourish. They formed Sikh societies across the rugged mountainous province of British Columbia, and by 1908 there was a *gurdwara*, or temple, in Vancouver. Four years later they built another in Victoria and in the same year a temple opened in Stockton, California. They published newspapers in *gurmukhi*, Urdu, and

English. The anxiety of their white neighbors soon verged on paranoia. Unlike the Chinese or Japanese who were docile and subservient, the arriving Sikh immigrants were considered a haughty group because they had a clear sense of what their legal and civil rights were. The Canadian and U.S. governments saw them as criminals and nationalist revolutionaries who had fled British government in India and planned to continue their fight in North America.

Har Dayal, a lecturer in philosophy at Stanford at the time, was already advocating violence and fomenting revolution in India from his base in Palo Alto, California. Har Dayal proselytized up and down the coast and was implicated in the attempted assassination of the India viceroy in 1912. Soon radical groups from India were recruiting guerrillas in North America. In British Columbia, men openly preached revolution and attacked British rule. They formed the Socialist Party of Canada and espoused a fierce militancy.

In California they rallied behind men such as Jwala Singh (a prosperous rancher known as "the Potato King"), Santockh Singh, Sohan Singh Bhakna and Bhagwan Singh Gyani. Sohan Singh Bhakna, a lumber worker in Oregon, and Har Dayal started the Hindustani Workers of the Pacific Coast group at Stockton. With money provided by Jwala Singh, they bought an office in San Francisco and began publishing a newspaper called *Ghadr* ("revolution"). Their organization came to be known as the Ghadr party, and the first issue of the paper proclaimed its aims: "Today, there begins in foreign lands, but in our country's language, a war against the British Raj. . . . The time will soon come when rifles and blood take the place of pen and ink."

Under the masthead, the newspaper boldly proclaimed itself: "Enemy of the British Government". The editors wrote about the expected war in Europe: "The Germans have great sympathy with our movement for liberty because they and ourselves have a common enemy [the British]. In the future Germany can draw assistance from us and they can render us great assistance also."

Politicians in Ottawa were under pressure from Britain to clamp down on the expatriate revolutionaries and from their own white constituents to curb immigration. In 1913, the situation became a crisis when thirty-nine Indians, mostly Sikhs, arrived in British Columbia on a ship called the *Panama Maru*. They were allowed to land after they successfully persuaded the Supreme Court of Canada to overturn the racist elements of the Immigration Act. The government, however, quickly issued new orders-in-council prohibiting Indian immigrants through British Columbia and reintroduced the two-hundred-dollar and continuous-passage restrictions in carefully drafted orders designed to skirt the Supreme Court ruling.

On May 23, 1914, the Japanese ship *Komagata Maru* docked in Burrard Inlet to take advantage of the court decision and the situation exploded. Gurdit Singh, a prosperous Sikh businessman from Amritsar, had chartered the vessel, picking up his passengers from India, Hong Kong, Shanghai, Kobe, and Yokohama. The B.C. newspapers had covered its approach daily and labeled it the "mounting Oriental invasion". Aboard the ship when it anchored were 376 Indians, all but 36 Sikhs; only the 22 who could prove they lived in Canada were allowed to disembark at Vancouver. The rest, most in multicolored turbans, white shirts, and ties, were told to go back. They refused.

Sikh laborers in Canada, who had raised $22,000 for the voyage, sent letters to the King, the viceroy, and Indian leaders around the globe complaining of the treatment. There were public meetings in the Punjab over the issue. But the Sikhs were facing a united racist opposition of federal, provincial, and municipal leaders. "To admit Orientals in large numbers would mean in the end the extinction of the white peoples and we have always in mind the necessity of keeping this a white man's country," thundered the provincial premier Sir Richard McBride.

A committee of Vancouver Sikhs took the case to court and a full bench of the B.C. Supreme Court ruled on July 7, 1914, that the new orders-in-council barred judicial tribunals from interfering with the decisions of the immigration department — in effect, the court held that the department was above the law. The passengers, near starvation, without water, and angry at the treatment, commandeered the ship and again refused to leave.

A second-hand British cruiser, which constituted half of Canada's navy, arrived from its base at Esquimalt, near Victoria on Vancouver Island. On shore, a force of about two hundred members of the local militia gathered. For hours federal officials tried to persuade the ship to leave before threatening to sink it. The passengers conceded, loaded the ship with provisions, and at dawn on July 23, the *Komagata Maru* weighed anchor. When it docked near Calcutta, it was met by British police and a riot ensued. Most of those returning were jailed, 27 escaped and were fugitives and 20 were killed in the riot.

Most of the Ghadr leaders left Canada before the outbreak of the First World War, and at a huge meeting in Sacramento, California, several thousand men volunteered to infiltrate India and overthrow the Raj. A collection was taken up and men began shipping out. The first band of would-be revolutionaries left for India in August 1914 but the British were on to them and when the ship docked at Calcutta they were arrested.

But the Ghadr movement continued and marked the introduction of the Sikhs to global revolution and the use of political terror as it has come to be understood in the latter half of the twentieth century. The lessons they learned would not be forgotten; the militant leaders would be revered as martyrs; and the networks they established would be tapped by the extremists of the 1980s. There were propaganda centers established in London, Paris, and Berlin. As it became clear that Great Britain and France would be on one side of the battle and Germany on the other, the Indian revolutionaries moved to Berlin. The German foreign ministry urged its consuls-general in the United States to provide whatever help they could.

There were only a thousand or so Indians left in British Columbia at the end of the war. The Sikhs and other Indians had learned their place and kept it after the failure of the Ghadr movement. Almost all would drop the outer manifestations of the Khalsa so they conformed and fit in with the rest of the society. At the Imperial War Conference, the Canadian government agreed to allow Sikh wives and children into the country. However, Sikhs were still denied the vote and were legally unable to join mechanical unions or to become civil servants, lawyers, or pharmacists. Nevertheless, they found work in the lumber camps, started small businesses, imported tea, and delivered firewood and coal. Although many prospered, at the outbreak of the Second World War there were still fewer than two thousand Sikhs in Canada.

In the United States the situation was much the same. With the collapse of Germany, many Ghadrites shifted their allegiance to Soviet Russia. In 1924, American communist Agnes Smedley recruited the remnants of the party and in 1925, a group of them traveled to Russia to attend courses at the Lenin Institute. Two years later, some crossed into India through Afghanistan to join the fight for independence.

The communist influence split the Ghadr party in the United States and Canada as most immigrant Indians were caught up in the same wave of anti-communist sentiment that swept the rest of society in the postwar years. Although several Sikh leaders were named in the report of the House UnAmerican Activities Committee, most had long before made a decision not to rock the boat because of the prosperity conformity promised. After India's independence, the assets of the Ghadr party were turned over to the Indian ambassador to the United States.

The Canadian and American governments were forced to reconsider their treatment of the Indians after the Second World War because they were about to become a free, independent, and sovereign nation. The human rights provisions of the United Nations Charter and amendments to U.S. law prodded Canada to give Indians the vote in 1947. Still, quotas for Indian immigrants remained in force in Canada throughout the 1950s. Even when Cabinet minister Ellen Fairclough introduced what were considered non-discriminatory regulations in 1962 the quotas remained. Most of the original Sikh immigrants to North America had over time adopted the practice of regularly visiting barbers and leaving their knives in the kitchen.

In spite of the lip-service politicians paid to multiculturalism, the country's white majority spent most of the century insisting Sikhs be stripped of their cultural heritage and transformed into swarthy Europeans. Although that history of racism was buried, it molded Sikh perceptions about Canada and intensified their feelings of insecurity. Stories of Ottawa's administrative treachery and the judiciary's complacency were recounted fervently within the temples where the men who died in the struggle against British government were revered.

The second wave of immigrants in the late 1950s and early 1960s was motivated not only by a search for affluence, but also by a desire to live in a more tolerant and less violent society. They left behind them an overcrowded land redolent of defeat and decay, where the water was often poisonous and where fewer than one home in twenty had even rudimentary sanitation. In its place, they came to a near-empty continent of unbounded opportunity, where the conveniences of the twentieth century were bountiful and the destitute received government handouts. Even the pittance provided to illegal refugees was far in excess of the salary earned by a man holding down an average full-time job on the subcontinent.

With civil rights and religious freedom the rallying cry of the day in North America, there was little pressure on the Sikhs to repudiate the traditions of the Khalsa. Indeed, the new arrivals were surprised to find most of the descendants of the original immigrants were North American in everything but skin color. The newcomers considered them traitors to the faith and the tension between the two groups soon turned into violence.

B.C. Supreme Court Justice Wallace Oppal is one of those second-generation Canadian Sikhs. "My father came over on the boat in 1911," the forty-eight-year-old said, heading for a fireside table at his favorite restaurant, The Wedgewood. He greeted Herb Doman, multimillionaire timber baron, who was lunching with Chester Johnson, chairman of the province's biggest crown corporation, the British Columbia Hydro and Power Authority. "You know," Oppal said, "Herb's dad was on the boat, too. They all came over from the Punjab, mainly farming families who had scraped enough together to send their sons here to work in the mills."

As he sat beside the fireplace amid Vancouver's establishment, Judge Oppal looked no different than any other member of the west-coast city's elite. "My dad's family was typical," he continued; "just well off enough to go to another country. The situation of most immigrants: If you're poor you cannot afford to go anywhere and if you're wealthy you don't want to go. We all grew up together over in Duncan, on Vancouver Island. For a while my dad and Herb's dad were even in business together but it didn't go anywhere."

Judge Oppal's father had dropped the manifestations of the Khalsa and his children grew up like any other Canadians. Judge Oppal refers to himself as an East Indian and is a Sikh but, like others of his generation, only by heritage. A bachelor, Oppal wears his hair closely cropped and sports only a neatly trimmed mustache. His father, Hari, he says, returned to India to marry his mother and both came to Canada in 1934. When Oppal was ten, his father died from cerebral hemorrhage. Hari Oppal had just received the right to vote.

Oppal's mother, Gurdial, raised him and his brother Harry by working as a housekeeper and babysitter. "She wouldn't even accept family allowance until I was fourteen," he said looking up from his menu.

While he fastidiously ignores the wine list and orders a soda water with his lunch, he does not hesitate about selecting the chicken swimming in a liquor-based sauce. Judge Oppal speaks in a casual, self-deprecating manner that belies his station. He is known as a ladies' man around the courthouse, and with his charm and his wit it is little wonder. He said he decided to become a lawyer because "I knew as an East Indian I wasn't going to be the president of [the giant B.C.-based forest firm] MacMillan Bloedel. So like a lot of immigrants, I went into the professions."

After Oppal graduated from the University of British Columbia in 1966, he paid a visit to India. "I wanted to see the old family house and things like that," he explained. Like many second-generation Canadian Sikhs, he's still a landowner in the Punjab — not much, he said, only about ten or twelve acres, a plot of land that has been passed down by his ancestors from father to son for generations. The Sikhs are a clannish people and their family name is often also the name of their villages: Oppal's father was from the village of Uppal.

He has not been back since.

When Oppal returned to Canada he quickly became one of

Vancouver's most prominent Crown attorneys and prosecuted some of British Columbia's most notorious murderers. One of his cases ended in the last death sentence to be issued in the province although it was never carried out. He was appointed a county court judge in 1981 and raised to the highest provincial bench only four years later. "[My mother] is very proud of me," he said. "She says she always knew I was the best criminal lawyer before but wondered why it took so long to make me a supreme court judge." None of the province's major newspapers mentioned that he was a Sikh: they called him an "East Indian".

It is little wonder. Oppal is part of the west-coast establishment. His friends are North American, or like Herb Doman, non-practising Sikhs.

"I have watched the turmoil and the events in the Sikh community during the last few years," he said, discreetly pausing until the waiter was out of earshot. "The militants picketed me a few years ago when I spoke at a Sikh convention in Calgary. I prosecuted a man who was jailed for murdering his daughter and her husband with a kettle bomb. He happened to be a Sikh. They didn't believe I should have prosecuted a Sikh."

He cannot understand such reasoning. "I think the community is still in a state of flux because of the very large number of immigrants who have arrived here since the late 1960s. I think in time all the issues will settle down and solidify themselves. It's a short-term period of turmoil. Economically at least the community has been a very successful group."

Herb Doman, for instance: he quit school at fourteen to support his family when his father died. Jobs delivering papers and picking berries on Vancouver Island paid for his first truck, and the trucking business eventually led him to form a lumber company that, within a decade, became one of B.C.'s top ten forest firms. With sales topping $250 million, Doman's company earned $22 million in profit in 1986. The ambitious, broad-faced fifty-five-year-old Sikh was indistinguishable from any other well-tanned North American executive. He was wealthy and connected — Doman was a long-time member in the Top 20 Club, the elite group of businessmen who were the power behind the Social Credit party, the conservative political movement that had governed the province for all but three years since 1952. He was one of the premier's closest advisers. He allowed senior government ministers to use his condominium on Maui and he was a director of the province's publicly owned development agency.

Oppal had just returned from a week in the sun at Doman's Arizona condominium, watching baseball spring training. That's his idea of a holiday now. He and Doman are Sikhs in the same way Canadians are Anglicans or Roman Catholics, mostly on special occasions.

But Sikhs such as Doman and Oppal have become a minority within the North American expatriate Punjabi community. They know more about the inner workings of the Vancouver Stock Exchange than they do about the modern Sikh community in North America. They contribute money to the right Sikh charities, attend the occasional high-profile celebration at a temple and stop by the Indian consulate's cocktail parties. Both were ill at ease among the working-class congregations of the largest Sikh temples in North America only a few kilometers away. For Oppal, the attack on the Golden Temple was the act of a government struggling — however heavy-handedly — to contain a threat to its legitimacy from armed separatists. Like other Canadians he has difficulty relating to the pain and outrage practising Sikhs say they felt at the army's violation of their religious sanctuary. "I grew up no different than anyone else," he emphasized. "I played baseball and did all of the other things kids in Canada do." He drained his cappuccino and grinned: "My mother even brought me chicken soup if I was sick."

The change in the character of Canada's Sikh community was a direct result of the federal Liberal government's decision to pull down immigration barriers in 1967. Indian immigration into Canada soared. By 1970, there were more than double the number of Sikhs in the country and the agriculturally based descendants of the Jats led the way. Like those who came at the turn of the century before them, the Sikhs found jobs in the sawmills and fields of the still largely undeveloped province. Weaned on the stories of the persecution faced by the earlier immigrants, and raised with the siege mentality produced by the language and religious struggles the faith had been waging in India, they kept to themselves.

Those who couldn't enter the country legally arrived by way of arranged marriages or as "tourists" on chartered planes. Once inside the country, the Sikh holiday-makers usually vanished only to appear later and apply for landed-immigrant status. Many of the new immigrants had fled India because of events there, especially during the Emergency imposed by Indira Gandhi in 1975. Most were chasing the prosperity that was out of reach in India. They brought their politics and their hatred for the Indian government with them, often marching through the streets of Vancouver and Toronto denouncing "the fascist dictatorship of Mrs. Gandhi".

But they discovered that over the course of seven decades Canadian attitudes towards them had changed little. The country espoused a multicultural philosophy in theory, but the residue of the institutionalized racism remained. The Sikhs were considered insolent by most Canadians for bringing their politics and grudges with them, while the new arrivals looked with distrust at the institutions of their new country. They congregated in specific neighborhoods. Their tribulations only fed their sense of being a separate and chosen people.

Unlike Oppal and Doman, the new immigrants were not prepared to abandon their Khalsa traditions. There were quarrels between the two groups over who should control the temple treasuries, and the disputes often flared into violence just as they did in India.

The community was ignored by the press except when police uncovered illegal marriage rackets or murders. But the Canadian government quickly realized the repercussions of its open-door policy and it quietly tried to stanch the flow of Sikh immigration by ordering its officials to scrutinize arriving East Indians.

The first indication, however, that something more sinister might be happening within the community came in 1978 when the corpse of a prominent Sikh realtor named Beant Dhalawi was discovered hanging in a vacant house in the Fraser Valley town of Mission, just east of Vancouver. The short, affluent, thirty-one-year-old who occasionally acted as a police interpreter, had been tortured to death by someone who had placed a large C-clamp on his skull and slowly tightened it. He was a casualty in the power struggle for control of the temple in the nearby valley town of Clearbrook. (His funeral was held at the New Westminster temple because of the tensions in Clearbrook.) Police were unable to identify Dhalawi's killers. With no officers who could speak the language or who had any ethnic training, law-enforcement authorities were impotent in this investigation. The connection between a political fight in the Fraser Valley and Indian politics was invisible to outsiders who were unaware of the cash-flow generated by the temples or the prestige and power temple positions conferred.

By 1980, what had been a discreet minority of only several thousand Sikhs had grown to a conspicuous community in Canada of nearly one hundred thousand — most of whom were living in British Columbia. There were racist clashes in Toronto and Vancouver as Sikhs were threatened, beaten, and their homes fire-bombed. Police struggled to keep the peace between white Canadians and the conspicuous immigrants. Not all of the anger was directed at Sikhs, but as the largest and most-easily identified group in British Columbia, they bore the brunt of the attacks. The turban, the sari, and the pungent smell of curry were too prevalent for a white majority feeling the pinch of an economic recession.

The Ku Klux Klan burned crosses for television cameras in southwestern B.C.'s lush Fraser Valley, where a majority of the Sikhs lived and worked. Its spokesmen denounced the new arrivals and its members sustained the hateful rhetoric with their fists and guns. There were bloody melees and shotgun attacks against Sikh homes. An embarrassed provincial government passed legislation outlawing racism and the promotion of hatred or contempt against minority groups. But the tide of immigration continued to rise and the number of Sikhs illegally slipping into the country began to increase dramatically, spurred by Indira Gandhi's re-election and her refusal to deal with Sikh grievances in the Punjab.

About 1,300 Sikhs arrived in Canada during the first several months of 1981 claiming refugee status and accusing the Indian government of genocide. In 1980, only 25 Sikhs had sought political-refugee status.

Not only did the growing number of mainly uneducated peasants fuel hostility among the whites, but it also added to the tensions within the Sikh community whose more established families continued to urge the newcomers to conform. They brought their renewed fundamentalism with them and saw in suggestions to conform the long arm of the Indian government trying to emasculate their faith. They began to use Canada as an overseas base for their fight in India, much as the Ghadrites had at the turn of the century.

Sikhs in Canada raised money to fuel protests in India, and Sikh separatist groups had opened offices. "Next will come direct action and then finally full-scale confrontation," said Gajender Singh, spokesman for one recently formed organization, the Dal Khalsa (the name of Bhindranwale's political party and of the Ranjit Singh's Sikh army). "Like the Palestine Liberation Organization, we are seeking international recognition, and at home we are prepared to use terror, the political language of the twentieth century." He quoted Guru Gobind Singh to justify the violence: " 'When all the peaceful means of reaching a settlement have failed, it is righteous to take hold of the sword'."

Thousands of Canadian Sikhs volunteered to travel to India to join the protests against the Indian government. The country's high commissioner to Canada, Gurdial Singh Dhillon, was pelted with eggs when he arrived at Vancouver International Airport. He was named to the post after being defeated in the 1980 Indian elections in which he had run as a Congress Party candidate and received support from Sant Jarnail Singh Bhindranwale. He had been shipping and transport minister during the Emergency and would later become agriculture minister under Rajiv Gandhi.

In response to the political activity and growing demand by Sikhs for refugee status, Canada introduced visa requirements for Indians entering the country. The Royal Canadian Mounted Police began to pay closer attention to the Sikh community. But the Indian government wanted tougher action and viewed the situation in Canada with the same alarm as that with which the British Raj had responded to the Ghadrites. Indian consuls were ordered to begin their own surveillance of the leaders of the Khalistan movement. They established networks of informers that reached into almost every temple. Hundreds of angry Sikhs demonstrated in Ottawa against the measures.

In March 1982, the situation deteriorated further. In the plush Queen's Bench courtroom of Osgoode Hall, the Ontario Supreme Court building, Mr. Justice John Osler had just ruled against Kuldip Singh Samra when the man pulled out a .357-magnum revolver. The Sikh sprayed the room with bullets, killing two men and wounding another. "As soon as I heard the shots, I ducked behind my desk," Judge Osler said later. "After that, the only noise I could hear apart from the shots were people saying, 'Oh, my God, oh, my God'."

Samra, a thirty-four-year-old real estate agent who was involved in the political struggle within a temple in Toronto's east end, fled to India with the help of an Indian consulate official, according to one investigator. Like the earlier killing in the Fraser Valley, the slaying was nearly impossible to understand without an appreciation of the political ramifications of the temple's treasury falling into the hands of fundamentalists. Samra's action was not that of an individual; it was a political act that many, including the Indian government, understood. He was defended as a misguided Indian patriot by those who opposed Khalistan and Sikh chauvinism. The Canadian government demanded he be returned but was rebuffed officially on the grounds that no extradition treaty existed between the two nations.

There would be similar fatal, bloody outbursts but police were powerless. Despite the warning signs over the previous two decades, neither the federal nor the provincial governments took steps to recruit Sikh policemen or to help the community integrate with the rest of Canadian society.

Like the courthouse where Judge Oppal presided, the Ross Street Temple was designed by Canada's most famous architect, Arthur Erickson. He put Justice in a dazzling glass ziggurat and the Sikhs in a concrete, marble, and chrome fortress surrounded by a moat. Even before the hostilities between India's central government and the Sikhs became a global concern, the Sikhs projected an image of a people under siege.

Outside the building, men in turbans lounged beneath the fluttering saffron-colored Sikh flag bearing the symbols of the wheel and crossed double-edged swords. Immediately inside the door, a numbered shoe rack that would look at home in a bowling alley is partly full of shoes. Several woman in pastel saris sit on the floor in a corner, chatting. The main hall is a scarlet-carpeted gymnasium of a room in which the Sikh's holy book, the Adi Granth, lies open on a silken bed of flowers on a low dais under a fringed awning. It is opened with an elaborate ritual in the morning, wrapped and put away in a repeat performance in the evening. A priest chants the soothing, sing-song verses of the sacred poetry while delicately brushing its pages with a peacock-feather fan.

Sikhs come here at dawn and dusk to pray. On special occasions, worshipers recite the hymns to the accompaniment of hypnotic drumming as a sign of devotion. They will take turns reading aloud for two hours at a time, often going on for 48 hours. There are only three rites for a Sikh — baptism, marriage, and cremation — and each primarily involves reading the requisite passages in the Granth.

In his basement office, Joginder Singh Sidhu strokes his gray-streaked beard as it curls on his chest and says quietly that the real problem facing Sikhs isn't terrorism or even the Indian government. It's Judge Oppal's attitude towards his faith. In Sidhu's eyes, Sikhs such as Oppal do not adhere to the dogma of Sikhism. Oppal agrees — he is unashamedly a secular Sikh.

Sidhu, looking stylish in a three-quarter-length coat bearing a black-and-white, herringbone design, was the temple president, a layman handling the congregation's budget of $650,000. Usually there were only four full-time, paid staff: the priests. Everyone else was a volunteer. Sidhu is a full-time woodworker in a local mill. But for him, his religion is everything. He has spent the last fifteen years working to save those whose devotion had faltered or whose commitment to the outward signs of the faith had waned. He counts Oppal among the prodigal sons who have yet to return. Every week, Sidhu estimates, he spends about forty hours administering the temple's affairs — sometimes in the early morning, sometimes at night, depending on his shift at the mill.

The fifty-two-year-old Sidhu arrived in Vancouver in 1970 with his wife and the dream of a better life for his children. He has achieved that: his eldest son is studying electronics at Lakehead University in Thunder Bay, Ontario, another has a B.Sc. from the University of British Columbia, and his youngest — the first to wear a turban playing highschool basketball in the province — is finishing Business Administration at Simon Fraser University. While Oppal frequents hair stylists and the city's finest restaurants, Sidhu stows his uncut hair beneath a black turban and lunches in the temple's *langar*, the communal kitchen that provides a free lunch to all comers regardless of faith.

The *langar* in Vancouver, Sidhu says a trifle embarrassed, isn't really a traditional Sikh kitchen. In Amritsar, for instance, he says nodding towards the sari-clad women dishing up the food, the poor are fed at the *langar*. But they are fed only two dishes — roti and dal: a bread-like substance and a mixture of grains, peas, and sometimes onions. Sidhu greets a pair of gray-bearded men on benches quietly eating. "Here," he says, "we also serve cooked vegetables."

He strides back to his tiny office, which is decorated with pictures of the ten Sikh gurus. What Sidhu remembers most vividly about coming to Canada was arriving at the temple. Everywhere were Sikhs who had cut their hair and trimmed or shaved their beards, he says. It went down from there, he said, they also swore, drank liquor, and smoked marijuana. "I didn't want to go inside because I didn't think it was a place of worship. I thought it was a club because everyone inside, except maybe two or three per cent, were bareheaded and totally against the basic tenets of the religion."

For the other Sikhs who were arriving at the same time, Sidhu says, the situation was equally shocking. He considers each word and delivers his sentences in a thoughtful voice. Immigrants like himself, he says, had left a land where Sikhs were struggling to prevent their faith from disappearing. To them the most insidious temptation to which a Sikh can succumb is assimilation. Sidhu says to lose his identity as a Sikh is to lose everything that matters to him. It binds his family and his friends; it is the glue that holds his world together. The second wave of immigrants defeated the temptation, albeit in many cases by staving in the skulls of those who tolerated western values. They quickly won election battles to control the temples, the center of Sikh cultural, religious, and political life, by intimidating or denouncing their opponents as unworthy Sikhs.

"Now you will never find a single person in the temple bareheaded," Sidhu says proudly of the largest Sikh congregation in North America. "There used to be a lot of fights here. We had to struggle a lot. For the older people the religion was just something of convenience and they had to struggle with the new people and eventually the people coming from India."

Across North America similar "struggles" took place, as the new immigrants arrived, Sidhu says. He does not like to talk about the brawls, the knifings, or the savage beatings administered to those who opposed the return to fundamentalism. These events are glossed over with euphemism. The violence, in Sidhu's opinion, was only a manifestation of the latest crisis of identity to rock the religion founded by the pacifist Nanak.

The two streams developed within Sikhism during the eighteenth and nineteenth centuries partly because the faith had no formal rules of entry, no priestly class, and no special days of worship. It admitted that other religions were equally valid paths towards God. The *keshadhari* Sikhs, however, became the dominant and most powerful group within the religion for several reasons: the benefits the British bestowed on the religion were directed to members of the Khalsa, and the Khalsa symbols were incorporated in the legal definition of a Sikh. The *sahajdhari* Sikhs were looked upon as *keshadharis*-in-waiting, people who would one day be baptised into the Khalsa. The fundamentalist revival that began in the religion during the 1960s was centered in the faithful's sense of separateness from Hinduism. They blamed the abandonment of the Khalsa identity for every social ill they faced: unemployment, drug addiction, poverty, and family breakups. As a result they demanded Sikhs embrace the "Five Ks" and they carried that logic with them around the globe.

Sidhu says it is the Sikhs' consciousness of their separate identity that fosters their self-reliance: because they believe they are different from everyone else they stick closer together as a community and aid one another lest they disappear as a people.

For Sidhu and most Sikhs in Canada, life revolves around the temple. Inside they find people from the same land, struggling with the same economic problems, revelling in the same martial episodes of Sikh history, and embracing the same conservative values. Sidhu himself, for instance, says he has chosen a bride for each of his sons — an estimated nine out of ten Sikh parents arrange their children's marriages, though some adult men return to India to find or buy a bride. Daughters continue to be shielded from the world and are often forbidden even to visit shopping malls on their own. That is how it has always been.

He points to a meter-long metal arrow in a case, kept under lock and key in the temple. "It belonged to Guru Gobind Singh, the last and tenth guru," he says. "There is a sword from the third guru, other *kirpans* stained with blood, pieces of clothing that supposedly belonged to someone centuries ago and other relics. They have been handed down from one generation to another." He says that he is giving up his temple job so he can devote more time to the political struggle for a Sikh homeland. "I will never again visit Punjab," he says. "But I hope to visit Khalistan."

Outside his office, a saffron-colored bumper sticker has been pasted to the wall. It reads: "Hands off our homeland." Saffron yellow is the Sikh color for martyrdom and the Hindu color of royalty. Those who are ready to die for the religion don a saffron-colored turban; Indira Gandhi strolled to her death wearing a saffron-colored sari. On the cars outside, other bumper stickers spread the message: "Catch the Sikh Spirit — Babbar Khalsa." There was no shortage of willing martyrs at the Ross Street temple. "The more martyrs, the better the nation, some would now say," Sidhu says. "Some have to sacrifice so the rest will wake up. A Sikh is supposed to sacrifice everything for his religion. That is the basic teaching."

Canadian Sikhs responded to the strife in the Punjab by contributing thousands of dollars, ostensibly for legal expenses of those imprisoned and to support the families of killed or jailed Sikh separatists. But, as with the money contributed to the Irish Northern Aid Committee in the United States to help families of killed or jailed Republicans, much was spent on procuring weapons.

When Indira Gandhi ordered Operation Bluestar, the invasion of the Golden Temple, Sikhs in Canada were staggered. They huddled around radios in temple basements listening to the BBC's World Service for information about the attack. They were horrified at the broadcasts.

For a people from a continent where the gestures of rebellion are trivial — driving cars, eating beef, drinking liquor — Mrs. Gandhi had struck a momentous blow at the masculine, martial beliefs of the Sikhs. There had always been leaders who claimed the religion was doomed unless Sikhs governed themselves. Mrs. Gandhi culled justification for the assault from the arsenal the army recovered from inside the shrine. For Sikhs around the world, however, a few hundred automatic weapons and a stockpile of explosives could not justify the killing of a thousand of their brethren and the arrest of nearly five thousand of their family.

Two saber-wielding men burst into Vancouver's Indian consulate and ransacked the office before surrendering to police. For three days crowds disrupted traffic in the financial center of the west-coast city, decrying the assault on the temple. More than 20,000 Sikhs arrived at the doors of the nondescript downtown building housing the Indian government office, screaming, "Death to Indira Gandhi" and "Indira Gandhi is a murderer". They burned an effigy of the Indian prime minister and incinerated Indian flags. Sari-clad woman wailed.

In the summer sunshine, women dressed in black to mourn the death of Bhindranwale and carried placards proclaiming him a saint and a martyr. The men waved swords and sported the bright saffron-colored turban that signified their willingness to die for their faith. They talked of Bhindranwale's death as a symbol of the persecution and genocide of the Sikhs. They drew analogies to the massacre at the Golden Temple in 1919 when General Dyer slaughtered hundreds and wounded more than a thousand.

Similar demonstrations occurred across North America. The crowds inevitably carried a bier with a mannequin representing the fundamentalist Bhindranwale. Placards read: "Blood will be revenged with blood" and "We want revenge". They cheered as speakers called for an independent Sikh homeland. In Winnipeg, a mob of Sikhs flailed at an Indian diplomat with fists and two-by-fours while shouting, "Kill the bastard." Hindu shopkeepers were beaten and threatened with death and their stores were damaged.

At the posh home of the Indian consul in a manicured subdivision perched on the mountains overlooking Vancouver, a mob of 250 Sikhs poured out of chartered yellow school buses and ran towards a line of riot police, screaming, "Shoot, shoot, we came here to die." They hurled rocks and eggs. One protester was bloodied by police and the consul's car windscreen was smashed.

"The demonstrators here do not represent the true Indian way," said consul Jagdish Sharma, a former Indian military intelligence officer whose last appointment had been in Kampuchea. He paced back and forth inside the house where empty artillery shells doubled as ashtrays. "The person who resorts to violence and undemocratic means to resolve a dispute," he said angrily, "I would describe as a coward of the first order. If the culprits were firmly dealt with there would be a precedent. I am worried that the impression is that anyone will get away with it."

In Toronto, there were riots and demonstrations. About five thousand Sikhs marched through downtown, burning effigies of Mrs. Gandhi at the provincial legislature and at city hall. One man stormed into the Indian consulate in Toronto and smashed at least one of the large portraits of Indian government politicians. But then something odd happened.

A radio reporter named Dana Lewis, alerted by a call over his police scanner, arrived on the scene within moments. According to his statement to police, there was only a small amount of damage in the fifth-floor reception area. Consul-General Surinder Malik spotted Lewis and asked if he was with a television station. "When I said no, that I had no camera crew," Lewis said later, "he proceeded to tell two guys who were with him to make it look better — for the TV cameras I suppose. I saw them tip over a chair, and they threw some magazines around the office. I think they broke another picture. Certainly they caused more damage."

In spite of the Indian government's outraged rhetoric, the cases never went to court. Consular staff refused to testify against the Sikhs. They also refused to press charges in Vancouver, feeding rumors that some of the accused were Indian government agents operating in Canada to discredit the legitimate Sikh political protests. "The really funny thing," Lewis recalled about the Toronto incident, "was that the Indian consulate people insisted the guy had a gun hidden behind his back while he was in their offices. But it turned out the fellow who was arrested only had one arm."

The rumors of *agents provocateurs* and spies disappeared as the Sikhs vanished from the headlines in the following months. Below the surface, however, emotions simmered.

Sikh artists painted a series of massive oil paintings depicting the siege. The hagiography — reminiscent of the patriotic Second World War propaganda posters that portrayed the Germans and the Japanese as monsters — pictured bronzed, turbaned warriors battling a hideous and deformed foe that advanced from the shadows. And the Sikhs planned revenge.

When the assassins struck on that Halloween morning, hundreds of Sikhs in Canada, the United States and Britain celebrated by dancing in the streets. In Vancouver, small groups distributed candy to children and passers-by. They set off fireworks in a frenzied celebration. "We're proud of it," one grinning Sikh told television cameras outside the Ross Street Temple in southern Vancouver. "Once you're suppressed you have to take blood for blood. We don't claim that we should take revenge at any time . . . but when you can only take so much, that's it."

Gurpartap Singh Birk, a computer wizard who had designed the Belgian parliament's electronic system and who was working to computerize U.S. toll gates, led the dancing on East Sixty-fourth Street in Manhattan. Dozens of American Sikhs on street corners cheered the killing, and in London they rallied and shouted that they had not yet begun to fight. In a single stroke, the Sikh separatist struggle gained instant credibility. No matter how small a minority the Khalistan supporters were, they had proven themselves capable of assassinating a political giant.

Three weeks later the World Sikh Organization, which represents a majority of expatriate Khalsa Sikhs, convened a meeting in the Fraser Valley town of Abbotsford. Amid the border-straddling farms through which the Sikhs were smuggling illegal immigrants and guns, temple leaders from around the globe met. They said they were preparing to protect their "faith from further desecration . . . our brothers and sisters in India are fighting a battle of survival. Not only have Sikh Temples been destroyed, but the Sikhs in Punjab no longer have the freedom of speech, demonstration, religion and vote. Now we are calling for a new state — Khalistan!"

In front of large crowds of immigrant Sikh laborers and a smattering of monied farmers and small businessmen, Lieutenant-General Jaswant Singh Bhullar urged armed revolution. The former Bhindranwale adviser said there was now no alternative for the Sikhs but to achieve their own state. Every Sikh society from across the province, from the isolated temples near the Yukon border to the lumber-town *gurdwaras* on Vancouver Island, endorsed the call for Khalistan.

Didar Singh Bains, a millionaire California peach grower with a personal jet christened "Khalistan One", exhorted Sikhs to rise up and fight for their rights. Bains was a U.S. Sikh with a Horatio Alger past who gave up shaving and haircuts after the attack on the Golden Temple. He had regularly met with Indian president Zail Singh and he operated businesses around the world protected by a private security force.

The convention ended with a communiqué: "For some thirty-seven years the Sikhs have tried all kinds of peaceful and democratic means to arrive at a settlement with the Indian government. Instead of replying to the Sikh demands the Indian army has been unleashed in order to destroy the foundations of the Sikh religion . . . . The call for Khalistan by Sikhs abroad is not a political demand but rather a religious call. We want to preserve our religion, faith and identity."

Engaged in their own private war, the fundamentalist Sikhs and the Indian government had opened a second front on the streets of North America. A Vancouver Sikh who sponsored a Punjabi-language radio program in the city was held at gunpoint in his shop for half an hour by two men. They were outraged that his program gave equal time to the Indian government's perspective. Two men, in the traditional dress of the Nihang warriors and brandishing meter-long sabres, surrendered to police. "I have been penalized for nothing," Sarbjit Khurana said afterwards. "If living in this country, you can't express your views, then these people don't deserve this country."

Several Sikhs were clubbed by turbaned thugs after being identified in the media as "moderate Sikhs" who opposed extremism. In March, a Sikh was arrested at Heathrow Airport when he stepped off a flight from Vancouver. In his suitcase was an Israeli-made Uzi machine gun he said he was taking to Pakistan to join the war for Sikh independence. Police in Vancouver had grabbed the man's uncle before he had a chance to board the flight after they discovered in his luggage parts of the dismantled automatic and two ammunition magazines.

Police said the supporters of Khalistan were engaged in widespread arms and drug smuggling. Immigration departments and various police forces in Canada and the United States were involved in massive investigations. They were trying to infiltrate Sikh gun-smuggling rings operating on Vancouver Island and down the coast into California. They were also tracking Sikhs with connections to the provincial cabinet in British Columbia, who operated an underground railroad network across the continent for illegal immigrants and heroin.

For those who sought nothing more than the right to choose their own lifestyle and live peacefully within the laws and mores of modern North America, the situation was a nightmare.

Ujjal Dosanjh sipped his after-dinner Scotch and dismissed with a wave of his hand the claims of those who would lead the faithful to the promised land. "I am surprised that these goons are getting into Canada without difficulty," he said, putting his feet up on an ornately carved coffee table in his modest livingroom. The Vancouver lawyer, who wears crisp business suits and prefers a regular haircut to a turban, said he's tired of hearing how different Sikhs are from other immigrants. "What responsibility does the Canadian government take for actually destroying the fabric of my community?" he said angrily. "These individuals are anxious to sacrifice themselves for the Sikh nation. They are five thousand miles away! If they went closer to the fires they have fed, they would be engulfed."

For holding such views, Dosanjh was beaten one afternoon as he left his law office by a Sikh wielding an iron bar. It took eighty stitches to close the wounds on his head. A death threat was stuffed under his door, he said calmly as if it were simply another piece of junk mail. The clean-shaven forty-year-old and his wife, Raminder, do not call themselves "Singh" or "Kaur". They consider themselves "secular" Sikhs.

Dosanjh is a man with political aspirations (he ran unsuccessfully for the New Democratic Party in the 1979 and 1983 British Columbia provincial elections). He says he won't be intimidated into silence as have many of his fellow immigrants in Vancouver.

"The problem here," Dosanjh said, "is that the community is alienated from the rest of society. It is becoming more isolated because of these individuals and it aggravates their sense of grievance. Their own insecurity lends credence to their sense of isolation. They're pampered. What discrimination are they talking about? What persecution? There were no injuries prior to 1984."

His wife, Raminder, a short woman wearing a pair of casual slacks and a pale yellow blouse, called to her three sons to do the dishes as she joined her husband in the living room. "The problem is that they are people from the Middle Ages," she said abruptly. "They are all male chauvinist pigs who are coarse old men. It's ridiculous."

Raminder, a college teacher who also worked as a social worker within the East Indian community, is a fiery activist trying to drag the majority of Sikh immigrants into the twentieth century. Their medieval attitudes, she said, are causing untold problems in North America. Teenaged girls are attempting suicide rather than face the marriages arranged by their parents. And the buying and selling of brides is not infrequent. There are three newspapers catering to Indian immigrants in Vancouver alone and advertisements for brides are common: "Brother, Jat Sikh, engineer, seeks Sikh match for sister, very pretty, 35, never married, employed. Canadian." . . .

"Match required for pretty, 5' 4", slim, fair, Sikh, never married."
... "Brother invites matrimonial correspondence for honorary
sister, 34, 5' 3", Punjabi Sikh, R.N., attractive, cultured, affectionate
and home-loving, innocently and issuelessly divorced." ... "Match
for Saini Sikh engineer, 30, 5' 8", 110 lbs., married and divorced
just in papers, well settled in New York, girl may be high school,
just for household, must be respectable like as Punjabi culture, any
caste from Sikh family."

"Ujjal still has people come to him asking for legal advice,"
Raminder said, "saying they can't understand what all the fuss is
about because they only slapped their wife around a bit."

Raminder smiled as her husband chuckled. But, she said, it's a
serious problem.

"I'm often shunned if I show up at a community meeting," she
said. "The others have left their wives at home and they expected
me to be there too. It's not just a battle with the fanatics. We have a
problem with some of the progressive men and getting women
involved. It's double standards everywhere. Women are bought and
sold there. We know a seventy-year-old man with a twenty-five-
year-old wife. . . . Things are frozen when you leave India. They
move ahead but your image remains frozen and therefore people in
India probably are better off. Women have it really bad here. You
invite a friend over and he arrives by himself without his wife. Ujjal
had to overcome some of the same attitudes.

"Before we were married, if Ujjal came home at midnight, his
sisters would get up and warm his supper. I wouldn't do that
although they expected it. There are other problems arising in
extended families, but it was hard when we got married to get him
to do things around the house. One of his friends came to the door
and I invited him in on Sunday when Ujjal was doing the dishes and
he couldn't believe it. He just couldn't believe that this outspoken
man would be doing dishes."

She helped found a one-hundred-member organization called the
India Mahila Association to ease some of the family violence. "They
have to stop," she says. "When a woman is in trouble, she won't
seek help because then she won't be accepted by her family."

Her group of volunteers has made inroads by manning crisis hotlines for women in trouble, she said. But the problem remains pervasive and her ability to help is hindered by the perception that she and her husband are Uncle Toms who have abandoned their heritage and faith. "But these are my people," Dosanjh says emphatically. "We're Jats. Part of me understands why they want to go out and break people's legs. Jats are crazy people you know. I've learned to control that. They have to fight that."

Dosanjh left the Punjab when he was seventeen to continue his education in Britain. He lived with relatives near Birmingham for three and a half years and then emigrated to Canada. He arrived in 1968 when there were still only a few thousand Sikhs living in Vancouver. He and his wife both had relatives in British Columbia, some of whom had arrived at the turn of the century.

"My uncle returned to the Punjab from Canada as a member of the Ghadr party, one of the Sikh-dominated groups fighting for independence," Dosanjh said. He was hanged from a British gibbit in 1916 for his activities in the rebellion. Dosanjh is proud of his family's history and involvement in Indian politics. His grandfather, Jarnail, he says, led a terrorist band of about forty Sikhs and later became the Congress Party's security chief in the decades before the British abandoned India. "He died here in 1982," Dosanjh said. "We've still got the old Russian commissar's uniform the party created for him."

As a result, Dosanjh said, he has always been involved in the political life of his community, even if he didn't share its fundamentalist convictions. "History doesn't begin with Bhindranwale, you know. You don't find educated Sikhs telling you he's a saint. He was a butcher. He did a lot of damage to the country. History doesn't begin with him — it begins much before Bhindranwale and his hooligans."

But Dosanjh agrees the events of the 1980s radically altered his community, both in Canada and in India. He said he began to notice the change as more and more immigrants arrived and claimed to be political refugees. "I went to India in December of 1983 for two months," Dosanjh said. "I wrote to all of the players and asked them to see me. I saw them all: Gandhi, Longowal, and Bhindranwale."

He vividly remembers sitting on the roof of the Golden Temple, arguing with Bhindranwale. His wife and three children sat anxiously while Dosanjh and the holy man debated. The Sant's heavily armed followers grew restless as Dosanjh's impertinence grew louder.

"All he wanted to talk to me about was why I cut my hair and beard," Dosanjh says. "It was an hour-long argument and there were heated words when he tried to play holier-than-thou with me. I simply trotted out my credentials and told him I was just as true a Sikh as he was. He didn't want to talk about the kinds of problems he was sparking with his hateful rhetoric. And he didn't want to talk about his mangling of history. Those Sikhs who fought the British didn't fight for a Sikh nation, they fought for an independent India. We parted company on not very good terms. He didn't like being challenged in front of about one hundred fifty of his people."

Later, he says, he visited Longowal and encountered an entirely different kind of man. "He didn't know me from Adam, but he spent two hours discussing the issues with me in an intelligent and articulate fashion. He said to me that he and Gandhi were very close to an agreement that would defuse the situation. 'But Bhindranwale has put a gun to our head.' Those were his words. 'The Congress Party put Bhindranwale up to it,' he said."

Dosanjh said as they parted, Longowal too mentioned his shorn hair. "But he said to me that if I kept coming to see him I might get to like a turban and beard."

His meeting with Mrs. Gandhi was polite, but he says not very satisfying. "She told me she saw a foreign hand in the disturbances. There was no call for Khalistan. She said they had evidence that Pakistan and the U.S. Central Intelligence Agency had a hand in it because they didn't like India's close ties to the U.S.S.R. The hope was that by causing unrest among India's religious minorities the country would be destabilized and move closer to the U.S. I asked her if she was simply whipping up Hindu chauvinism, as people said, to maintain power. She said people said all sorts of things, but denied it."

Dosanjh, however, believes that the Indian government's insensitivity to the feelings of the Sikhs eventually touched off the powder keg. "They were worried about the unity of the country, but they didn't address the grievances whether real or imagined. The assault on the temple gave fundamentalist Sikhs support for their false sense of grievance."

It also forced Dosanjh to re-examine his own view of the immigrant community of which he is a part. It is far more fundamentalist, he says, than he feared before. Before the assault he had believed only a few hundred Sikhs in Canada supported the call for Khalistan. "It won't be over soon," Dosanjh says now.

"We're destroying our position in this society," Dosanjh lamented. "We're giving all the arguments to the racists that they've always used. I really feel sad that freedom of expression in my community is being strangled and there is no outcry in the larger Canadian community. It's not just an issue that affects me and other Indians. It affects our whole life as a Canadian community. We have tended to form islands unto ourselves. Today we're seeing the results of that isolation. There aren't enough bridges to Canadian society. We told the federal government that the temples are being turned into centers of violence and hatred, hate-mongering continues there incessantly. Nobody listened. I believe there is a perception, 'Let the East Indians fight among each other as long as they don't hurt the mainstream, white Anglo-Saxon Canadian.' But, if tomorrow Canadians don't want to awaken to a violent ghetto, they'd better wake up now."

5. CANADA'S BHINDRANWALE

Talwinder Singh Parmar was Canada's Sant Jarnail Singh Bhindranwale. The Indian government considered the forty-one-year-old British Columbian the most dangerous of its expatriate opponents and had been trying vainly for years to have him extradited from Canada. But while the country's domestic spies watched his every move, the federal government refused to deport a citizen.

Intelligence agencies from around the globe had compiled thick dossiers on Parmar's travels and politics. Those who agreed to talk about him inevitably said they had come to the same conclusion about the barrel-chested man with eyes like two clean bullet holes. They say he is an uncomplicated, friendly man with a genuine talent for leadership, who was born out of his time.

Parmar scoffed at their deductions and at the vans parked down the street from his home containing men with binoculars. He ignored the nosey, ordinary-looking people who always seemed to be hanging around everywhere he went. He wasn't an educated man but he had wise blood and he talked to God. "Between eight and twelve hours a day," he said.

He called himself a Sikh priest. "I have been given the title 'Jinda Shaheed' by the priests of the Akal Takt," the dark-eyed man explained in halting English. "That means, 'living martyr'." He had been involved in the modern Sikh struggle for a homeland since the days following the Emergency. From 1980 until 1982, Parmar said, he lived in Punjab — baptising people into his understanding of the faith and rallying the faithful alongside Bhindranwale. But he had been forced to flee.

Parmar now had associates worldwide and frequently contacted them to arrange money transfers and other business. He used international airlines the way most people used the local transit system.

In 1983, as the situation in the Punjab slipped towards civil war, he jetted to England to rally support and preach his secessionist message. From England, he traveled to the Netherlands. After meeting with Sikhs in Roermond, he boarded a train to West Germany, where half a century before O'Dwyer's killer, Udham Singh, had found support before embarking on his assassination mission. When Parmar crossed the border on June 29, however, he was arrested at the first train station, Monchengladbach, by West German police armed with an international murder warrant. The Indian government had tracked him around the globe and waited until he had entered a country prepared to treat its charges seriously.

Parmar spent almost a year in prison while the courts waited for the Indians to provide evidence for his extradition. But while New Delhi was willing to pay a reward for his capture, it failed to convince the court that he was guilty of anything other than proselytizing. No charges were ever laid and he was eventually released.

When Parmar stepped off the plane at Vancouver International Airport on July 7, 1984, the newly formed Canadian Security and Intelligence Service followed his every move. Like most Khalsa Sikhs, Parmar was fairly easy to spot. He made the job of keeping tabs on him easier by wearing a fluorescent saffron-colored turban coiled nearly a meter-high atop his head. He also liked to wear slippers with upturned toes and the electric blue battle dress of a

Nihang. He led a major Sikh extremist organization, orchestrated its movements from his home behind the screen of his Canadian citizenship and was proud of it. Talwinder Singh Parmar believed that he had been anointed: "God awakened me."

Parmar emigrated to Canada from Punjab in 1970. Parmar was clean shaven then, and his hair was clipped. He joined other relatives who were already living in British Columbia, and moved in with his brother in Vancouver. He worked at a local lumber mill. But amid one of the largest concentrations of Sikhs outside of the Punjab, he found faith.

His $350,000 home in Burnaby is mortgage free. Inside its spacious living room hang portraits of Bhindranwale, and Parmar's father. His fire screen depicts the Indian army's assault on the Akal Takht in florid colors. Sitting with his wife and three children, Parmar says that "God [first] spoke to me in 1973." He made a series of trips to Pakistan and India over the next few years. On one trip, he was introduced to Pakistani defence officials, who wanted to encourage Sikh aspirations in order to create a buffer state between Pakistan and India, and to key Sikh separatists.

The trip was arranged by Ganga Singh Dhillon, a U.S. Sikh millionaire who had close ties to the Pakistani administration and dabbled in international politics from his base in Washington, D.C. Bhindranwale's nephew, Jasbir Singh, was also part of the group, as was Parmar's close associate Surjan Singh Gill, an affluent B.C. farmer.

Religion and the quest for a Sikh homeland became an obsession for Parmar after the trip. He became active in the Akhand Kirtani Jatha, the fundamentalist organization that promoted hymn singing and secession. His devotion and commitment attracted the attention of his religious brethren and they began to see in his prescient, piercing look, the gaze of a holy man. In public, he wore an expression usually seen in medieval paintings, in which the martyr's limbs are being sawed off but the face says he is being deprived of nothing essential. He has not held a job other than preaching since then.

"I no need money," he said. "I was able to buy and sell a lot of houses, making a lot of money. Our mortgages were paid off — two houses with clear title. And two cars. Plus, I was able to take $35,000 to India with me to baptise and preach ... I got a house, cars, money, family. They all work. There's no cinema, no drink, no meat. I have too much money."

His involvement with the Akhand Kirtani Jatha introduced him to Amarjit Kaur, whose husband was killed in the 1978 clash between the Sikhs and the heretic Nirankari sect. Through his contacts with her and the other Punjabi politicians, he developed a following in the Indian state. He said that during one trip to India he and several priests he paid to accompany him baptised more than 10,000 Sikhs. His supporters called themselves the Babbar Khalsa, or "tigers of the true faith". Parmar registered the group outside of the Punjab as a Sikh charity to take advantage of tax laws and to facilitate funding.

"We were all very young," his twenty-year-old daughter Rajinder Kaur added. " I was in Grade 6 or 7, they," she said, indicating with a nod her brothers, Naswinder and Jaswinder, "were in 5 and 3. It was tough when he went to do his religious duty." The Babbars made no secret of their aims: to protect the purity of the faith and to meet Hindu aggression in kind. Their name was a reference to the Babbar Akalis, the Sikhs who, during the 1920s supported the Akali Dal party in the same way that the IRA backed the Sinn Fein: through random bombings, beatings, and assassinations. Spokesmen for Parmar's group who called themselves his followers boasted of having killed more than forty Nirankaris and other enemies of Sikhism since 1978.

The Indian government painted the Babbars living on the subcontinent as criminals racing through the Punjab on motor-scooters, wreaking havoc wherever they went.

"[The Babbar Khalsa] looks upon the Jewish struggle for the creation of Israel and the National Liberation struggle of the Kurds as models for organizing its activities," the Indian government's white paper on the Punjab agitation explained. "The Babbar Khalsa was established in 1978 in India. Its branch in Canada was set up in 1981. Talwinder Singh Parmar is the Jathedar [leader] of the overseas unit. It is trying to extend its activities to the USA, the UK, Holland and West Germany.... The members of the organization have been talking about plans to organize a 'Khalistan Liberation Army'. .... [at a meeting in which British Sikhs were urged to boycott Air India flights they were] warned that the names of Sikh passengers and Sikh travel agents in the UK who do not cooperate with the committee would be passed on to representatives of the Babbar Khalsa in Punjab and New Delhi so that they could be killed."

While in India between 1980 and 1982, Parmar met and discussed strategy with the fundamentalist leaders. "Bhindranwale's mistake was playing politics in the beginning," Parmar said. "When he woke up to what they were doing, that they were breaking promises, then he began to break away from them and think in religious terms. That's when they said he was a terrorist. .... There were two men — Bhindranwale and me."

In August 1981, at the economic summit conference in Nairobi, Mrs. Gandhi and Prime Minister Pierre Trudeau discussed the situation. But there was little Ottawa was prepared to do.

The arrest of Bhindranwale that September and the hijacking of an Indian Airlines jet by Sikh separatists highlighted the problem. The skyjackers were friends of the Canadian separatist leaders, many of whom, including Parmar's wife and sister, flew to Pakistan to coordinate the legal defense and offer support. Parmar was underground.

Akali leader Harchand Singh Longowal's battle with Mrs. Gandhi was degenerating into a religious gang-war at the time. Parmar disappeared into its vortex shortly after the murder in September of newspaper editor Lala Narain and the arrest of Sant Bhindranwale. He was wanted for murder.

In November 1981, Parmar was hiding in the Indian state of Uttar Pradesh. His wife, Surindar Kaur, feared the worst when none of her letters to relatives were answered, and she pleaded with the Canadian government to help locate her husband. By December, Parmar had a price on his head: the Indian police offered a 50,000 rupee (about $5,000 U.S.) reward for his capture. They accused him of killing two policemen and another man from his father's village, Panshta, a charge that has never been proved.

Parmar says the police ransacked his ancestral home, beat his family, and persecuted even distant relatives. "Fifty members of my family were arrested," he said. "One had his legs broken. Another, broken arms. One spent nine months in jail. How can I forget that. We wanted to live peacefully, but they forced us to fight . . . We are fighting to defend ourselves. We were forced to."

Parmar arrived home to a hero's welcome at Vancouver International Airport on May 2, 1982. Among the chanting supporters was his daughter, Rajinder Kaur, who was celebrating her fifteenth birthday. "This is the best birthday gift I ever got," she said with a grin after hugging her dad.

Gill, the vegetable farmer from the Fraser Valley and one of Parmar's closest friends, said Parmar was smuggled out of India through Nepal.

The Indian government demanded his extradition immediately upon hearing that he had returned. But the Canadian government maintained that it couldn't extradite one of its own citizens. Parmar stayed for a year in Canada before jetting off again to England to meet with British Sikh leaders in London and Birmingham.

His message was straightforward. He maintained that the followers of the five-hundred-year-old warrior faith deserved a homeland in the Punjab because their ancestors were born on the broad plain, their gurus taught there and, for a short stint more than a century ago, the Sikhs had governed it. The Jews won Palestine; the Muslims won Pakistan; the Sikhs will win the Punjab, Parmar argued with all the conviction of a logician articulating a tautology. The Sikhs are about as numerous as the Jews. They had won Palestine when a minority of only 600,000 lived in the Arab-held territory. There were twelve million Sikhs living in the Punjab. The other two million around the globe made the expatriate community as numerous today as the Palestinians, who were trying to win a homeland with far fewer resources.

His friend and supporter, Gill, had opened a "consulate" for the new nation in a sparsely furnished suite in Vancouver, which was dominated by a portrait of Maharaja Ranjit Singh and the saffron-colored flag of Khalistan. Inside, Gill issued propaganda and threats. "We can't forgive the Hindu government of India any more," said Gill, who called himself the consul-general of the Republic of

Khalistan. "There were no plans to hurt anyone [in the September hijacking of the plane to Pakistan]; it was designed to tell the government of India that we mean business."

The Malayan-born Gill lived in Surrey, a sprawling rural municipality on the eastern outskirts of Vancouver. He emigrated to Vancouver in 1969 after spending ten years in Britain. He said Khalistan would be a buffer state between India and Pakistan running from the Chinese border in the north to the Arabian Sea. "All Sikhs in Canada are involved," claimed Gill. "It's a community job to get things done. The message we get from the Sikh temples in B.C. is that we have their full support."

The burly Sikh arranged through a Seattle printing company to produce worthless Khalistan currency, blue five-dollar bills that identified him as the "governor of the Bank of Khalistan". He mailed them to Indian members of parliament along with Khalistan postage stamps and passports. Supporters of the secessionist movement also opened offices in Toronto, Winnipeg, and Calgary.

Dr. Jagjit Singh Chauhan, the former Punjab cabinet minister who was leading the separatist fight from his base in London, visited in a show of support. "Takeover is never without arms," he said shortly before the Canadian government ordered him out of the country. "We shall continue to pursue peaceful methods, yet we are training our young — in Canada and the United States — in martial prowess. We shall raise our own army, our own units. There are fifty thousand Sikhs who are ex-soldiers in India whom we can prepare in ten days. We have training in the latest guerrilla warfare tactics with the most modern weapons."

Parmar's circle of friends and supporters included other wealthy and influential Sikhs such as Raminder Singh Malik.

Malik was one of "midnight's children", a man like Bhindranwale born in 1947, the first generation ever born in the political entity created at midnight on August 15 of that year: India. A united and independent India had never existed before. His family was from West Punjab in what is now Pakistan and he had been a student at the University of British Columbia in the 1970s. His faith was as strident as Parmar's, and his business acumen or luck had also earned him a fortune. He remained in the background, however, and when questioned about his dealings he shrugged: "I was successful and made money."

The Vancouver businessman was president of the Satnam Educational Society which produced audio tapes of Sikh music and sermons. While Parmar was jailed in Germany, Malik looked after the financial arrangements for his family. (Gill arranged for Parmar's lawyers.)

Malik would also help create the first Sikh credit union and the first Khalsa school in North America. More than a hundred Sikh children attend classes from kindergarten to Grade 6. "We are isolating them from sex at ten, from smoking and from drugs," Malik said expressing his disdain for what he considers the corruption rampant in Canadian society. "In this society, the family structure is pretty weird. I want to separate my children from that and teach them to respect themselves and their own parents. We can be successful and be isolated. We don't need to learn the bad things from your society."

There were others in Parmar's circle of separatist agitators such as Sodhi Singh Sodhi, an excitable thirty-three-year-old who was one of two saber-brandishing Sikhs who trashed the Vancouver Indian consulate after hearing about Operation Bluestar; and two Sikh separatists from Kamloops, a city in the interior of B.C., who helped found the Babbar Khalsa: Satnam Singh Khun Khun and Ajaib Singh Bagri. One of the most curious, however, was a school janitor who had helped arrange Parmar's trip to Pakistan in 1978. He was one of Parmar's conduits to the powerful politicians in Punjab.

Only a few blocks from the heart of the city's East Indian community, inside his spacious home, Hardial Singh Johal sat in his shirt-sleeves and work pants, playing coy. He smiled at his questioner's consternation. "Yes, I know," the Vancouver School Board engineer said. "It's a little odd. I know some good guys and some very bad guys."

He has seen the Sikh struggle from the inside, and he required little prompting to spin his stories. Since 1920, when the Sikhs formed their own political party, the Akali Dal, his family has been at the heart of the fight. First they fought the British to win independence for India and now they are trying to wrest power from New Delhi. Johal's involvement began at age fourteen, when he was imprisoned for joining a demonstration demanding official recognition for the Sikh language, Punjabi. "It was a lot like the movement in Quebec for French rights," the forty-year-old man says.

He shrugs off as a rite of passage the few days he served in an Indian jail. He emerged and went on with his education, obtaining a degree in civil engineering. In 1968, because of his family's ties to the Sikh establishment, he was hired by the SGPC, the body that maintains Sikh temples in the Punjab.

Johal became the committee's head of public works and maintained the shrines and temples. It was a job he held for four years until his second term in an Indian prison, this time for his role in Sikh agitation. "We could see the future," he says of his decision to emigrate. "My wife had a good job, we had land. We knew we could survive. But for my children? We knew it wasn't going to be bright."

They chose to come to Canada because, like the thousands of others who came in the same year, they had relatives on the west coast. A grandparent had come in 1906, he says, and two of his uncles were born in New Westminster's Royal Columbian Hospital in the 1920s.

Johal brought his politics with him. He was a leader in the fundamentalist drive launched by the new immigrants to rid the temples of those who had become westernized. He liked to keep one foot in each nation, even though they are separated by an ocean. He has adopted Canadian citizenship. His spacious house was in a neighborhood of modest, single-family homes, but to step inside is to journey inside Indian politics. Sikh warrior pictures adorn the walls. An aging relative sits quietly off to one side, rising occasionally to utter what appears to be his only line of English: "It's the Indian government who are the culprits."

"In 1982," Johal continues, "when I spent three and a half months in the Punjab, my impression was that Sikhs were on the right track, and I was hoping the Indian government would consider their demands and the problem would be settled. They didn't."

Johal's wife appears, delivers a glass of orange juice to him and disappears demurely back into the kitchen, his two children in tow.

Powerful Sikh leaders from the Punjab stayed with Johal regularly. Hardial Singh Longowal, once the most important of the Sikh leaders, visited for several days in 1979 and again in 1982. Johal moves back and forth between the Punjab and Canada for several months every other year. He helped raise money in Canada for Longowal's crusade in India. In 1982, he traveled to his homeland to campaign for Longowal.

"The Longowal group, who were pushing for political compromise," Johal says, "found themselves unable to please their own constituents while Mrs. Gandhi bolstered her own party's fortunes by keeping the Sikhs divided. Face it, it doesn't matter where you go, those who speak loudest and more violently — people will listen to them. Lebanon, Vancouver or Punjab — it doesn't matter. Those who speak loudly and irrationally are listened to and attract more attention."

Bhindranwale's audacity and the inability of the Indian police to quell the violence he counseled bolstered every faction within the Sikh community. The resurgence of Sikh chauvinism in the Punjab was reflected in the expatriate communities. The more militant temple politicians in the Fraser Valley of British Columbia provided money, support, a haven for fugitives and recruits. "The Congress Party pushed Bhindranwale in the beginning but some hard-hearted people came in after and pushed him farther," Johal says.

He leans back in his chair, sips his orange juice, and smiles sphinx-like when asked who were the hard-hearted and blood-thirsty advisers who encouraged the Sant to wage war on Mrs. Gandhi. "Khalistan, a separate nation as far as Longowal was concerned," Johal says somberly, "was just a bargaining position. We were pushing for political compromise."

But in fact, Parmar and his associates were an integral part of the rebellion in the Punjab. They maintained their ties to those waging war in India and provided moral and material support to the struggle.

"The Khalistan movement announced . . . on March 20, 1981, is the start of our association," imprisoned Sikh hijacker Gajinder

Singh wrote to Parmar in a letter the priest treasured. "Since this meeting, enough has passed by and the Khalistan movement has covered a bloody trail. Even after spending more than four years in Pakistan we are still behind the lock and you after [spending] time in German jail must have reached Canada. The dream of Khalistan that I have been dreaming for the last sixteen, seventeen years, I would like to know the present situation of that battle that is being waged for the achievement of that Khalistan. Please make an attempt to send your Khalistan date and emotional feelings on this subject."

During Parmar's imprisonment, Bhindranwale's political tactician mailed letters to Sikhs around the globe urging them to rally around the imprisoned Vancouver priest. When he was freed, Parmar spent most of his time raising thousands of dollars to help men like Gajinder Singh and the families of those who were suffering as a result of the fight. In Vancouver, he and his friends collected about $34,000 during one drive — $5,000 from one man's brother, $2,500 from a sister, another $5,000 here, $10,000 there. He helped raise millions for the Sikh campaign. After the Indian government confiscated $13,000 en route to the Akali Dal leader, he and Malik were forced to begin legal maneuvers to get it back and find other ways of transferring funds.

Occasionally too, the group squabbled. Despite Parmar's assumed status as priest, those who helped him complained of his "big ego" and said that "one day that ego was going to sink him". They were doing the running around, they said, neglecting their families, suffering the inconvenience, yet Parmar didn't show any appreciation. "These Singhs, who under his command laid down their lives, became martyrs, were all poor," said one disgruntled disciple. "Now that they are gone, their families are completely ruined. No one cares about them . . . . Parmar never appreciates the sacrifices of other people."

At a B.C. Sikh wedding attended by Parmar and several of his lieutenants from across the country the animosity between the priest and a former member of his group, Mohinder Singh, became apparent when they quarreled openly. Despite his abrasive personality, however, Parmar commanded enormous loyalty and devotion because of his own commitment.

"You know that guy who was with us, Amarjit Singh, a policeman," he would tell his supporters. "His wife has written. It is so sad that it is hard to read. She says she has two children, no home, and her father's been badly beaten by the police. 'His legs are broke and he's bedridden and the police keep us hopping from the police station to the village. We have no money, no home and no one willing to help the poor.' She said we don't know who to turn to."

Parmar wanted to provide that help.

Canada's novice domestic intelligence service had kept Parmar under surveillance since he arrived from his cell in Germany. On June 4, 1985, the spies were at their usual vantage point, about a mile away from Parmar's home, watching his comings and goings through binoculars.

The pending arrival of Rajiv Gandhi for his first official visit to the United States had them jittery. Indian intelligence added to the anxiety by asserting that one of his mother's assassins, Beant Singh, had made calls to Vancouver shortly before the killing.

The Federal Bureau of Investigation had arrested a number of American Sikhs for plotting to murder the Indian prime minister but two members of the group escaped. Not only were the Canadians worried that they might seek Parmar's help, but there had also been warnings that Sikh separatists planned to mark the first anniversary of Operation Bluestar with a spectacular and violent offensive. Airport security across the continent had been increased and law enforcement agencies around the globe were on alert.

The Canadian agents followed Parmar that day as he made his regular visit to his temple, but they lost him. It didn't matter; they knew his routine and could pick him up again at his home. Later that day they tailed Surjan Singh Gill as he drove Parmar and a man the spies didn't know to the B.C. ferry terminal at Horseshoe Bay on Howe Sound. The ferries regularly plied the Georgia Strait, carrying cars and passengers back and forth between Vancouver Island and the province's southern mainland. Gill dropped his passengers off.

Parmar, wearing a blue turban and a blue-and-white sports jacket, and the unidentified man strolled aboard the *Queen of Oak Bay* with the spies close behind. During the trip, Parmar made two telephone calls within earshot of the intelligence agents and arranged to be picked up when the ferry arrived in the coal-mining town of Nanaimo.

Joginder Gill, a local island temple leader, met Parmar and the unidentified man at the ferry terminal and drove them to Inderjit Singh Reyat's home in Duncan, a small lumber town nestled amid the island's rugged hills. Reyat had got to know Parmar, Johal, Gill, and the others through his own involvement in the faith. He played tabla drums and joined the Akhand Kirtani Jatha shortly after he and his wife moved to Vancouver in 1972.

He had left India at thirteen and moved to Britain where he lived for seven years and met his wife. She had moved to Britain from East Africa when she was ten. Reyat moved to Vancouver Island in 1980 and worked as an electrician in the local Auto Marine Electric shop. He was heavily involved in local Sikh politics and was well-liked in the community where he and his family put down roots.

At about 5:00 P.M., shortly after they arrived from the ferry, Parmar, Reyat, and the unidentified man left the modest two-story home and drove to a secluded wooded area west of town. As several spies peered or listened in the bushes, Parmar and Reyat removed something from the trunk of the brown Mercury with "I REYAT" vanity license plates and walked into the forest. Reyat maintained that the powder, light-filament and .22-caliber bullet he used to make the device whimpered when detonated. The spies said they heard a loud explosion.

"It scared the hell out of me," Larry Lowe, a hulking, grey-haired Canadian Security and Intelligence Service (CSIS) agent, said later. He bent low, believing someone was shooting. His partner back in one of the hidden surveillance cars, Margaret Lynne McAdams, says it made her "jump off of the seat".

Moments later, Parmar and Reyat emerged from the bush, rejoined the unidentified man in the car, and drove away. Lowe and McAdams made a quick search of the area where the car had been parked, found nothing, and headed back into town. They did not go into the forest to see what might have caused the noise that startled them. Lowe, a big-game hunter, was sure it was a rifle shot. His partner agreed that it must have been although she had never heard a rifle discharge. They informed senior intelligence officers in the Royal Canadian Mounted Police, who were also keeping tabs on Sikh separatists. Under the law, the security agency's role is to only gather intelligence; the national police force handles arrests and criminal investigations. Despite the CSIS information, the senior Mounties did not order a search of the area Parmar and Reyat visited. Much later, Reyat told police he liked to play with dynamite as a hobby. He had obtained more than a dozen sticks illegally from a local driller. He said that he intended to use it to clear some land. He later confessed that he had been asked to make an explosive device that could be smuggled into India and used in car bombs or to destroy "a bridge or something you wanta blow." He failed, he said.

Parmar returned to Vancouver that night with the spies in tow. The unidentified man stayed with Reyat. The two went to a local Woolworth's store the following day and bought a stereo tuner. Reyat paid the bill because the other man didn't have enough money. He said he gave the man the tuner as a present. When questioned by police later he couldn't remember the man's name, but he thought it might have been "Surjit Singh" but he could not positively identify him.

Parmar flew to Toronto a few days after his trip to Duncan to preach and meet with his eastern Canadian supporters in southern Ontario. On June 10, three of his B.C. Babbar Khalsa members tried to cross into the United States to protest Rajiv Gandhi's visit but they were turned back as undesirable aliens at the Blaine border crossing in Washington State.

During his visit, Gandhi railed against Canada for harboring "terrorists" who were implicated in the conspiracy that led to his mother's death and that threatened his democratically elected government. The rookie Conservative government in Ottawa, run by industrial-relations lawyer Brian Mulroney, feared his anger would jeopardize Canada's attempts to improve business relations with India. The Canadian government authorized the broadest and most expensive national-security operation the country had ever undertaken. Parmar and the Babbar Khalsa were at its core.

Aside from the physical surveillance of Parmar and his supporters, the intelligence agency was also electronically intercepting their telephone calls. During the month, they monitored a flurry of early-morning phone calls between Reyat, Johal, and Parmar.

On Thursday, June 20, while the spies watched Parmar, a large, bearded man in his late thirties wearing a saffron-colored turban approached Canadian Pacific Airlines ticket clerk Gerald Duncan in downtown Vancouver. He wanted to pick up tickets booked the day before for Mohinderbell Singh and Jaswand Singh. The man wanted the arranged ticket to Bangkok changed from a return to one-way fare, and the name changed from Mohinderbel Singh to L. Singh. He also changed the name on the second ticket for an Air-India flight heading out of Toronto from Jaswand Singh to M. Singh. He then paid $3,005 in cash for the tickets and left.

Duncan, who would later be put under hypnosis by police to try to remember details of the transaction, paid little attention to the well-spoken customer, but was fascinated by the beard net the man wore. The ticket buyer left a local telephone number for the airline to call if there were any problems. The number had belonged to Hardial Singh Johal. Another number used in the transactions was a line into the Ross Street Temple.

The following evening, Reyat traveled to Vancouver by ferry.

On Saturday morning, about 6:30 A.M., a man identifying himself as Manjit Singh called the CP Air reservations office and asked if he was still on the waiting list for an Air-India flight out of Toronto. He was. The man then asked if he could still send his luggage through from Vancouver to New Delhi. He was told that unless his seat on the Indian government-run airline was confirmed, he and his luggage would stop at Toronto, where his CP flight ended.

Two hours later, a slender, clean-shaven man in his mid-thirties approached check-in counter number twenty-six at Vancouver International airport. He was carrying a medium-sized, burgundy vinyl suitcase. The gray-suited man presented M. Singh's ticket to CP Air clerk Jeannie Adams. She gave him seat 10b for the flight to

Toronto, but told him he was still wait-listed on the flight to New Delhi. He asked her to check his luggage straight through but Adams explained it was against regulations to tag bags for loading on connecting flights for wait-listed passengers. In front of a long queue of waiting passengers, the man firmly pressed her to check his bag. He ignored her pleas to be reasonable, and Adams remembers giving up in frustration, thinking, "You jerk, you're taking up my time. I said, 'Okay, I'll check it through but you have to check with Air India when you get to Toronto'."

The CP Air jumbo carrying M. Singh's bag lifted off, heading for Toronto just after 9:00 A.M., eighteen minutes late. The man wasn't in his seat, but his luggage would nevertheless be loaded aboard the connecting Air-India flight in Toronto. The Air-India plane was guarded by five Mounted policemen as it sat on the tarmac. Security had been tightened around Indian planes for the last month because of threatened terrorist strikes. Inside the terminal, the guards under contract from Burns International Security Service to screen Air-India baggage-checked suitcases with an explosives sniffer that the RCMP later described as "useless".

When they held it close to a burgundy suitcase that was being transferred from the CP flight, the sniffer beeped. The noise, however, didn't match the high-pitched whine they had been instructed to expect if explosives were present. The bag was loaded aboard the Air-India jet.

A few hours after the man checked M. Singh's suitcase though the Vancouver airport, another man approached Jeannie Adams's check-in counter and presented a ticket in the name of L. Singh for flight 003 to Tokyo. Adams assigned him seat 38h and checked his gray bag. When the jumbo lifted off seventeen minutes late, at about 1:30 P.M., L. Singh was not on board.

Nearly ten hours later, L.Singh's bag exploded as it was unloaded at Narita airport, seventy-two kilometers northeast of Tokyo. Two baggage handlers were killed and four others injured by the bomb that had been hidden inside a stereo tuner. Had it detonated minutes earlier it would have knocked CP Air flight 003 from the sky, killing all 389 people aboard.

A team of more than three dozen investigators combed through the debris. Jacques Girard, head of a Quebec trade delegation in Tokyo, was waiting to assist a Quebec cabinet minister with customs and immigration formalities when the blast rocked the airport. The minister for citizens' relations had arrived on an earlier flight. Girard said the entire terminal building shook.

"There was a big bang and suddenly police and firemen were running everywhere," he said later. "I waited to see what would happen next. Even after the minister landed we had to wait nearly three hours while everything was checked before we could leave."

The country's forensic scientists established that the bomb was hidden in a discontinued Sanyo stereo tuner model number FMT 611K. Three thousand of the tuners had been sold in Canada — one to Reyat only a fortnight earlier. The Japanese police also believed the powerful bomb was probably meant to explode after the bag was loaded aboard the connecting Air-India flight to Bangkok. The luggage loaded aboard the Canadian plane had not been screened.

"There are some countries who want close scrutiny of their luggage, such as Air India," an embarrassed Transport Canada spokesman said. "But there was never any particular scrutiny given to bags on board a Canadian plane heading to Japan."

Less than an hour later, half a world away, on a sunny Sunday morning, the Air-India plane carrying M. Singh's bag plummeted from the skies as the plane cruised towards London for a refueling stop.

Stunned air-traffic controllers in Shannon watched impotently as the plane's green radar image faded from their screens at 7:14 A.M. Captain H.S. Narendra, a former pilot for Indira Gandhi with thirty-five years' experience, had been telling a steward to bring an excited boy forward for a promised visit to the cockpit in a "few minutes".

The police believe a massive explosion ripped through the cargo hold, lifted the passenger floor from its stays, and severed electrical power and the oxygen supply to the pilots. Frantic radio calls from Shannon went unanswered. Most of the 329 passengers and crew died instantly, but some survived to drown in the choppy, frigid waters of the North Atlantic.

A four-jet Nimrod reconnaissance plane was scrambled out of Kinloss Royal Air Force Base in Scotland moments after flight 182 vanished from radar screens. Twenty-five minutes later, about two hundred kilometers off the southwest coast of Ireland, the twenty-nine-year-old pilot looked down on the carnage scattered across the heavy swell. "There was an oil slick and we could see wreckage from the undercarriage. Bodies were floating in the water," Flight Lieutenant Neil Robertson said. "We could see aircraft panels, seats, and pieces of interior trim. We also located some survival dinghies only partially inflated, which had no one in them."

Sixteen minutes later the first of eleven British helicopters lifted off and three U.S. HC-53 Jolly Green Giant helicopters joined the effort along with two other Nimrods. By nightfall, an armada of ships and helicopters had plucked from the shark-infested sea 131 corpses, most beyond identification. Only one other body would be recovered weeks later, washed ashore. The jetliner's black box was located on the ocean's bottom.

Seven Sea King and two Chinook helicopters from the Royal Air Force ferried the dead back to the airport hangar that served as a temporary morgue. Later, the remains were shuttled to Cork Regional Hospital. A ten-member Irish guard of honor saluted each body as it was carried past.

There were 279 Canadians aboard the seven-year-old plane, but Prime Minister Mulroney insensitively offered condolences first to India and Gandhi, instead of to the next-of-kin in Canada.

The tiny Irish town was overrun by the rescue and investigation crews and anguished families. Five top Indian aviation experts arrived to lead the inquiry that would include experts from Canada, the United States, and Britain. With the help of mini-submarines and specialized ships, the investigators conducted a $10 million, summer-long salvage operation. They discovered the red-and-white remains of the plane strewn across an eight-kilometer swath of the ocean floor, six kilometers beneath the surface.

The flight deck and first-class compartment were lying shattered two hundred meters from the rest of the twisted wreckage. The nose appeared to have broken away just behind the plane's forward door, and investigators said they believed the blast in the forward luggage hold had severed the plane's electrical spine, knocking out all instruments and controls.

At a later official inquiry in New Delhi chaired by Justice B.N. Kirpal, one expert hypothesized that the pilots may have survived the initial explosion and tried vainly to regain control of the crippled craft before it slammed into the sea upside down and at a steep angle. But it was more likely they passsed out in the thin, icy air of the upper atmosphere. Kirpal concluded that a bomb destroyed the plane and blamed lax security in Canada as a contributing cause.

A man called *The New York Times* and admitted responsibility for the 331 deaths on behalf of the "Sikh Student Federation, 10th Regiment". Another called a Bombay newspaper and said the Babbar Khalsa were responsible for the two explosions.

The disaster sent a shudder through the intelligence community of North America. It was only the twelfth Boeing 747 to go down since the first of the hump-backed airliners went into service in 1970 — and half of those crashes had been claimed by terrorists.

As they sat in a briefing that Sunday morning listening to what the Canadian security service knew about the Sikhs, the RCMP investigators realized they had underestimated the Sikh separatists they had been monitoring. The Mounties were told that the spy agency believed a well-organized revolutionary movement was operating in cells across Canada. They pointed to Parmar as one of its leaders and told the Mounties to concentrate their investigation on him and his supporters.

Parmar was eventually acquitted of charges that he was involved in the Air-India disaster. In March 1986, the explosives charges that had been brought against him were dismissed when the prosecution offered no evidence.

6. AGENTS PROVOCATEURS

Senior Canadian intelligence officials and politicians were furious that Sikh terrorists were able to use the country to launch their attacks on the Indian government. For months, their agents, along with undercover policemen, had been watching those in the Sikh community believed capable of orchestrating such destruction. But they had failed to prevent the death of 331 people. They had been warned, and still they underestimated the Sikh separatists.

The first real evidence that a Sikh terrorist network was being created around the globe came from a U.S. police operation that began about the time of Mrs. Gandhi's assassination. It ended shortly before the Air-India crash.

About a month before the experimental bomb was detonated on Vancouver Island, U.S. police captured a linchpin of the international Sikh extremist movement. The documents they seized at the time indicated that cells of Sikh terrorists were being established in Toronto, Montreal, and Vancouver more than two months before the Air-India jet went down.

Frank Camper, a thirty-eight-year-old Vietnam veteran and sometime mercenary who had served with the Long Range Patrol, the fearsome "Lurps", approached the Federal Bureau of Investigation with the tip that changed the way North American law-enforcement agencies handled the Sikhs. Camper operated the Recondo Merc School in the pine woods of Dolomite, near Birmingham. He offered a two-week course in which people paid to be beaten, sprint across rivers under live machine-gun fire, fight each other with clubs, and watch while one of their number was interrogated while suspended naked over a campfire. "I tell guys they don't really want to do it," he said. "It's not lucrative, it's not romantic — don't get involved."

There wasn't much Camper wouldn't do for money. He and two of his associates, for instance, fire-bombed two cars in 1985 after they were paid to intimidate two California teachers. His contact with the Sikhs began with a telephone call to his "bunker" two weeks before Mrs. Gandhi's assassination on October 31, 1984. The men duly arrived wearing turbans, three-piece suits, and tennis shoes. One also wore a metal badge: "Sikhs Seek Justice".

A man who called himself Balraj Singh introduced the others as Sukhvinder Singh, Avraj Singh, and Lal Singh. He joked about their concealed identities: "You see, we are all named Singh." All had visited Toronto and Vancouver and had friends or relatives in those cities.

A few days into the training program, as the three stood shivering in their underwear, Camper says Balraj asked for his help in staging a revolution. It was conspiracy at first light. Later in the week, when Balraj nearly had his eye knocked out in one of Camper's mock ambushes, the mercenary trainer had a chance to go to the FBI while surgeons worked on the Sikh. An FBI agent and Camper talked about Sikh terrorism and, from that moment on, Camper considered himself a G-man. He told the Sikhs he could get them anything they wanted.

The Sikhs with their heritage of martial myths were easy fodder for the mercenary. In the back woods of Alabama, he fed them fantasies and dreams culled from the magazine Soldier of Fortune, and bolstered their belief that it was more effective to blast away at one's enemies than to lobby or wave placards.

The Sikhs graduated from the combat training course and

arranged to meet Camper in New York's Sheraton Center Hotel to discuss the arms and munitions they needed. Camper had an Ingram submachine-gun loaded with a short, sixteen-round magazine hidden in the desk drawer. He wanted to be able to produce it with a flourish at the appropriate moment to impress them. "I wanted it there when I came back to the room," he later recounted. "I would sit on the bed near the drawer as I talked to the Sikhs."

Gurpartap Singh Birk, a well-built thirty-five-year-old in a good suit, gave his name as John. He held a PH.D. in computer science and was a former technical envoy with the European Common Market who had designed the Belgian parliament's computer system. Birk's wife and two children still lived in London where he was vice-president of Data Application International. The computer expert was in America working with an associated company called Automatic Toll Systems, of White Plains. He was also a leader of the International Sikh Students Federation. He celebrated in the streets of Manhattan after Mrs. Gandhi was killed.

Neither Birk nor twenty-five-year-old Lal Singh Lally introduced the short elderly man in a white turban with a handlebar mustache to Camper. He was Major-General Jaswant Singh Bhullar, the former military adviser to Sant Jarnail Singh Bhindranwale, who had fled to the United States just before Operation Bluestar was launched. He fomented armed revolution and openly discussed strategy with representatives from the Mujahiddin and the Kashmiri Liberation Army, a subcontinent separatist group that murdered an Indian diplomat in Birmingham in January 1984.

Bhullar's role at the hotel-room meeting was to inspect the weapons and the arms merchant. The Sikhs would later accuse him of being an agent provocateur, an Indian government plant who had infiltrated Bhindranwale's group and now spied on the expatriates. He was the most vociferous in his call for military action. Unlike the others, he would not be arrested or charged by U.S. police. When his separatist colleagues accused him of being an Indian agent, he fled the United States under threat of deportation.

Except for Bhullar, the Sikhs lived together on the second floor of a red-brick apartment house in the New York borough of Queens. Lal Singh Lally, who had been at Camper's school, and thirty-four-year-old Ammand Singh Dhaliwal worked as laborers. The six-story building was in an area crowded with immigrants, about ten blocks from Shea Stadium where they watched an occasional baseball game. They were remembered as quiet tenants who promptly paid the $400 monthly rent. There were often as many as five Sikhs living in the apartment.

During the meeting in the hotel room, the Sikhs told Camper they wanted more specialized training. They also wanted enough explosives to blow up a thirty-six-story skyscraper, the FBI says. Camper said he could introduce them to just the man they needed, an expert in urban guerrilla warfare. Camper didn't tell them Tom Nichols's real name was Thomas Norris and that he was working for the FBI and the U.S. Secret Service.

On January 26, in the New York Hilton Hotel on Sixth Avenue, Lally and Birk were introduced by Camper to the ex-U.S. Navy commando. The men discussed the merits of Mach 10 machine-guns and c-4 plastic explosives in conversations that were videotaped by police. Camper at one point asked: "What about going after Rajiv right there in India, going after him personally?" Birk replied uneasily. "Uh, we thought about it . . . . You see, what would happen is that . . . . Okay, he's eliminated, another person of the same type is going to take command. Okay, because, remember, he's been elected by . . . I think he got eighty-five per cent of the votes."

Later, he said: "So, we cannot . . . dictate, uh, democracy over there or anywhere. Democracy is in the majority."

The second meeting was on February 15, 1985, at the Island Inn, Westbury, Long Island. Ammand attended the meeting but not Camper. Birk said the Sikhs needed six or seven passports and Norris said they would cost $300 each. Birk gave him a check. He also said he wanted enough explosives to destroy bridges about the size of New York's Triborough and Brooklyn spans. When the FBI informant asked if the Sikhs had any source of explosives at all, Birk told him, "I'll tell you straight. We steal from the Indian government itself."

Lal Singh Lally and Birk later took Norris to a four-hectare farm in Columbia, New Jersey, where they said they were going to set up a guerrilla training site. But on May 4, two days before the undercover man was to begin training the Sikhs at their New Jersey camp, New Orleans police arrested Birk.

A gun bought from Camper's store was found in his car. Three other Sikhs were arrested loitering on the sidewalk outside a New Orleans hotel. Inside the hotel was Bhajan Lal, the Hindu chief minister of Haryana state and Mrs. Gandhi's staunch ally. All four Sikhs were held without bail on charges of planning to assassinate Lal, who had flown from India to Louisiana for surgery at the Louisiana State University Eye Center. After two years in jail, all would plead guilty in a plea-bargain arrangement.

The sudden arrests forced the hand of the Americans. They tried to collar the others involved quickly. But when they arrived at the New York apartments, Lally and Ammand Singh had fled with the furniture. Three other Sikhs who were part of the group were also on the run.

The secretly recorded FBI videotapes showed Birk talking about establishing a guerrilla training camp, detonating bombs, and causing an industrial accident such as the chemical leak that killed at least 1,700 people in Bhopal, India.

"I want to cause injuries," he said at one point; "that is the price of our revolution." Birk had dozens of contacts in Europe and North America and moved back and forth between the two continents, organizing. At one point he said the two Sikhs who gunned down Mrs. Gandhi did it under orders from "our organization". It was a statement that appeared to confirm the Indian government's claims that the conspiracy reached around the globe.

Police also seized documents from his briefcase that included a "Proposed Training Schedule" covering such items as "principles of explosive ambush" and "electrical delay firing systems".

"My New Year resolution is to make Khalistan," Birk wrote:

In a nutshell what we have to do is to defeat India economically. Many different ways are available. What I am propagating is make India financially so poor that it falls on its knees. Stop each and every industry in each state of India . . . . Select five commandoes for each state. One as the organizer and four blowing the shit apart. Start with big industries by bombing the industry on same day, same time. Four people further divided into two groups. I have found that groups of two are most effective.

One of the main target[s] is the Baba Atomic Power Station. I have the information that by simply contaminating the water they use we could blow the atomic power station. How easy it can be done . . . . The next target is chemical firms such like Union Carbide. Once the poisonous gas leak takes place, let the nature take its course. All I need is one hundred people and I could bring the Indian puppet government to its knees for God . . . . I can get one group of five people from N.Y. R. Sheregill should be able to get the second group. This makes ten . . . . Balbir should also be able to get five people from Montreal. Vancouver is another five people. I myself will have to go to Toronto to raise five . . . . This makes six groups and thirty people. England has a rich resource of people . . . . Can it be possible that we can get seventy people from there? When we have done this then we have to have three workshops. The first for the coordinations which includes everything from making time bombs, contaminations, poisonings of food crops, biological warfare, to organization. Bhullar is army advisor and should be used as such.

Another letter outlined the goals of the International Sikh Students Federation: "the liberation of Sikh land . . . to fight against the Indian government . . . to work out plans to get assistance from other governments in particular from USA, Canada and British; to revenge the murder of Sant Bhindranwale and other two thousand Sikhs in the Golden Temple . . . to start a Sikh homeland Liberation Army from abroad (USA, Canada, Britain)."

The U.S. authorities — from President Reagan to the head of the FBI — trumpeted the arrests.

But the publicity and the strident rhetoric of the law-enforcement officials on both sides of the border galvanized the fundamentalist Sikh community. The men who had been arrested were well known and respected leaders among the expatriates. Birk was a sophisticated, well-educated man with powerful connections.

The Sikhs refused to believe that he or the others would be involved in mass murder. The use of unscrupulous informers who encouraged violence, and undercover police plants bolstered the feeling that the Sikhs had been framed. It had happened to the Sikh community before. At the turn of the century, spies who worked for the British Raj were utilized by the Canadian and U.S. governments to infiltrate and divide the Sikh community. The media spotlight sparked an outpouring of money from the faithful for the Khalistan cause and led to well-heeled, politically astute Sikhs coming forward to help their brethren.

The Sikhs hired the best lawyer they could find to fight the charges Birk and his fellow conspirators faced. The defense was orchestrated by the World Sikh Organization's Dr. Gurmit Singh Aulakh. A turbaned man with a white beard and waxed mustache, the Harvard professor believed that there were five hundred trained Indian agents within Canada and many more in the United States. He and other Sikhs accused the law-enforcement agencies of North America of preying on emotionally distraught Sikhs at the urging of the Indian government. Aulakh hired William Kunstler to handle the case.

The sixty-six-year-old Kunstler was a forty-year veteran of courtroom skirmishes and his career was built on defending civil liberties. The lawyer had defended the "freedom riders" who protested racial discrimination in Mississippi, and had been special trial counsel to Dr. Martin Luther King Jr. Later Kunstler defended other unpopular civil rights cases involving anarchists and militants such as the Black Panthers, Stokley Carmichael, Rap Brown, and the Chicago Seven. He represented the Indians at Wounded Knee and Pine Ridge, and the inmates involved in the Attica prison riot. He was also hired by Philippines president Corazon Aquino to help retrieve the wealth Ferdinand Marcos had siphoned into the United States.

He had been in the midst of almost every important legal battle between the state and its dissenting citizens for three decades when he agreed to take on the Sikhs. They would pay for his services even though Kunstler often worked for free in his role as a lawyer for the Center of Constitutional Rights, a civil rights organization he helped to found.

"I think it's a consummate fraud," Kunstler said about the case against Birk. "The government has all these video and audio tapes on which you would expect to hear incriminating statements. But all

I hear Birk saying on the tapes is, 'No, no, I won't do it. It would be wrong. It would hurt innocent people. It would hurt our cause in this country.' It seems to me that the only reason he is being tried is to make an example of him or as a sop to the government of India."

The expatriate leadership of the Sikh community agreed. Every day, scores of Sikhs filled the courtroom to support Birk who was accused of plotting to kill Gandhi and of violating the U.S. Neutrality Act, the law used earlier in the century to prosecute the Ghadrites and other Indian nationalists. Their faith in him, however, counted for little in the eyes of the jury when the case came to trial. It was swayed by the cumulative effect of the video tapes, the documents in his briefcase, his politics, and the knowledge that an airliner had been bombed by Sikh terrorists.

The jury agreed with the defense lawyers that Birk had not specifically planned to kill Rajiv Gandhi. But it did conclude that he and his friends were organizing a military expedition against India. Birk got seven years in prison, two years less than the maximum allowed, and Kunstler called it "harsh and animalistic". Kunstler argued that Birk got more time for thinking about the crime than he would have received if he'd carried out all of the acts he discussed.

"A perusal of the transcripts will unequivocally reveal a wholly indecent scheme by government agents to provoke a grief-stricken young Sikh into agreeing to the murder of Prime Minister Gandhi, so that he could be prosecuted," Kunstler later wrote. "That any civilized society, much less one that professes to give the very highest priority to human rights, should utilize the services of a man like Frank Camper to strike a sham and meaningless blow against 'terrorism' is perhaps the most accurate measure of our unfortunate times."

After Birk's arrest, the FBI and the U.S. Secret Service traveled to Canada with the information gleaned from the documents and tapes. The Canadian Security and Intelligence Service and the Royal Canadian Mounted Police were told that most of those arrested in the United States had traveled extensively in the Sikh communities in Canada. They were concerned that Canadian Sikhs had received similar training provided by Camper from a mercenary operating in the Fraser Valley of British Columbia. They also wanted to snare the Canadian extremists Birk had been working with.

The American information confirmed for the Canadians that Sikh terrorists had targeted Air-India and other Indian government offices for attacks that would coincide with the anniversary of Operation Bluestar. They were convinced that any serious terrorist strike would be planned by the International Sikh Youth Federation — the overseas arm of the radical All-India Sikh Youth Federation, a group briefly banned in India for terrorism. The federation had the manpower and resources to wage a campaign of sabotage, and Birk was a senior official in the organization. Parmar and those who formed the Babbar Khalsa were considered too unsophisticated and too loosely organized to coordinate a major attack against New Delhi.

But although Canada was involved in tracking Sikh separatists for at least two years, its law-enforcement agencies had built no bridges to the moderate Sikh community. They had few competent translators and only a handful of Sikh officers.

The police and intelligence agents got nowhere. Less than two months later, the Air-India jet plummeted into the North Atlantic and the bag bomb exploded at Narita. The man who picked up the tickets had used the names "L. Singh" and "M. Singh". The Indian government told journalists they were a reference to Birk's fugitive friends. Why, asked the fundamentalist Sikh leaders, would anyone involved in the Khalistan movement blow up a plane and leave their own names or names that would further incriminate Birk?

The disaster forced the RCMP and the CSIS to reconsider how they analyzed the Sikh separatist threat.

Canadian authorities were ill-prepared for the fallout of the Indian government's assault on the holiest Sikh shrine, the Golden Temple at Amritsar, and the Air-India disaster made the country's intelligence gatherers look incompetent. The Sikhs were one of Canada's largest ethnic groups. Their influence reached the highest levels of society, yet the police believed the community was harboring a network of terrorists under the noses of the country's top security officers. The development of the radical organization followed clearly established historical precedents within the Sikh community, but most law-enforcement officials were ignorant of the events or their contemporary significance.

The initial reports of the Air-India disaster said many of the victims were Sikhs. In fact, only a few dozen Sikhs were aboard the plane. The faithful had been warned for more than a year not to fly the state airline. In the days after the crash and the bombing in Japan, the manhunt focused on two B.C.-based Sikh militant groups: the Babbar Khalsa and the International Sikh Youth Federation.

With no legitimate pipelines into the Sikh community, the country's law-enforcement agencies were forced to rely for information on sleazy tattletales who inhabited the shadowy criminal world of drug dealers and gun-runners.

Paul Besso, a twenty-three-year-old small-time drug dealer, was involved with a group of Sikh separatists on Vancouver Island. Cashiered from the Canadian Navy with few skills, Besso bought illegal narcotics from the Sikhs who were also trafficking in guns. When he learned they were plotting armed robberies and contemplating bombing various buildings around B.C., he says, he went to police.

But most of his information was bar room bravado. He worked as a paid informer for almost nine months, from May 1985 to January 1986, receiving almost $20,000 from the RCMP, and not a single charge was laid. He was fired, but not before police used his tales to obtain sweeping wire-taps on numerous Sikhs who disliked the Indian government.

Police also relied on information provided by Roy Maia, a middle-aged Portuguese martial-arts instructor who fancied himself as a Canadian Frank Camper. Maia, who had trained groups of Sikh separatists in unarmed combat and how to jump out of moving cars, was a veteran of African bush wars and hired himself out as an expert in terrorism. He had a long relationship with the police, and several Mounties had taken hand-to-hand combat lessons from him.

Maia was involved in late-night talks with members of the ISYF about obtaining heavy-caliber weapons and organizing a guerrilla training camp in B.C. He passed on all the information.

The Canadian Security and Intelligence Agency used such

information to obtain warrants that authorized eavesdropping and mail interception on a massive scale. The warrants were so broadly worded that they could be used against citizens raising money for the United Jewish Appeal in the wake of the Israeli invasion of Lebanon. The agency even surreptitiously tape-recorded discussions between lawyers and clients. Police were prohibited under the Criminal Code from listening to such conversations unless they reasonably believed the lawyer was a crook. But the CSIS was exempt from such civil-libertarian shackles.

After the Air-India crash, however, the Mounties realized how little they knew about the Sikhs. One of the Horsemen went to see the movie *Gandhi* in the hope it would help him understand what was happening. Others simply concluded that they just hadn't watched the right person carefully enough beforehand.

Canadian police and the CSIS spent millions of dollars over the next several months trying to prove Talwinder Singh Parmar was the terrorist who masterminded the two bombings. They followed him, taped his telephone calls, and intercepted and opened the letters of his friends. They learned of the extensive network Sikhs maintain around the globe.

The RCMP paid for Besso to lead a group of Sikh gun-runners from Vancouver Island to California where they went shopping for Uzi automatic rifles. When they turned up at the door of a Los Angeles heart surgeon who was a prominent separatist leader, he told them they were crazy. Didn't they know about Air-India? Didn't they know they were being watched? They left empty-handed.

There were numerous men in Quebec, Ontario, Alberta, Manitoba, and British Columbia working for the cause of Khalistan, just as their fathers and grandfathers had joined the fight for Indian independence. But in the course of their investigations, police also discovered the scope of Indian intelligence operations in Canada.

After Operation Bluestar, Indian diplomats and intelligence officers had conducted a disinformation campaign by downplaying damage to the temple, by underestimating the death toll and by denying that there was any substance to the Sikh grievances. Almost immediately after the bombings, the Indian diplomats and spies began manipulating the press in similar fashion.

They gave false and misleading information to reporters. A Toronto newspaper, *The Globe and Mail*, for instance, initially published stories that blamed Sikhs for the crash and suggested the bomb was smuggled aboard the Air-India jet by the co-pilot, a known separatist Sikh sympathizer. Later, the paper published stories implicating the Indian government itself in the disaster. If the newspaper of Canada's establishment was confused, there was little wonder: the country's security and police agencies were equally perplexed.

Four months of the largest, most expensive Canadian police investigation ever undertaken produced scant evidence. They still couldn't prove that a bomb knocked the Air-India plane out of the sky. Only some parts of the recovered wreckage indicated that an explosion might have ripped through the plane's belly: blisters on a fiberglass panel believed to be from an overhead luggage rack; a section of carpet riddled with holes apparently made by particles blasted up from the front baggage hold; a piece of interior paneling embedded with hundreds of shards of glass; a two and one half meter section of the forward baggage compartment that appeared to have been pierced in fourteen places from inside; and a shredded burgundy suitcase similar to the remnants of the bag that had contained a bomb that brought down another jetliner several years before. "There was no evidence of any explosion found on any of the bodies ... no burning, no evidence of noxious fumes or explosive substances," said Cuimin Doyle, the pathologist who led the team of doctors who performed the post-mortems.

The circumstantial evidence, however, pointed to about a dozen individuals in British Columbia and Ontario. The man who purchased the airline tickets that police believed were used to smuggle the bombs aboard the planes had provided the Canadian Pacific Airlines clerk with two contact numbers: one belonged to the Ross Street Temple in Vancouver and the other was a former home number of Hardial Singh Johal. There was also the trip Talwinder Singh Parmar had made to Duncan and the loud noise the CSIS agents had heard in the bush. Four days after the crash, Parmar's house was searched but nothing incriminating was found.

The police grew worried that their leading suspects — Parmar and Inderjit Singh Reyat — were about to flee. Reyat had placed an advertisement in a local Vancouver Island newspaper offering his furniture, waterbed, car, and trailer for sale. A for-sale sign had also sprouted on the lawn of Parmar's home.

In desperation, the eighty-member Air-India Task Force mounted a series of highly publicized raids across British Columbia on November 5, 1985, under the direction of a Department of Justice lawyer from Ottawa. Mounties and municipal policemen rummaged through the homes of Sikhs who were active in the Babbar Khalsa or friends of Parmar, including Surjan Singh Gill, Hardial Singh Johal, and Ajaib Singh Bagri. They rousted prominent members of the International Sikh Youth Federation.

In the glare of television lights and photographic flashes, the Sikhs were hauled to jail. Parmar was arrested and his home thoroughly searched again. Police found nothing in his house and Parmar refused to talk to them.

Reyat was arrested on Vancouver Island as he sat in his brown LTD with the vanity license plates, "I REYAT". The soft-faced, burly electrician was heading home for dinner at the end of his day at the Duncan Auto Marine Electric Store, when the tall, lean police corporal approached his car. Reyat had previously met Corporal Doug Henderson to discuss the local animosity between Khalsa Sikhs and those who had come to Canada in the early part of the century and become westernized. He was not expecting Henderson to lean inside the car and accuse him of blowing up the Air-India jet. "No, no, what are you talking about?" Reyat stammered.

Henderson and his partner, Corporal Glen Rockwell, did not handcuff the young Sikh but rather asked him to drive to the nearby RCMP office. There, they interrogated Reyat over the following six hours, and then questioned him again early the next morning. The three men sat in a three-meter-by-three-meter interview room in the small building that housed the detachment. A copy of the Canadian Charter of Rights and Freedoms was pinned up on a bulletin board, and there was a tape-recorder on the table.

"Carry on here, Mister Reyat," Henderson began. His partner

Rockwell threw off his jacket so Reyat could see the .38-caliber Smith & Wesson snub-nose detective model pistol he wore on his hip. "You're under arrest for conspiracy to commit murder," Henderson said.

"What murder? What are you talking about?"

"Okay. What I'll do is I'll go through these things that you're under arrest for and then I'll explain to you what these offenses relate to, okay?" The lanky detective paused for a moment before continuing. "What I'm talking about Mr. Reyat is the, the, um, Air-India disaster. . . . I'm talking about the explosion at Nor-Narita Airport in Japan. . . . You're aware of both, right?"

Reyat mumbled that he'd heard something about the two events and acknowledged that he understood he had the right to call a lawyer and had the right to remain silent if he wished. The policemen stressed that Reyat shouldn't worry about being tortured. "Like, I'm not going to, we're not going to retaliate against you or your family or anybody else," Henderson said. "Like you related to me before that back in India the police take you in and they beat you and stuff like that. Well, do you understand, we don't do that in Canada?"

"I know that," said a confused Reyat, who had lived in the country for more than a decade. "I know . . ."

Henderson cut him off. "You shouldn't, I don't want you to feel threatened in any way."

With Reyat apprised of his legal rights, Rockwell said: "May I please trouble you for the keys to your car and your knife please?"

For the first time since he entered the room, Reyat asserted himself. "It's not a knife," he snapped. "This is a sword. Okay."

He tried desperately to convince the two policemen not to take the elaborate ceremonial dagger he carried. He asked to call his wife, and Henderson agreed. But the detective brought back the subject of the Air-India disaster before letting Reyat use the telephone. He ran through the evidence that had been compiled and said that he had drawn the conclusion that Reyat was part of a plot involving Parmar and other Sikhs.

Reyat denied everything, including knowing Parmar. He maintained that he didn't know the Burnaby priest even as

Henderson recited one damning fact at a time from intelligence surveillance reports and records of surreptitiously tapped telephone calls between the men. Reyat broke down and admitted the two had met through their activity in the temples. They played music together, drumming and chanting for days. They were active in the Akhand Kirtani Jatha, the Sikh organization devoted to the hymns and singing that are central to the faith's rituals.

"We're going to be talking for a while here, Reyat," Henderson said. "If you wanna take your coat off so you don't get so hot, or just relax."

He impressed upon Reyat that he had "facts here, like we're going to be talking facts here . . . . I indicated to you [that] there's six or seven different parties involved in this matter. And I wanna straighten out what each person's actual involvement is in it. Like maybe some people weren't involved. Maybe some people didn't have the whole idea of what was gonna happen with what their part in this incident was. I just want you to think about that, just keep that in your mind. Okay? Now, now do you want to make a phone call to your wife."

The well-liked director of the town's main Sikh temple was led to a telephone just outside the room in which he was being questioned. Reyat was close enough for the microphone of the table to pick up a snippet of the conversation that followed. His wife told him the Mounties were rifling their home. The police search team discovered a plastic bag filled with brownish-green gelatin atop a shelf in his basement. It was dynamite. In a locked desk drawer, they found a .357 magnum revolver with the serial number erased from the butt. They also seized ammunition, a receipt for a stereo tuner, a partially filled red-and-white can of smokeless gunpowder, and a collection of family snapshots and letters. During the interrogation, the Mounties insisted Reyat was the bomb-maker.

Henderson kept coming back to the events of the previous summer. "How do you explain then, that this tuner that you bought for Surjit Singh shows up in half of one guy's body in the airport in Japan, and half in the other guy's body at the airport?"

"I can't," was all Reyat could muster.

"What does it look like to you? I'll tell ya what it looks like to me," Henderson said. "It looks like you knew what was going on, what was happening. You put some kind of explosive device into that tuner, gave it to them and said, 'Here ya go boys.' Okay?"

But Henderson was fishing. His accusations were founded on speculation and coincidence, not fact. When one listens to the tape of the interrogation afterwards, the questioning begins to sound comical as the policemen run into the wall of Reyat's professed ignorance. The two policemen tried good-cop-bad-cop, with Henderson urging Reyat to confide in him using lines culled from a TV script.

"There's some reason why you're sitting here talking to me as far as I'm concerned," Henderson said as if he were about to recite a Christian parable about a prodigal son who could still be saved. "Somebody, maybe somebody up there says there's a reason why you're here talking to me, Reyat. I, I believe that. I just can't explain it otherwise like there's gotta be some reason why that happened. Maybe the reason is that the guy, maybe that guy up there says, 'Okay, I want these two guys to get to know each other', which we did. 'I wanted Reyat to believe in this policeman so that when he talks to him on this particular day he can tell him the truth and there's gonna be some reason [for] all that. I know he's got some reason for it.' I think that and I think that is your faith . . . . This is our destiny. It's strange that we ended up like this. I think you're a nice person."

But Reyat insisted he didn't know what Henderson was talking about. He changed stories, he vacillated, he contradicted himself, he got confused, and he pleaded that he couldn't remember the name of the man who had stayed with him for a week in June. In the end, despite the sometimes bizarre but relentless interrogation, Reyat stuck to his story.

The father of three children said he had nothing to do with the Air-India crash or the explosion at Narita and that he had no idea whether Parmar or anyone else did. He even agreed to take a lie-detector test. As Mounties were about to send him by helicopter to Victoria for the test, Reyat's wife arrived and vetoed the trip. She told her husband to say nothing more until his lawyer arrived.

Parmar and Reyat were charged with general explosives offenses that made no mention of the Air-India crash or the bombing at Narita Airport. They hired one of the most expensive criminal lawyers in Vancouver, David Walter Gibbons.

Since his graduation from the University of British Columbia law school in 1969, the short, rotund Gibbons had acquired a mansion-like home with a magnificent view of the Strait of Georgia, the arm of the Pacific separating the southern B.C. mainland from Vancouver Island. "The view always justifies the means," he quipped.

Gibbons was well acquainted with the Sikhs. He had visited India, liked the spicy food, and had a feeling for the Sikh perspective. He had successfully defended nearly two dozen Sikhs who were charged in connection with an immigrant smuggling ring. He liked to joke that he won the case by persuading the judge that a male transvestite involved couldn't testify against his husband because the prosecution hadn't demonstrated that the marriage certificate was illegitimate. Afterwards, the lawyer with a taste for fine wine and contemporary art was put on a retainer and made an honorary member of the temple. He posed in front of the temple with the saffron-colored turban of the Sikh martyr draped over his arm for a photograph to accompany a magazine profile.

The Air-India case opened a window on a world for Gibbons that he once thought only existed in spy novels. Over the following three years, he would find himself in courts around the world, battling accusations against Sikhs that were based on little more than an angry outburst or an attempted police sting operation. He would defend accused Sikh terrorists in Montreal, Vancouver, Hamilton, and fly to Britain to defend a Vancouver Sikh heading for Pakistan with an Uzi in his suitcase.

Gibbons would catch glimpses of undercover intelligence agents lurking outside of his law office in Vancouver's trendy Gastown district, and joke about his telephone lines being tapped. He and many Sikhs came to believe that the religion's expatriate followers were being set up by undercover agents working for the Indian government who urged Sikhs to commit violence in order to discredit them.

"We have to keep in mind," Gibbons said, "the Canadian Sikhs have the same rights as Canadian Jews, Irishmen, Russians, Arabs, French, Nicaraguans, or whatever, to be actively and peacefully involved in the affairs of their religions and nations of origin. That's the meaning of the free world. By the same token, the Canadian government does not have the right or mandate to put itself at the service of foreign governments, to spy on and in other ways interfere in the legitimate and peaceful activities of Canadian citizens. That's arbitrary and unilateral prejudice."

When Parmar and Reyat finally appeared in court in the spring of 1986, the spy agency had artists sketching for TV news programs barred from the hearing. A court order prevented publication of details until the trial had ended. Spectators — who included a score of reporters, Sikhs, Indian government representatives, and a handful of Reyat's friends — were frisked every time they entered and were forced to pass through an airport metal detector before entering the courtroom.

The two CSIS agents — Larry Lowe and Margaret Lynne McAdams — told the court that they followed Reyat and two other men the previous June to a wooded area outside of town. They did not see Reyat commit any crime. They wrote in their notebooks that they believed he had probably discharged a rifle while in the bush. But after the Air-India crash and the bombing in Japan, they told the court they changed their minds, and now believed he had detonated an explosive device.

At a series of police noise tests only a few weeks before the trial, the agents identified the report of an exploding stick of dynamite as the sound they had heard nine months earlier. They had found no evidence of an explosion when they searched the area immediately after Reyat left, however. When they admitted, under cross-examination, that other security agents had also been skulking in the Vancouver Island bush, Gibbons wanted to know how many. At that point, a man named Joseph Wickie startled the court by rising among the spectators and ordering the questioning stopped. The tiny, jammed courtroom watched in amazement as the balding, rumpled man stood in the gallery and read from a folded piece of paper that trembled in his hands.

In a scene more befitting a John le Carré novel, the west coast's Smiley had raced to Duncan that morning from his Lower Mainland office. He arrived late and flustered at the preliminary hearing. He had sat down quietly and unobtrusively. Wickie, who identified himself as the deputy-director of the British Columbia region for the CSIS, said the agent would not answer the defense attorney's question because it would jeopardize Canada's national security.

The spectators murmured in disbelief as provincial court judge Robert Metzger was told he was now powerless to compel the witness to answer. "I'm *functus*," he said, using the legal term for impotent, as he put the cap on his Mont Blanc Diplomat fountain pen. "It matters not what I think."

The Big Brother feared by civil libertarians had appeared in the small town of Duncan less than two years after Canada established its civilian spy agency. If he was the avuncular Wickie instead of a scarlet-clad policeman, his appearance was no less troubling: he was still spying on Canadian citizens. And he was hiding behind the same shield of national security used by the Mounties to cover up illegal or awkward operations when they had doubled as spies before the creation of the CSIS. The only difference was that this time the targeted citizens were Sikhs instead of the French-Canadian separatists of the 1960s.

The agents who accompanied Larry Lowe and Margaret Lynne McAdams into the Vancouver Island bush tailing Reyat and Parmar were all possible witnesses to the alleged crime. "This does not meet any test of fairness that we have in our system of justice," Gibbons said after the CSIS agents were muzzled. "Is our body politic so flimsy that it is threatened by this innocuous question on cross-examination? Our nation is much stronger and I think it can withstand the perceived threats by Mr. Wickie that it might be threatened."

The McDonald Royal Commission of inquiry into the RCMP security service (the precursor of the CSIS) discovered the Mounties used "national security" as an excuse to illegally torch a barn, open mail, and burgle the offices of those whose political views were anathema to the ruling Liberals. The commission — which heard Gibbons deliver a brief as the lawyer for the Federation of Civil Liberties Associations — tried to curb such abuses by separating the policing and intelligence-gathering functions of the government.

The Canadian Security and Intelligence Service was established on June 28, 1984, with a $116 million budget and roughly 2,000 agents, mainly ex-Mounties. It immediately began tracking the Sikh separatists within the country. The case in Duncan promised to embarrass the rookie James Bonds. They claimed to know who had masterminded the Air-India crash and the bombing in Japan. By their own admission, however, they had bungled the investigation.

They let the culprits plan their bloody scheme while being watched, and they failed to get the necessary evidence to prosecute them later. Their Keystone Kops antics would have been laughable had the mistakes not left 331 people dead.

After the disaster, agent Larry Lowe directed police to the site where Reyat carried out the alleged test on June 4. They said they found no evidence of an explosion. Yet, when the investigators returned on July 2, an officer on a cigarette break looked down and a tiny object "miraculously appeared" at his feet: a small square of yellowing, weathered paper. Then, in a "most remarkable coincidence", his partner looked down and discovered a piece of twisted wire in the gravel. The items were described in court as key pieces of evidence: the tell-tale remains of a "shunt", a small safety device attached to a fuse to prevent premature detonation. But, nearly nine months later, police still could not prove Reyat and Parmar were doing anything more than setting off a homemade firecracker.

The intelligence agents and police had only suppositions and innuendo. There was no evidence to support their contentions, and as this fact sank in, the Crown offered to drop the more serious charges. Reyat pleaded guilty to possessing the restricted handgun and the 530 grams of dynamite. He was fined $1,000 on each charge and placed on probation for five years.

The charges against Parmar were dropped. About fifty Sikhs, wearing ceremonial robes and brandishing sabers, surrounded Parmar as he left the courtroom. His son Naswinder sported a shield and bells on his turban. Security agents snapped pictures of the crowd as they burst saffron and blue balloons, which exploded like the sound of gunfire. In the Punjab, they would have fired rifles into the air. Reyat, in a camel-hair jacket, embraced his wife. Parmar, in his Nihang costume, pointed and smiled at the undercover police. "It makes no difference to me whether they keep following me because I believe in God and I live a clean life. God is above my head always," he said.

He was asked if he denounced violence in his quest for a Sikh nation. Parmar pulled the gray blanket that was part of his costume more tightly around his shoulders, clutched his saber, and said no. "The objective of the Babbar Khalsa is to promote Sikhism in the world, and to protect Sikhism throughout the world from the tyrannical government of India, and to defend ourselves to any degree, depending on the circumstances."

Then, he and his retinue, dressed as for the court of Ranjit Singh, boarded the ferry back to Vancouver. Reyat moved back to England to live with his relatives.

But the effect of the high-profile arrests, the rhetoric of terrorism and North American trials backfired. The legal maneuvers by the Canadian and U.S. governments intensified the faithful's feelings of persecution and legitimated their cause. A year later, the Sikhs learned that the charges the courts had dismissed, and other specious or false accusations against the separatists were used to obtain a number of wiretaps. The security agency continued to listen to their conversations for another year even though the warrants authorizing the bugs were illegal. When the information became public, the head of the csis, Ted Finn, resigned, and other senior officers in the B.C. region were disciplined.

Fundamentalist Sikh leaders took solace in the knowledge that some members of the intelligence community were whispering that the Indian government itself might be behind some of the violence. Many of the most vociferous Sikh separatists had been financed by the State Bank of India — including Parmar's friend Raminder Singh Malik — and the Indian government funneled cash into newspapers published by Sikhs who supported Gandhi.

Parmar himself was accused of being a double agent. According to this theory, the Indians hadn't provided evidence to the German courts because his disappearance in 1981 and the murder charges were intended to establish impeccable separatist credentials for an Indian mole. The international political intrigue created another distorting layer of glass behind which those responsible for murdering the 331 people were hiding.

The Canadian government grew so fearful that the Sikh extremists would strike again that Indian consulates were guarded constantly by the RCMP. Behind two locked doors and a picture of Mahatma Gandhi, Vancouver consul Jagdish Sharma affected mystification about the charges against his country. His eyes were closed as he spoke and he held his hands in front of his chest, as if in prayer. "We are the world's largest democracy," the trained military intelligence officer intoned.

He was in the middle of a three-year posting, having come from Kampuchea, and said languidly that Canada was "a challenging and difficult assignment. There have been some unfortunate developments. We don't have any doubts in our minds that the overwhelming majority of the Sikh community in India and abroad does not support this so-called Khalistan . . . . Only a fraction, a very small fraction of the Sikh people abroad are working for this so-called Khalistan. As far as we are concerned it's quite clear that it's a handful of people. Certainly they don't represent the Sikh community. It's most unfortunate that because they do negative things they attract more attention."

Sharma was living comfortably behind armed guards supplied by the Canadian government. They chauffeured him to lunch at a nearby Indian restaurant. There, he was waited on personally by the owner, who had lost his daughter in the Air India crash. The two Mounties in plain clothes and aviator sunglasses waited outside while Sharma tried his favorite buffet of spicy meats. He sipped his tea and chuckled at the accusations by the Sikhs and *The Globe and Mail* that Indian spies were running rampant in Canada and may even have instigated the bombing of Air-India to discredit the Sikhs. "Highly imaginative," he said.

India didn't need to discredit the Sikhs in his mind; they were doing a good enough job on their own. The Babbar Khalsa and the International Sikh Youth Federation had little political credibility outside of Sikhdom because of the rough-hewn character of their members. Their arrogant refusal to build bridges to western society and their steadfast insistence on self-sufficiency kept them isolated, and the Sikh fundamentalists lacked an invitation to the power centers of Ottawa, Washington, and London.

In contrast, there are a large number of politically connected people in North America who by wealth, livelihood, and history are associated with the ruling elite of India. There are hundreds of "old boys" from Rajiv Gandhi's alma mater, Doon School, India's fifty-year-old, upper-class training center whose graduates are scattered throughout the world's investment and commercial banking houses, the World Bank, and high-technology firms.

Sharma's home and office had been placed under siege for days and his lawn turned into a riot zone by outraged Sikhs after his government ordered the attack on the Golden Temple. But Sharma spoke in mellifluous tones about the Sikhs. As far as he was concerned, the extremists had lost the battle for the hearts and minds of North Americans. Just as the Ghadr movement was crushed by the coordinated efforts in the subcontinent, North America, and Britain, so would the Sikh separatists be eliminated. "The Sikhs are nothing," he said confidently. "If they think they can influence politicians in Canada or the United States, they're foolish. We can turn out five hundred resident citizens who are university professors tomorrow."

With little knowledge of Indian history or the complicated background of the rift between the Sikhs and New Delhi, North American leaders chose to side with those whose perspective and goals seemed modern, secular, and westernized. It was much easier to see the fundamentalist Sikhs with their medieval costumes, Samson-length hair, and quaint customs as the villains, and the soft-spoken representatives of New Delhi in their well-cut suits as allies in the global war against "terrorism".

Besides, Fabian-socialist India was now run by a new young elite and, like communist China, appeared to be eager to attract western capital. It was the next largest potential market in the world behind the Middle Kingdom and Rajiv Gandhi said he wanted to do business. India presented itself not as a hostile foreign power but as a potential customer and the customer was always right as far as Canada's political leaders were concerned.

Behind the scenes, Canada was trying to win a share of the contract for an $833 million, 1,600-kilometer-long gas pipeline which New Delhi was tendering. Canada extended to India almost $200 million in credit for oil and gas equipment, and promised $5 million in technical aid. India ranked fourteenth in importance among Canada's trading partners, but business between the two was growing and, in the eyes of the Canadian government, needed to be protected.

In the interests of maintaining good relations with India, the Department of External Affairs torpedoed a multicultural grant of $300,000 that was to support a university education program in Sikh studies. The grant would have allowed the University of British Columbia to establish a chair in Punjabi literature, but External Affairs said such a move "would likely be misunderstood by the Government of India, and might well cause damage to our bilateral relations with India."

Similar grants had been used to establish ten academic chairs since 1978, including one for Estonian studies. The Sikhs complained loud and publicly about the inequity, but the chair in Sikh Studies was approved only after the Indian pipeline contracts had been awarded to other nations.

In Toronto, India's consul-general Surinder Malik spoke with the same unctuous assurance as Sharma when questioned about his government's position. He smiled indulgently at the accusations that were leveled at him and his officials: that they used their diplomatic cover to infiltrate the Sikh community, and that they agitated in the temples urging young, impressionable Sikhs to violence. "Utter nonsense," he said boldly.

Although there were sworn statements from a reporter and security guards, Malik also denied having helped smash up his office for television cameras after the initial damage was done by a Sikh enraged over Operation Bluestar. He rejected out of hand the allegations that Indian spies were operating in the Sikh community. But it was only a question of semantics.

The consulates provided money to groups that opposed Khalistan. Indian government-ordered surveillance on external groups increased dramatically starting in 1983. Additional intelligence agents from the Research and Analysis Wing of the Indian prime minister's office (RAW) were posted in key embassies in Toronto, Vancouver, London, Washington, New York, Bonn, and Paris. They relied on Sikhs who were Indian government sympathizers to keep track of the separatists and to undermine the Khalistanis. People supported by the Indian consulate in Toronto had organized a counter-demonstration at Yonge and Bloor streets that ended in the bloody shooting of a policeman in November 1982. Indian intelligence agents often paid for information and sometimes attended meetings themselves incognito.

Bri Mohan Lal, who was posted to Toronto, was a former brigadier in the Indian Army who worked for the Secret Service Bureau of India's defense ministry and boasted of having led a squad of marksmen whose job it was to shadow Bhindranwale. Gurinder Singh, of the Vancouver consul office, was a senior police intelligence officer and claimed to control a network of more than fifty informers within the Sikh community.

Inderjit Singh Bhindra, a member of the Toronto consular staff, requested asylum in 1986, and gave the lie to the bland reassurances that emanated from the consuls. The fifty-seven-year-old clerk was at the end of his three-year posting and refused to return home. He said his bosses had wanted him to infiltrate Sikh temples, and he feared for his life if he returned to India because he had refused the assignment. He acknowledged visiting the temple, but claimed to have told his superiors nothing.

"I said nothing," Bhindra said. "I have sympathy for the Sikhs. I am a Sikh. My life and the lives of my family are in danger in India. My main reason for asking for asylum is not because I fear what is happening in India. It is the fear of what will happen to me for not doing what I was told and because of what I know to be happening here."

The twenty-five-year veteran civil servant said the consul operations were designed to discredit the Sikh community. His wife, twenty-two-year-old daughter, and seventeen-year-old son also asked for asylum.

Their names were on a list of those of more than a dozen Indian consular officers the Canadian Security and Intelligence Service labeled as suspected intelligence agents. There were others who entered Canada disguised as Sikh separatists wanting asylum, but whose real assignment was to infiltrate the Sikh community.

Two immigration cases highlighted the problem the rookie Canadian intelligence service faced. In the first, a twenty-four-year-old who went by the name of Kulwant Singh Sidhu arrived in Vancouver from India carrying a forged Swiss passport. When he was detained and questioned, he claimed to be the adopted son of the renegade Indian army general Shabegh Singh, the military aide to Jarnail Singh Bhindranwale. He begged to be allowed into Canada as a refugee, and spun a story of traveling through Europe running guns for the Sikh separatist movement. He traveled on fake documents, he said, and spent cash transferred into secret Swiss bank accounts. The young man claimed to be able to fly helicopters and planes.

In spite of Kulwant Singh Sidhu's apparent sincerity, his comrades-in-arms within the World Sikh Organization refused to recognize him. No one would corroborate his story and he could provide no evidence to substantiate his claims. When suggestions became public that he was an Indian intelligence agent snared by accident, he went home. In the middle of the refugee-determination process, his lawyer was surprised to learn one day that his client had returned to the country he claimed to be trying to destroy.

Another case involved Harpal Singh Gumman, a twenty-five-year-old Sikh accused of having links to India's Central Bureau of Investigation, the umbrella agency in charge of the country's intelligence gathering. He acknowledged to reporters that he had a clutch of aliases. But he shrugged at the charges that he was not a pure Sikh. "Let him give proof," he demanded. "I have no connection [to the CBI]. Most of the time I stayed with Sant Bhindranwale."

He said he was the son of a Punjabi police inspector and was studying law at Rajasthan University at Jaipur, about five hundred kilometers from the Golden Temple, when he joined the militant All-India Sikh Students Federation. During his final year at law school in 1983, he was jailed several times. "I left the temple on June 3 at midnight. The army attack had started and bullets were flying. Bhindranwale had said that whoever has no weapons or his bullets are finished should leave and organize outside. My weapon was finished so I left."

The World Sikh Organization and the ISYF were initially leery of Gumman. He was rumored to have been involved with the Indian abduction of the federation's international leader, Jasbir Singh, a nephew of Bhindranwale. Jasbir Singh, who had travelled to Pakistan many times and who had met with Parmar, was grabbed by the Filipino government and bundled aboard an Air-India jet and flown to India where he was imprisoned. His brother fled to Canada where he sought refugee status and assumed control of the separatist group. Gumman said he had nothing to do with the Indian government's kidnapping of Jasbir Singh. He claimed Filipino security officials arranged it for a $100,000 fee from the Indian government.

Gumman said the Indian government wants him for three murders it says he committed and that he was tortured during a short spell in prison — all before he turned twenty-four and fled the country. He arrived in Canada from England in February 1985, and was sponsored by people related to members of the Akali Dal government in the Punjab. Gumman married a Canadian and now lives in Vancouver. The Sikh separatists confirmed his status and he is considered by many in Canada to be a priest.

Canada's intelligence agency had little hope of getting to the bottom of such cases, especially when most of its Regina-trained officers had neither traveled outside North America nor been present when shots were fired in anger except on television. A man who is related to the victims of torture or who has faced an enemy with a gun is apt not to be intimidated by law-enforcement officials bound to uphold the rights and freedoms of a democracy. The inexperience of the CSIS allowed the Sikh extremists and Indian spies to operate with ease within the country.

The internecine squabbling between the RCMP and the CSIS aggravated the situation. The CSIS had withheld information from its police partners and, in retaliation, they blocked the agency's direct access to the Canadian Police Information Centre. It forced them to waste time routing requests for background information through the correct channels.

After the aborted case in Duncan, Solicitor General Perrin Beatty ordered measures to prevent the CSIS agents from testifying at trials or its documents from being improperly disclosed publicly on the grounds of national security. The measures seemed to be designed not so much to protect the country's integrity but rather to shield the much-touted civilian intelligence gatherers from ridicule.

The federal government also began drafting an intelligence-sharing pact with the Indian government and letting the spies whose cover had been blown by the CSIS quietly leave the country. The surreptitious intelligence gathering was seen as an irritant, not a major issue. The Canadians were much more concerned about the Sikhs they too considered "terrorists".

Canada announced it would lift its ban on deporting Sikhs in November 1985 (shortly after Parmar's arrest), and later signed a bilateral extradition treaty with India, although India's capital-punishment law may yet make extradition difficult. The government also promised to keep separatist Sikhs in Canada under surveillance and to establish formal links with India's intelligence services.

The CSIS planned to spend almost $7 million of its $134 million budget in 1987 on counter-terrorism. The RCMP was spending $17 million to protect diplomats and diplomatic missions. Ottawa also planned to establish a special SWAT squad akin to the famed British SAS at an initial cost of $48 million, and an annual operating budget of $30 million. Solicitor General Beatty said it was obviously needed because Canada could no longer remain aloof from the war against terrorism.

"Those who threaten or kill innocent people to achieve their goals are not freedom fighters," said Beatty. "They are extortionists and murderers whose actions mock the principles they support. These foreign fights have no place in Canada. For the benefits of living in this country, we ask one price — to obey the laws of the land and to respect the rights of others. No one — no one — has the right to kill or maim as an expression of opinion or to use violent intimidation as a political device."

The Canadian security and police establishment pursued the Sikh separatists with a fervor that bordered on an obsession. Only a few months after the CSIS had been embarrassed in Duncan, B.C., police arrested five men in Montreal. On Friday, May 30, the five were charged with plotting to blow up an Air-India jet scheduled to take off the following day from John F. Kennedy International Airport in New York. All were members of the Babbar Khalsa and were close associates of Parmar, who had visited them on May 25.

When Parmar was informed of the arrests, he was outraged at his followers. "We told those bastards to stop it," he exclaimed before sending his Hamilton lieutenants racing to Quebec to help the jailed Sikhs. David Gibbons would be their lawyer.

The charges stemmed from a story told by another petty criminal who worked as an informant for the Quebec provincial police. The drug trafficker, code-named "Billy Joe", said the Sikhs were interested in blowing up another airplane. The Canadian police quickly imported an FBI undercover agent to help them.

Billy Joe introduced FBI agent Frank Miele to the Sikhs during a fifteen-minute meeting in a restaurant, saying Miele was a Vietnam veteran and explosives specialist. Billy Joe vanished before the men went to trial and most of the evidence against the Sikhs came from meetings between them and Miele in a hotel room a few days later. The Sikhs again complained of entrapment, but to no avail.

Still, the Crown's case was disorganized. One of the five Sikhs was quickly released because police had mistranslated wire-tapped conversations. Only the two Sikhs who attended the hotel-room meetings were committed to stand trial. They claimed the plot was all in Miele's imagination.

Although the meeting was recorded by hidden police microphones, no one in the hotel room on May 19 and May 22 actually mentioned blowing up a plane. Instead, Kashmir Singh Dhillon, a forty-one-year-old Babbar Khalsa leader, wrote codewords on a piece of paper indicating "mobile home" meant "plane", and "ship it to us" meant "destroy it", according to the New York-based undercover cop. The defense rested on the assertion that the Sikhs thought they were involved with a stolen-car ring and could purchase cheap automobiles.

The courtroom was ringed with heavily armed police, many of whom stood with their guns drawn when Miele gave his testimony. Dhillon and twenty-four-year-old Santokh Singh Khela "continually used code and gestures to indicate they wanted the airliner destroyed," the G-man testified. "I asked him [Khela] if he was interested in destroying an aircraft and having me do it. He motioned with his hand like this, rising up and then dropping to the table. I asked if he wanted it to contain cargo and he said, 'No, the other.' I said, 'Passengers?' He said, 'Yes, many passengers'."

Miele said he believed he had a deal with the men to blow up an airliner in exchange for twenty kilograms of heroin. No such words can be heard on the tape. Miele said the Sikhs offered him $20,000 for completing the job, and a bonus if the plane destroyed was a Boeing 747. During the second tape-recorded meeting on May 22, Khela talked about "our plane", but he said it was a slip of the tongue because in Punjabi the same word can be used to mean a plane or a car. Miele said the Sikhs agreed to meet him in New York at a later date to complete the deal with the exchange of high-grade heroin. They didn't show up.

Khela, a baker who came to Canada from a village in Punjab, and Dhillon, a machinist from the Montreal suburb of LaSalle, said they were entrapped and that the FBI man even offered to destroy embassies for them. They told the jury of seven women and five men that they were involved with the mysterious drug trafficker named Billy Joe because he offered to supply them with inexpensive stolen cars and illegal guns. Billy Joe, who had been a police informer for more than a decade and had received substantial favors for his imprisoned friends as a result of his work, was to have attended the May 19 meeting with Miele but failed to arrive. Khela said Dhillon had gone to the meeting with him only to act as a translator.

They said they never sealed any deal because they believed they were being manipulated. They testified that Billy Joe concocted the story about them so he could abscond with the $8,000 they paid him for an undelivered stolen car, and win an early release for one of his jailed friends. Billy Joe wasn't around to tell his side of the story.

"I have no guilty conscience whatsoever," Dhillon, the former president of a Montreal Sikh temple, told the court. "I am innocent."

The Quebec Superior Court jury deliberated for about eight hours before finding the two men guilty of three charges each, of conspiring to destroy an aircraft and murder the people on board by planting explosives on the plane. The two Sikhs sat looking grim in brightly colored turbans and Nihang warrior skirts. Outside the courtroom a solemn group of Quebec Sikhs criticized the verdict.

They shook their heads and told reporters that already they had collected and spent $150,000 in legal fees for the three-week trial. Madam Justice Claire Barrette-Joncas sentenced the two men to life imprisonment. She told a stunned courtroom that "the crime is so mind-boggling that the primary end of this sentence must be deterrence. Terrorists must know that such acts will not be considered lightly in Canada."

The two Sikhs were impassive. "The fact that you chose to conspire to kill hundreds of innocent people for terrorist purposes has brought you [into] the category of the worst offenders," she told them.

At worst, the two Sikhs had done nothing more than utter dangerous thoughts in the presence of an undercover policeman. But they had received sentences more severe than those meted out to Front de libération du Québec terrorists who kidnapped a British trade commissioner and murdered a provincial cabinet minister in October 1970. They were also treated more harshly than some members of the Squamish Five, a self-styled urban guerrilla group that operated in Canada during the early 1980s. The young anarchists caused millions of dollars' worth of damage in Ontario and British Columbia and left several people maimed. Two of the five saboteurs were out on parole after serving fewer than forty-eight months in prison. The Sikhs launched an immediate appeal and there was a bitter residue of distrust and cynicism left among the Sikh community at the way the two men had been treated.

The anxiety of those Sikhs who clung to their Khalsa identity and Punjabi roots had become rampant paranoia a fortnight after the arrests in Montreal. Almost two years to the day since Mrs. Gandhi ordered the storming of the Golden Temple, and one year after the Air-India crash, police raided Sikh homes in Brampton, Hamilton, Kamloops, and Vancouver. Parmar and six of his friends were again arrested on June 14, 1986, and charged with participating in a wide-ranging conspiracy to commit terrorism in India.

The swoop was precipitated when one of the men discovered an ultrasensitive microphone on the gas tank of his truck and thought it was a bomb. Tejinder Singh Kaloe called Hamilton-Wentworth Regional Police on June 7 to say he had found a stick of dynamite with wires and a timer under his truck. Police arrived, ordered the thirty-five-year-old leader of the Ontario chapter of the Babbar Khalsa into the house, and removed the sophisticated bug.

Fearing the "get-Parmar" operation they had been working on was blown, the intelligence service and police moved in. They launched their cross-country raids on June 13. Kaloe, who had lived in Canada for twelve years and had three children, and two other Babbars were on their way to London on Worldways Flight 912. Specially trained intelligence agents tailed them recording their conversations. The three planned to tell police they were traveling to Britain for an arranged marriage but they were arrested on arrival at Gatwick Airport.

The police called the men a "suicide squad" for Khalistan and said they were heading for India via Pakistan. They were deported back to Canada where four other Sikhs had been arrested in the raids. Other conspirators were being hunted in Holland and India. One would be killed by Indian police a few days later.

The men were accused of a Guy Fawkes-like plot that bore striking similarities to the plans of Birk and his associates. Police said that between June 1, 1985, and June 14, 1986, the Sikhs conspired to blow up the Indian parliament buildings, an airport, railway lines, an oil depot, and to kidnap the child of an Indian member of parliament. In taped conversations translated from

Punjabi, transcribed and distributed to reporters by police, the group appeared to discuss plans to shoot down a plane and leave an attaché case full of explosives in an airport. The charges bore a startling similarity to the sort of sabotage the U.S. Sikh separatists had contemplated. The intelligence agents who followed Parmar everywhere had watched him and two of the others as they strolled through a Hamilton railyard apparently examining the tracks and switching devices.

There was little physical evidence against the men, but lots of rhetoric. Police snipers equipped with automatic weapons lined the rooftops around the court in downtown Hamilton. Rush-hour motorists peered up at the men wearing olive baseball caps turned backwards who were scanning traffic through binoculars. Intelligence officers videotaped everyone entering or leaving the courthouse and two airport-style metal detectors were used in repeated searches of everyone attending. Inside the court, there were more heavily armed police with machine-guns.

Again, charges were dropped against two of the seven Babbars arrested. One was Ajaib Singh Bagri, the thirty-seven-year-old priest from Kamloops who was Parmar's chief lieutenant. He came to Canada a year after Parmar and worked for fifteen years at Balco Forest Products Ltd. He had been to Pakistan several times, twice in the past year, and three times to India.

The other man freed was Rampal Singh Dhillon, a twenty-seven-year-old Brampton man. The landed immigrant arrived in Canada two and a half years before and was unemployed. He had a wife and an eight-month-old child and he was a regular worshiper at four southern Ontario Sikh temples. As a result of the charges against him, however, Indian police jailed Dhillon's sixty-year-old father on the suspicion that he might also be involved. "He's still sitting in jail and I am mad," fumed Dhillon on his release. "I hope the RCMP send the Indian CIA the two hundred letters my father wrote that they seized from my house. That will show how innocent he is."

The defense lawyers — again headed by David Gibbons — were astounded to learn that police were relying mainly on translations of a May 15 conversation between Kaloe and Sadhu Singh Thiara as they sat in a bugged van in a traffic jam. Thiara, who wore a steel-blue turban that was the emblem of the Sikh's Akali Dal party, was a forty-four-year-old businessman who bought and sold grocery stores for a living. He too had traveled to Pakistan in 1985.

The conversation between the two men was transcribed by a Sikh Metropolitan Toronto police constable who added words such as "kidnap", "plan", and "bomb" to make certain sentences understandable. Constable Avininder Chadha said he also sometimes reversed the sentences when translating them into English.

The Crown's case was further compromised when it was learned that the police lied to obtain the authorization for a wiretap. The police had been given the false information by the CSIS, most of which could easily have been checked. Gibbons told the Ontario Supreme Court that police had given the judge who granted their request the impression that Parmar was a dangerous criminal facing explosives charges in B.C. when the charges had been dismissed long before. They also suggested to the judge that Parmar was in Canada to evade six counts of murder in India when, Gibbons told the court, Parmar had been a Canadian citizen for "some time and that's why he was living in Canada like the rest of us".

Gibbons said the judge who authorized the wiretap should have been informed that the murders in India occurred in 1981 while Parmar was in Nepal, and that the Indian government had failed to convince a German court that there was any substance to its allegations.

Crown attorney Dean Paquette, who complained that the CSIS was withholding information even from him about the Sikhs, argued that Parmar was the general who issued orders and directed the distribution of the money the terrorists collected. He weaved his story from phrases and epithets gleaned from the taped conversations.

Kaloe, the owner of two health-food shops in Hamilton called Khalsa Foods, was Parmar's lieutenant and the other five were his soldiers, said the Crown attorney. The prosecutor drew sinister conclusions from a call Parmar made to Inderjit Singh Reyat after his conviction in which he told him "to get strong now — now we will pull the moon down to the earth," and that the Babbar Khalsa would pay his $2,000 in fines.

Paquette inferred a suicide mission from Kaloe's actions. Although regularly behind in his mortgage payments, Kaloe arranged to sell his house the month before he was arrested. He bought $500,000 worth of life insurance before paying just over $1,000 for three round-trip tickets to London from Toronto. The travel agent he bought them from, Joanne O'Brien, was asked to identify him in court, but pointed to the wrong Sikh in the prisoner's dock that was crowded with bearded men in turbans. "It may be the other Sikh," she said. "They all look the same to me."

Afterwards, when witnesses at the preliminary hearing were asked to identify any of the Sikhs, Paquette pointed to each by name and then asked the question. But his case was falling apart. Gibbons accused the prosecution of being racist when it placed an expert witness on the stand and tried to prove that the violent climate in India was an indication that the men in the courtroom were likely to have a propensity for violence.

Stephen Keller, an American associate professor at Memorial University in St. John's, Newfoundland, was a former Peace Corps worker who would more properly have been described as an expert on refugees, not Sikhs. He gave a brief, flawed history of the Sikhs, and testified that the Indian government had hitmen in its law-enforcement agencies who were "somewhat equivalent to the death squads in Latin America." His testimony was unintentionally germane.

Kaloe's brother, Balbir Singh, was gunned down in India only a few weeks after Canadian police intercepted a call in which the two men discussed the arrival of the Babbars in India. Indian police claim the he was killed when he and another Sikh tried to murder a Hindu politician. His family, with supporting evidence from an autopsy that indicates the fatal shot was delivered from point-blank range, say twenty-seven-year-old Balbir Singh Kaloe was executed by the Indian police acting on the information from the telephone call supplied by Canada.

In temples across the country, the accused terrorists had more credibility than either government. The congregations had little doubt that a nation in which the police acted as self-appointed executioners would have no scruples about sending spies overseas to discredit and destroy the Sikhs. They were appalled at the racist attitudes displayed by condescending investigators who didn't know what they were talking about, by prosecutors who asked in court for permission to use "the accused's Christian names", by judges who imposed extraordinary bail conditions and handed down severe sentences, and by federal cabinet ministers reluctant to recognize Sikh separatist aspirations as a legitimate political expression.

The official ignorance and lack of appreciation for the predicament of the Sikhs alienated nearly all those who could have helped. Professor Hew McLeod, an historian from New Zealand who is among the world's most respected white Sikh scholars, was teaching at the nearby University of Toronto but refused to get involved. The wiry gray-bearded scholar feared jeopardizing his access to Sikh leaders and literature. Police responded by signing up for some of his lectures.

McLeod could have presented to the court a more even-handed and more accurate picture of the Sikh community in India and abroad. He said the ethnic group had been misinterpreted and maligned even by responsible people. McLeod said that Sikhs generally took up armed struggle against tyranny after exhausting all other means of redress. He blamed some elements within the Sikh community of evading and cleverly misinterpreting Nanak's teachings in such a way as to contribute to the community's being branded as violent. These elements downplayed the pacifist teachings of the first five Sikh gurus and the non-violent tradition of political action the mainstream Sikh community had endorsed for more than a century. But because the atmosphere surrounding the community had become so polarized and volatile, the Canadian courts were deprived of McLeod's perspective.

Despite a thin case built solely on wiretap evidence, Parmar, Kaloe, and Thiara were refused bail. In Sikh temples across the country people protested the treatment of the arrested men. Parmar was housed in the Hamilton-Wentworth Regional Detention Centre's solitary-confinement unit. Policemen continued to insinuate to reporters that the sawmill-worker-turned-preacher planned the Air-India bombing.

Rooftops and hallways were lined with anxious SWAT team cowboys dressed in flak jackets every time he was moved. Parmar said as many as ten Indian agents were trying to kill him, too. Whenever a van carrying him came or went from the court, small knots of Sikhs wearing swords stood at the driveway waving their fists and shouting support.

Parmar had been convicted of no crime and was welcomed as a preacher in temples around the globe. Despite police attempts on three continents to convict him of terrorism, Parmar maintained an unblemished record. "If I did it, they should charge me," he said adamantly.

It was a gauntlet thrown down before the security agents. Parmar was only too aware that if police had any evidence against him, he would still be in jail. So much time had passed since the bombings that anyone who came forward to testify against him would lack credibility. Police would have to link him or his friends to the physical evidence that existed in Japan — tiny particles of a stereo tuner, fragments of a can that contained a fire accelerant, shreds of green tape and the chemical composition of the explosive — or amid the wreckage on the bottom of the Atlantic Ocean.

Parmar gained credibility not because his fellow Sikhs believed him innocent, but because they accepted his word over that of law-enforcement officials who had relied on information from questionable sources and the unsubstantiated charges of the Indian government. They also believed that police informants and undercover cops who urged Sikhs to violence were manipulating unsophisticated people who were emotionally distraught after the attack on the Golden Temple.

Parmar gained stature because the intercepted conversations could be read not only as the talk of a sanguinary extremist, but also as the talk of a man whose family has been butchered, whose friends have been imprisoned without trial, and who could no longer stomach it. He had spent nearly a year in jail waiting for his trial as a result of charges based on the word of anonymous accusers the Sikhs believe were Indian government agents. His stoicism and unwavering faith throughout such ordeals marked him as a leader.

At his trial, Gibbons said that a Canadian citizen had a right to know who his accusers were. The judge agreed and Parmar's trial abruptly ended. The federal government refused to reveal its questionable sources and the case was thrown out.

As he stood outside the court and proclaimed that he was innocent of any wrongdoing save being a true Sikh, Parmar said: "I can sleep at night. I did not kill three hundred and twenty-nine people. I am a man of God."

But he acknowledged he was a threat to the Indian government. "That's why they want to kill me," he said. "Bullets are only fired at a lion. Have you heard of bullets being fired at a chicken?"

7. TERRORISM AND CRIME

The charges against Talwinder Singh Parmar were dropped and he was released from jail in April 1987, and returned to a hero's welcome in Vancouver. There was a white stretch limousine waiting at the airport and he was described by his legion of supporters as a "high priest".

Canadian and U.S. prosecutors had alienated the Sikh community by describing it as violence-prone. Government attorneys were forever smashing "international conspiracies" and rooting out "the cancer of terrorism". Ordinary laborers, truckers, farmers, and small businessmen who were Sikh didn't agree. They preferred to believe the bulk of their troubles were caused by the Indian government's meddling.

Thirty-four Sikh societies in British Columbia — representing the faithful from urban Vancouver to the isolated northern community of Mackenzie, about 70 per cent of all Canadian Sikhs — had endorsed the call for Khalistan. In the United States, Parmar's affluent allies had established links to the conservative Heritage Foundation and a growing list of congressmen. They also forged ties with Pakistan, a nation only too happy to support the creation of a buffer zone between it and the country that has twice defeated it in war. And they were lobbying to get the same status at the United Nations as the Palestine Liberation Organization.

Sikh separatists, who commanded a majority within most North American temples and who had formed several national and international organizations, made large donations to the campaigns of sympathetic congressmen and senators. They began full-time lobbying in Ottawa and Washington. They called those who died fighting for Khalistan "freedom fighters", emphasized India's bonds to the Soviet bloc and began publishing newspapers that promoted friendly politicians and attacked those sympathetic to India.

The fundamentalist Sikhs received endorsements from U.S. politicians such as Jesse Helms, Dan Burton, George Miller, and William Lipinski. They met President Reagan and Republican presidential nominee Jack Kemp. Their allies attacked the Indian government from the floor of the House of Representatives and the Senate for "committing genocide against innocent Sikhs" and for providing aid to Nicaragua. Congressman Robert Dornan, a Republican from California who had received campaign money from the Sikh separatists, pledged his full support to counter what he called the unfair branding of Sikhs "as an irresponsible and destructive group".

The ex-Air Force pilot who was part of an exchange program between the United States and India in the late 1950s and early 1960s had visited Amritsar. He said the Sikhs should take "a cue from the Armenian and Jewish communities in protecting yourselves against defamation by hostile groups. Don't let the faith and religion you revere be slandered and smeared by being branded terrorists."

As in Canada, the influx of Sikh immigrants to the United States occurred when they began to have doubts about living within the Indian federation. In the early 1960s, there were only two Sikh temples in the United States. In 1980 there were two in New York alone and another sixteen operated in the country's largest cities. Nearly two hundred kilometers northeast of San Francisco, some Sikh families had lived in Stockton and Yuba City for three generations farming cotton, walnuts, and kiwis and other fruit.

The Sikh separatists emphasized the split between India and the United States on global political issues such as Afghanistan, the Middle East, and Latin America. They also drew particularly on the power of the Jewish lobby in Washington. There were once fifty thousand Jews in India, mostly in Bombay. In 1986, there were perhaps seven thousand. The Sikhs drew an analogy between their struggle for Khalistan and Zionism. They impressed upon the U.S. politicians that they were a similarly minded people: hard-working, affluent, democratic. There were also about as many Jews in the world as Sikhs.

As they sought North American allies, much more marketable and educated Sikh spokesmen gained prominence. The main national organizer was a senior executive of the Gillette Company of Boston called Manohar Singh Grewal.

At the end of 1986, the small intense-looking man waited at the Boston Airport wearing a blue turban, pale blue sweater, and a burgundy ski jacket. He and his wife were meeting another jet. They did it regularly as Sikhs came and went after conferring with him before heading around the globe to promote the cause. Grewal emigrated to the United States in 1963 and his wife, Gurmit, arrived a few years later. With a doctorate from MIT, he handled steel supplies for the multinational firm.

As he wheeled the plush, dark-blue Delta 88 into the freeway traffic, he gave a guided tour of Boston between short, set-piece stories about the Punjab. "There's a revolution happening," he said. "We feel conservative measures are now needed to properly channel that revolution."

The Grewals live in a colonial enclave called Hanover, about thirty-five kilometers from downtown Boston amid the rolling countryside of truck farms, family sawmills, and the remnants of the American Revolution. They live in a quiet subdivision where the price of homes began at $400,000.

Grewal owns a large, two-story home with automatic doors on the two-car garage. The couple have two teenage daughters, the oldest working in the neighborhood Friendly Ice Cream shop. They are all practising Sikhs and, as in the homes of most devout Sikhs, a room inside their home was set aside for prayer.

Every morning, Grewal rises at dawn and performs the elaborate ritual of washing and then coiling his waist-length hair. He regularly travels the world for Gillette and often combines the trips with politics. There is a telephone in every nook and cranny. "Our telephone bill is staggering," his wife said. "Sometimes more than the grocery bill with the calls to India, Britain, and Canada. That's even when we wait for the discount hours."

Their involvement with Sikh politics began after Operation Bluestar. The storming of the temple was such an egregious affront, they and many other Sikhs began to give credence to the message of the fundamentalist preachers.

Sant Jarnail Bhindranwale had warned that the Hindu majority would turn on them. Devout Sikhs feared his prophesy would be fulfilled after hundreds of pilgrims were killed in the government's assault on the Golden Temple. Their anxiety was fueled when the government failed to charge the organizers of the riots in which thousands of Sikhs were killed after Mrs. Gandhi's assassination.

The Grewals and the vast majority of practicing Sikhs judge every event since June 1984 against the bloody background of Operation Bluestar. On the large console color television set in the wood-paneled basement, Grewal runs through a library of videotapes that are the annals of the crusade for Khalistan. There are special reports on Bhindranwale, smuggled footage of the fighting during the battle inside the Golden Temple, gruesome documentary accounts of Mrs. Gandhi's assassination and the riots in New Delhi, and propaganda films for Khalistan.

"Look at some of these lies," he said, fast-forwarding with the remote control to footage of India's U.S. Ambassador K.S. Bajpai after the attack on the temple. "The Indian security forces did not storm the temple," the diplomat is saying serenely under a vitriolic commentary by Grewal. "The central part of the temple was not touched. We have tried as a government to find a solution through negotiations . . . . Those negotiations were always sabotaged by the extremists . . . . There was no alternative to flush them out — the holy of holies was not touched."

"They stopped talking to us," Grewal said. He zipped ahead and stopped at one of the last interviews Mrs. Gandhi gave, and he chuckled as she spoke. "I've lived with danger all my life and I think I've had a very full life," the late prime minister was saying. "It makes no difference whether you die in bed or die standing up . . . . The Golden Temple itself has some bullet marks but it is not otherwise damaged."

He then inserted the videotape recorded during the attack. It was a short, dark film with a confused din for a soundtrack: shouts and screams, the pock-pock-pock of automatic gunfire, the muffled thud of mortars, weeping, and the sound of grinding metal and stone. "That's the tanks," Grewal said staring at the shadowy subjects occasionally illuminated by explosions of red, green, violet, and white flashes. It ends abruptly. Still photographs taken later in the daylight and video-recorded after the battle revealed the damage. The Akal Takht shrine, the symbol of Sikh political authority, was smoking rubble. The film ended with a picture of a globe with a tiny version of the saffron-colored flag of Khalistan sticking out of northwestern India.

The next scenes Grewal is proud of are the home movies the separatists took of themselves. "There's Didar Bains," he said pointing at the burly man shouting "Down with India" through a megaphone.

Like the proverbial immigrant, Bains stepped ashore in 1958 and became a farm laborer. Within four years he had earned enough to buy 10.8 hectares, and subsequently, through the sweat of his brow, built a farming empire that embraced more than 14,000 hectares of orchards. There was other property, large tracts in British Columbia, and oil interests. Now, he was reputed to be the world's richest peach farmer.

Bains owned a fleet of Rolls-Royces and controlled a large, private security force. He helped organize the itinerary of Zail Singh when he went to the United States for surgery and the ties had led to the Indian intelligence agencies questioning the president's loyalty.

Operation Bluestar and the events that followed it had pushed Bains into the fundamentalists' camp and he became a zealous convert to separatism. He grew his hair and beard and helped organize demonstrations at the L.A. Olympics to embarrass the

Indian government. He became the international president of the World Sikh Organization and christened his saffron-colored jet Khalistan One. But Bains was only one of the numerous affluent North American Sikhs who joined the crusade.

Grewal's daughter arrived with a cup of sweet Indian tea. "That's Birk and them," Grewal said stopping the film again. Birk is in a T-shirt bearing the motto of the "Tenth Regiment", a group formed by the International Sikh Youth Federation members. After the Air-India bombing, an unidentified man called *The New York Times* and claimed responsibility on behalf of the "Sikh Student Federation, Tenth Regiment".

Birk was shown dancing in the streets of New York after the assassination. There are other pictures of him at a later demonstration. "The U.S. government just made a big show (at the trial) to show India what they were doing," Grewal said of Birk's trial. "They're good people," he added. Grewal knew Parmar too, although they had not met. "A very holy man," he said.

In Grewal's mind those Sikhs who have turned to violence should not be condemned: it was an understandable reaction given Mrs. Gandhi's desecration of the Golden Temple. He forgave the assassins. "Sometimes you need men like that. It takes all kinds to make a revolution."

He inserted a videotape made surreptitiously inside the shrine as Sikhs worked to repair the damage to the buildings, clear the rubble, and purify the sacred pool, which had to be drained so that bodies and debris could be removed.

Later, at lunch, Grewal explained that he and other Sikhs in the northeastern United States decided it was time to get involved immediately after the assault, and they began meeting at his home. They became printers and publishers, disseminating pamphlets and propaganda on Sikhs and what is referred to as the genocide by the Indian government. On weekends, several often stayed with him. Over lunch — an Indian buffet of chappaties, rice, curried vegetables, and pickles served with virgin strawberry daquiris — the Sikhs plotted strategy and argued politics.

Sukhinder Bajwa, a young senior engineering manager from Digital Equipment Corporation and a long-time family friend, said he was one of the first to get involved. He helped create a computer bulletin board on Indian issues. In his mid-thirties, Bajwa was single and considered himself a non-practising Sikh. He wore his hair short and his beard neatly trimmed. He grew up in India and was trained at an expensive college run by MIT.

"It is the same here as in India," he said. "It doesn't matter what you did or didn't do, it's who you knew and who you have bribed that will get you out. Everything can be done for those with connections. We need to create more connections."

The son of a retired Indian general, Bajwa traveled to India every year for several weeks at a time and because of his position and Digital's prestige, he had access to the top political leaders. He considered them all to be corrupt. "The graft, the hypocrisy, the vote buying. I went to see [Chief Minister Surjit Singh] Barnala. He is a dead man. He shook like a leaf all the time I was with him.

"Fat, dumb and happy," Bajwa continued, "is how to describe Sikhs before Bluestar. We weren't watching what was happening. But anywhere else in the world quotas are used to raise minority representation in various sectors of society; in India the Hindus were using it to reduce our participation. We formed our cell here after the attack."

Already, however, he said the concern about Indian agents provocateurs, spies, and undercover cops made everyone wary. "We made sure everyone had a history," he said.

Bajwa, for instance, said Bhullar was under suspicion. The retired officer had served under Bajwa's father and he believed Bhullar was working for the army's intelligence branch. "Or, maybe he's just incompetent," Bajwa said, helping himself to more curried beans.

After the North American arrests, he said, the Sikhs realized that their public spokesmen must be seen to be above reproach. Bhullar, who had become secretary general of the WSO after arriving in the United States on a tourist visa shortly after Operation Bluestar, was removed. Grewal and the others disliked his too-public militant rhetoric and the mysterious manner in which he left India on the eve of the assault on the temple.

Bhullar was ordered out of the United States for overstaying his welcome on the tourist visa he used to get in. He disappeared after his deportation hearing began and the Immigration and Naturalization Service issued a warrant for his arrest. It was withdrawn after he turned up in Brussels in October 1986, and reported to the U.S. embassy to halt the deportation hearing. He was coy when asked how he left the country. The retired army officer would have been forced to surrender his landing card if he traveled by regular airline as he had neither an American passport nor a green card. Bhullar had decided not to contest the deportation order because he normally would have been banned from returning to the country had he lost. Voluntary departure allowed him to apply for a visa later.

Bhullar's main accuser among the Sikh separatists was Ganga Singh Dhillon, the man in charge of the Sikh Sri Manhar Sahib Foundation in Washington. The son of a wealthy East African Sikh family, Dhillon was a key separatist organizer and had pressed the case against India in front of the Senate Foreign Relations Committee. He was responsible for introducing Parmar and other Sikh separatists to Pakistani officials. Dhillon had access to Pakistan's leader, General Zia ul-Haq, and also maintained ties with Zail Singh. One of his letters fell into police hands after he met the Sikh president in Karnal, Haryana, in 1981, and was a source of some embarrassment for the man who had been Mrs. Gandhi's main Sikh adviser.

Dhillon himself was elbowed aside as head of the WSO amid complaints of financial irregularities. He was replaced by Grewal after a rowdy meeting in Stockton, California, in which Dhillon's supporters ripped off Bhullar's turban. The accusations relating to Indian spies and the mistrust threatened to destroy the organization. Grewal arranged a meeting at the secluded Marriott Hotel in Saddle Brook, New Jersey. Dhillon arrived with his bodyguard for the meeting which was attended by twenty-nine of the thirty-one members of the WSO board of directors, including Didar Bains.

Grewal, who was endorsed by Dhillon, was unanimously chosen to take over. The new leader swept away the charges against Dhillon and said the group had settled its differences. The new leadership appointed Naunihal Singh, of New York, general secretary; Autar Singh, of New Jersey, G.S. Brar, of Houston, Dr. S.S. Dhillon, of Cleveland, and G.S. Pumma, of Yuba City, were renamed vice-presidents. Dr. Arjinderpal Singh Khalsa, director of the cardiopulmonary unit at Good Samaritan Hospital in Mount Vernon, Illinois, became the spokesman for the International Sikh Youth Federation.

"We've always had a problem with leadership," Grewal said. "In the Punjab it is the same. They have locked up the only man capable of filling Bhindranwale's shoes: Simranjeet Singh Mann. We need more men like him."

Bajwa nodded at the mention of the former Punjab policeman's name. He said he understood the revulsion that compelled him to resign and send the missives to Zail Singh after Operation Bluestar. They excused the exaggerations and inflammatory rhetoric of the letters by saying Mann was overwrought at the breadth of the persecution of the Sikhs.

Amerjit Singh, a wiry, elderly Sikh with a fiery disposition, sipped a glass of orange juice and joined the discussion. He was a trained lawyer employed by the Connecticut workers' compensation board who spent his spare time proselytizing for Khalistan. Like his friend Grewal, Amerjit Singh moved to the United States in the 1960s and described himself as an "economic refugee". He sent anonymous letters to women widowed by Sikh extremists urging them to repent for their husband's sins so they might be forgiven. "Now you know how thousands of Sikh mothers felt," he said in a screed to the wife of a murdered Indian general who helped plan Operation Bluestar.

Amerjit Singh carried an elaborate *kirpan* which hung at his side on a saffron-colored sash. "It is said in India that one's religion is worn on one's sleeve. I say it is worn on the hip in a scabbard," he said. "I'd never move to India because I've never felt secure there. Sikhs have no rights or freedoms. I would have killed Mrs. Gandhi myself."

Gurmit Grewal put down her fork and added calmly. "I would have too." She paused for a moment as the table fell silent. "I mean it. If she were here now I would kill her."

It was that sort of talk that sparked charges against the Sikhs in

Canada. As they sat around a dining room table outside Boston, the group of executives were preaching treason and sedition. They knew it, acknowledged it, and asked only that their motives be understood. They did not consider themselves terrorists; they saw themselves as patriots waging a new version of the American Revolution.

"My only regret is that I have only one life to give to my country, Khalistan," Amerjit said. "But that I will gladly give. I do not fear death. But I would have killed her. Really, I would have. First we must get out of this unholy union and then we must negotiate as equal partners in some kind of federation of states perhaps. But first we must get out."

The fringe, nationalist movement within the expatriate Sikh community had become a mainstream crusade within three years of Mrs. Gandhi's death. Like all aspiring revolutionaries, the fundamentalist Sikhs had begun with little money, questionable support, and only vague rhetoric when it came to policies and proposals. With the assassination of the Indian prime minister, the bombing at Narita airport, and the crash of the Air-India jet, they achieved the international recognition that made it easier for them to gather donations. They had a haven in Pakistan next to their main area of operations and, according to the Indian government, the Sikh militants were running a parallel government in Punjab whose edicts were widely followed. Now they were chasing the international support needed to build the infrastructure to withstand the pressure from the Indian government and force it to negotiate.

The heavy-handed and sweeping measures the Indian government adopted in dealing with the separatists alienated the mainstream Sikh community. In its attempts to curb terrorism, New Delhi stripped Sikhs of their legal rights in the name of national security. If they were detained by police under the sweeping anti-terrorists laws, they were presumed guilty. Sikh participation in the army and in the civil service was reduced; they were disenfranchised by the imposition of martial law. And special border laws were passed forcing even Sikhs to request special permission from the Congress Party administration to return to their homeland.

The fundamentalists capitalized on the disenchantment. They gained control of the many overseas temples and their sizable treasuries, which allowed them to bolster the struggle for Khalistan. This support was supplemented by organizations the fundamentalists founded, such as the World Sikh Organization, Babbar Khalsa, and the International Sikh Youth Federation.

What concerned law-enforcement authorities in North America, however, was the accompanying rise in drug trafficking, illegal immigration, insurance frauds and other crimes involving Sikhs. In the view of many police and intelligence officers, much of the money in donations that paid for the guns, munitions, family support, and legal fees and services came from crime. The police feared such a situation could be exploited by the unscrupulous. Members of nearly every Sikh separatist group — from the ISYF to the WSO — could be found in jails around the globe, convicted or accused of complicity in terrorism or crime.

In Detroit, the FBI followed Sikhs as they met with underworld arms brokers. On Vancouver Island, there were several Sikhs under surveillance for drug dealing and weapons smuggling. There were guns being illegally traded in Toronto and Windsor. Inderjit Reyat had been caught with an illegal magnum with its serial number removed and admitted that he was shopping for other guns.

It was believed by some that the Sikhs were running arms on the scale of the rear-echelon support provided to the IRA by sympathetic North Americans. Sikhs who claimed membership in the WSO and other separatist groups were caught in Britain and in India smuggling guns. A Canadian Sikh who was a member of the WSO was caught in the summer of 1987 when he was nabbed by Indian police shortly after he smuggled a cache of machine guns into Punjab.

Members of the ISYF were also heavily involved in smuggling people out of India. Canada became a sanctuary for the Sikhs in April 1985 when the Supreme Court of Canada ruled that anyone claiming to be a political refugee deserved a hearing. Anyone who arrived without documents could invent a history and a past knowing that he could remain within Canada for between three and five years exhausting the appeal process. Among those who subsequently took advantage of the ruling were Sikh separatists, Indian spies, and ordinary immigrants.

Lakhbir Singh Brar, a nephew of Bhindranwale, arrived from Dubai shortly after his brother Jasbir (both Sikh separatists) was arrested by the Indian government. They had operated a contracting business in the United Arab Emirates. Jasbir, who had accompanied Parmar on his trip to Pakistan in 1978, had left Dubai in 1984 and flown to London.

On December 22, 1984, he left England for the Philippines. According to one intelligence agent's account, Jasbir was taking a roundabout route into North America via Manila and Mexico. The Indian government persuaded ex-president Ferdinand Marcos's security forces to arrest Jasbir Singh on arrival. They did.

Although the Sikh separatists hired a Filipino lawyer who tried to see the imprisoned leader of the ISYF, they were refused access. On December 26, a special plane arrived from India and Jasbir Singh was flown to New Delhi less than an hour before his lawyers were to appear before the High Court with a petition of habeas corpus. Jasbir Singh had been deported without a hearing. He was imprisoned in India, but not charged.

As a result, his brother Lakhbir Singh Brar assumed the international leadership of the ISYF. He arrived in Toronto from Abu Dhabi and asked for asylum. Already, he said, sixteen members of his family had been killed in India. The Indian government responded by saying the ISYF was one of the most notorious groups committed to spreading terrorism in India. Brar traveled to Vancouver where he met with Satinderpal Singh Gill, the Canadian leader of the ISYF. They had met in Pakistan during 1984 and Gill was preparing to go again with a group of other ISYF members.

Numerous other Sikh fugitives followed Brar into Canada, which they favored over the United States because it had less stringent border controls and its refugee determination process was in chaos. Still, they were infiltrating the United States too.

Almost two hundred Sikhs were caught trying to sneak into Florida. "They were seeking a safe haven in the United States because they had committed a crime in India, such as the murder of a police officer, or this type of thing," said Dwayne E. Peterson, district director for the Immigration and Naturalization Service and chief of investigations. "They were ordered by the Sikh organization of which they were members to shave their beards and remove their turbans to fit in with the Bangladeshis and with other Sikhs coming into the U.S."

Peterson said twenty of those who were detained confessed to being "terrorists". Many of those had tried to gain admission to the United States by coming through the Bahamas after flying from London. All were part of the global transportation system the separatists operated. They were provided with documents, told where to go, who to see, and promised a warm welcome. "We had lawyers from New York, California, and other places that would, within hours or days of the Sikhs being taken into custody, post their bond, and call on their behalf," said Peterson.

The INS was also picking up Sikhs coming in through Mexico. In 1985, the San Diego border patrol alone grabbed 203 Indian nationals, mainly Sikhs, using well-trodden "wetback trails" into the United States from Central America. The Punjabis had begun using the routes in the 1920s. They were also coming into the United States from Canada.

The arrest in 1984 of a Sikh political activist in Vancouver on charges of smuggling $35 million worth of heroin led to the smashing of an underground railroad that had operated in the Pacific Northwest since 1980. It generated more than one million dollars in profit just from the illegal immigrants who used it.

It worked this way: The mainly Punjabi Sikhs would obtain a visa to visit Canada. Once in Vancouver, they would contact well-known travel agent Malkit Singh Parhar, and be guided into Washington state across border-straddling farms at Sumas and Lynden, Washington, about forty-eight kilometres east of Vancouver. The police nicknamed the operation the "Punjabi pipeline". The same route had been used when the *Komagata Maru* was under siege in the city's harbor at the turn of the century.

Inside the United States, the immigrants were met by Seattle lawyer Dominic Santiago. Charging fees as high as $10,000,

Santiago would arrange for the immigrant to marry an American. The women received about $3,000 and a divorce once the immigrant received permanent-resident status. Santiago told them how to lie to immigration agents during interviews.

Authorities posed as brides, ministers who performed sham marriages, and would-be immigrants. The smuggling network extended across the continent, into Sikh communities in Memphis, San Francisco, Los Angeles, Boston, and New York. The illegal aliens were able to begin reconstructing their lives within familiar communities. They arrived to join relatives or friends within the brotherhood of their faith. The men who had helped them into the country were well-known in the temples.

Parhar was a wealthy man, and was prominent in British Columbia's East Indian community. He was a close friend of Grace McCarthy, the province's deputy premier and one of its most powerful cabinet ministers. When he was arrested, he was in the midst of inviting two thousand guests to a banquet in her honor. He was released on bail after McCarthy's husband, Ray, and other friends extolled his honesty in letters to the court.

Later, Ray McCarthy said he couldn't remember who Parhar was until a questioner reminded him of the letter he sent to the Seattle court. When Mrs. McCarthy was asked about her relationship with Parhar, her secretary said that she was too busy to bother with the question. The couple had known the man for twenty-five years.

The rest of Vancouver and British Columbia's establishment was equally squeamish when questioned about the smuggler who was on a first-name basis with the rich and powerful. "When Parhar phoned me, I agreed to come [to the banquet for Grace McCarthy] but this latest event poses some very practical difficulties," said Liberal senator Ray Perrault. "Now I'd like to know who is going and the format of it. I'd say it might not be wise to go ahead with it if there's any concern about who's organizing it. But that's up to the guest of honor."

Parhar was arrested along with more than one hundred others — most of whom were detained as material witnesses against the kingpins in the elaborate scheme that involved bribery and falsified documents. One undercover agent got $30,000 in bribes. On

February 20, 1985, in Gene Coulon Park in Renton, near Seattle, Parhar, Trilochan Singh Dillon of El Centro, California, and Hardev Singh Panesar of La Mesa, California, paid $20,000 to an undercover U.S. Immigration and Naturalization Service agent for Panesar's immigration file. As the Sikhs burned the file, the entire incident was recorded on videotape by the police.

All twenty-eight accused pleaded guilty to conspiracy charges or turned state's evidence. Parhar pleaded guilty to two felonies including conspiracy to defraud the government and trying to cover up a sham marriage. Santiago also pleaded guilty. The deal Santiago and Parhar struck required them to pay fines and serve three years in jail followed by five years' probation.

The Sikh separatist fraternity cared little for the legal niceties of the modern nation-state such as immigration law: they believed they were a persecuted people deserving of refugee status. The Sikhs were simply joining their families. Long before Marshall McLuhan coined the phrase, some Sikhs treated the world as a "global village".

For Canada, the problem became a crisis in 1987 when 173 men and one woman disembarked at night from a tramp freighter and landed on a foggy beach on the southern shore of Nova Scotia. All but a handful were Sikhs. Many had been sent from India by the ISYF; others were separatist supporters who had been living in Europe but faced deportation back to India; and some were simply people who had left India looking for a better life. Many admitted they had no idea when they left India where they were going. Their leaders gave them instructions and sent them. Many had relatives in Canada, some of whom were high-ranking members of the ISYF. Some wore jackets emblazoned with the crest of the Babbar Khalsa International.

Within hours of their arrival, Talwinder Singh Parmar was on hand with one of the country's top immigration lawyers, Mendel Green, to help the illegal arrivals. David Gibbons's law office would also be involved in the legal work. Their arrival had been anticipated.

Intelligence wiretaps on Sikh separatists in Toronto had warned

Canadian authorities of the ship's approach a few days beforehand, but police and the immigration department had been unable to intercept it. The refugees were found by the local residents shortly after they waded ashore. Some carried briefcases and wanted to hail a cab to Toronto, more than 1,400 kilometers away.

The Canadian government recalled Parliament and rammed through a tough new refugee law to seal the borders. In 1981, only 1,600 people had arrived in Canada and claimed refugee status; the government expected 30,000 to make applications for such status in 1987. It estimated that 70 per cent of such claims would be bogus. Ottawa also ordered ISYF leader Brar out of the country saying it considered him a threat to national security. But his separatist supporters said they would fight the deportation through the courts — a process that could take years.

Many of the Sikhs who claimed refugee status freely acknowledged that they would do almost anything for their separatist leaders including assassinating members of the Gandhi family. Their commitment to those who had helped them escape India was unquestioning. And authorities had reason to fear an upswing in violence as a result of the increased separatist politicking.

In Britain, two Sikhs who opposed Khalistan were murdered with sawed-off shotguns in 1985, two others were knifed, and one died in a fire-bombing. Another moderate Sikh leader was gunned down in December, 1987. All of the crimes were believed by police to be politically motivated. Rival demonstrations on English streets between those who supported the Sikh separatists and those who backed the Indian government often degenerated into gang clashes with swords, clubs, spears, spiked cudgels, and guns. There had been similar outbreaks of violence and political intimidation in Canada.

Sikh activists were responsible for ambushing a Sikh Punjabi cabinet minister on May 25, 1985, on a remote Vancouver Island logging road. The "hit" had been ordered by fundamentalist leaders who wanted to send a message to Sikhs who cooperated with the Indian government or criticized the terrorists operating in Punjab.

The fifty-six-year-old, gray-bearded lawyer had arrived in Canada to attend the wedding of his nephew at the New Westminster Sikh Temple, called Sukhsagar. He was a member of the Akali Dal government in Punjab, which was dominated by Sikhs who had agreed to cooperate with the Congress Party in order to hang onto power. They were opposed by more militant members of the Sikh party and the fundamentalists who favored armed insurrection. But the moderates, too, would be ousted by New Delhi in the spring of 1987 when it became apparent that they could do nothing to quell the violence. Members of the ISYF targeted Sidhu for the same reasons its members had assaulted short-haired Sikhs: it considered him a traitor.

During the ceremony in front of about four hundred people, Sidhu was spotted by Jaspal Singh Atwal, a millworker with two young sons aged twelve and eight. A burly thirty-one-year-old, Atwal was an ISYF enforcer. (He was the man, Ujjal Dosanjh claimed, beat him up. Atwal was acquitted of the charge.) He quickly informed the other members of the militant federation of Sidhu's presence. In spite of the bugs and tails the intelligence service had on many of the extremists, they were still within hours able to formulate an assassination plot.

Atwal's associates were either temple leaders or senior members of the youth federation. They carried out their plot while Sidhu visited Vancouver Island with his nephew's family to see other relatives in Tahsis, a small, isolated lumber town where about 135 Sikhs lived.

They waited on a side-road until the car carrying Sidhu passed them at about 8:15 A.M. Sukhdial Singh Gill, wearing a burgundy turban, spun a rented black sedan out of its hiding place and raced after Sidhu's Mazda. When Nachhattar Gill (Sidhu's brother-in-law), who was driving, saw the speeding car in his rear-view mirror, he slowed and pulled over to the side of the gravel road and waved the Pontiac Grand Am past. Instead, the black car veered in front of the blue Mazda, smashing its front fender.

"What the hell's going on?" Gill remembers shouting as the doors of the Pontiac sprang open and the assailants sprinted towards his car. Gill managed to open his door and briefly grapple with one of the attackers. "What's wrong with you guys? Tell us what we've done."

He ripped a white mask from the face of twenty-five-year-old Amarjit Singh Dhindsa before being knocked over. "I could see his little mustache," Gill said. Dhindsa swung a short length of chain that shattered the rear, side window of the Mazda on the driver's side. At the same time, another man was smashing in the other side windows with an ax handle. Someone yelled, and a man leaned out of the Pontiac and emptied a .32-caliber handgun into the Mazda. One bullet lodged in the windshield, but two ripped through Sidhu, the Punjab State planning minister who was huddled in the back seat with his wife. He crumpled onto her lap. "You've killed my husband," a hysterical Manmohau Sidhu shrieked. "You've killed my husband."

With that, the assassins jumped back into the car and sped off, leaving the cabinet minister wounded but alive. Moments later, Nachhattar Gill flagged down a passing pick-up truck. The driver, Paul Griffiths, had just seen the speeding Pontiac and quickly used his citizen's-band radio to contact police. Warned that there was a group of armed East Indians fleeing an attempted murder, Campbell River RCMP parked two cruisers across their only escape route, Highway 28. Ten minutes later another Mountie found the black sedan. At about 9:30, less than ninety minutes after the attack began, Mounties with guns drawn stopped a gray van and arrested the thugs.

Although Indian diplomats were routinely protected by the RCMP and the Canadian Security and Intelligence Service, Ottawa had arranged no protection for Sidhu and he had requested none. Justice minister John Crosbie later told the House of Commons that he had been completely unaware of Sidhu's presence in the country. It was a claim that, if not false, indicated another serious failure by Canada's national security apparatus.

Indian visitors needed visas to enter the country, and the Indian consulate knew of Sidhu's presence four days before he was shot. During a telephone conversation that was recorded by the CSIS fundamentalist leaders discussed attacking him. But the intelligence agency was hampered by the lack of skilled translators and Punjabi-speaking officers. In the normal course of events, it took roughly a fortnight from the day a recording was made for intelligence analysts to receive a translation of a tape. It was only after the shooting, when the RCMP asked the intelligence service to check its tapes for evidence of a conspiracy, that the incriminating conversations were translated.

David Gibbons, who again came to the defense of the Sikhs, told the court that the accused all had exemplary family lives and were pillars within the Sikh community. Provincial court judge Anthony Sarich freed the men on $50,000 bail saying they posed no danger to Canadians. He characterized the assassination attempt as a "stupid, emotional and spontaneous single act". He prohibited the men from traveling outside the province, possessing firearms or ammunition, or from coming within a mile of the Vancouver International Airport or within ten blocks of Expo 86, the world's fair being staged at the time in downtown Vancouver.

The decision was appealed when the CSIS wire-taps were finally translated. Using the information, Crown attorney James Taylor argued that the ambush had occurred with the blessing of the highest members of the ISYF. (A total of nine men would be charged with conspiracy in connection with the ambush). As a result of the surreptitiously recorded conversation Taylor insensitively asked the court for permission to refer to the men by their "Christian names" to ease his confusion when talking about their roles in the attempted assassination. The B.C. appeal judge reversed the decision to grant the four attackers bail and ordered the others jailed too until their trial, citing the international repercussions of the attack.

After a short trial, Jaspal Singh Atwal, Jasbir Singh Atwal (no relation), Amarjit Singh Dhindsa, and Sukhdial Singh Gill were each sentenced to twenty years' imprisonment. "It was a cowardly and heinous attack," said Justice Howard Callaghan of the B.C. Supreme Court. People in the courtroom gasped at the severity of the sentence. "They had assumed the power of life and death over a visitor to Canadian soil," the judge continued. "Every such act can only diminish Canada's image abroad. Acts of violence are not to be perpetrated on Canadian soil in order to pursue a foreign cause. They tracked and stalked Sidhu like a hunter who stalks his quarry."

The other five Sikh separatists, who were refused bail because the government claimed they helped plot the May 1986 ambush, were released in September 1987. None of the information contained in the tape-recordings was admissable evidence because the CSIS misled the court to obtain the eavesdropping warrant, and the conspiracy charges were dropped.

The CSIS had relied on information supplied by sources such as Paul Besso and Roy Maia that proved to be false, to obtain permission immediately after the Air-India disaster to wiretap dozens of Sikhs. The intelligence agency knew from the aborted prosecutions of Parmar and the Babbar Khalsa that the authorizations for its listening devices would probably be deemed illegal and that any evidence gathered as a result would be tainted and inadmissible in a court. When the information became public in September 1987, the head of the intelligence agency accepted responsibility and resigned. Although no legal evidence existed against them, the five separatist Sikhs had been held in jail for about a year.

For police and Canada's intelligence agency, the collapse of this case was another devastating blow. In their view, there was little difference between the activities of the Sikh separatists and organized crime. In British Columbia, where an estimated 70 per cent of the Sikhs chose to live, the provincial government released a report in 1987 indicating that one in five refugees would be engaged in crime within five years. The three-year study had been carried out by officials with the federal immigration department and the Coordinated Law Enforcement Unit — a provincial umbrella group that handles investigations involving more than a single police department. The problem with illegal drugs was particularly acute.

The Sikhs come from a region where opium and heroin production have been legitimate and lucrative economic activities for centuries. The opium fields in India and Pakistan once helped sustain the Moghul empire and now supply the world's pharmaceutical companies. In the isolated and rugged tribal areas, the narcotic is freely available in bulk. It is a commodity that is compact, has a high profit margin and is marketable around the globe. Aside from the Sikh separatists, the Indian government had caught other insurgent groups smuggling drugs to raise money for their campaigns.

The northwestern corner of the subcontinent has become one of the main sources of hard street drugs. In Britain, the United States and Canada, Sikh separatists had offered to provide high-grade heroin to undercover policemen as payment for weapons or illegal services.

Punjabi finance minister Balwant Singh admitted the situation was bad but asked people to understand that life in rural India was different than in modern cities of North America or Europe. "Smuggling is an integral part of politics," he said. "Some members of parliament from those areas cannot keep away from the smugglers."

The implicated Sikh politicians included such highly placed figures as revenue minister Major Singh Uboke, who was attacked for his ties to one well-known arms and drug smuggler in particular. "How can I keep away from smugglers when a large number of my constituents are smugglers?" he asked rhetorically in his defense. "I come from a border constituency where smuggling has been an integral part of life and politics for many decades. I cannot change all that now. I have to eat with the people of my village. I am not denying that several of these smugglers worked for me during the election. What is smuggling after all? It is the consequences of our excessive misplaced idealism. In the quest for high morals and ideals we have resorted to controls on liquor, opium and various other things .... I support people fighting repression."

Even Punjab's chief minister, Surjit Singh Barnala, refused to step in because of "the forty-six major smugglers in the border district, only six are with us while the rest are with the Congress (I) Party."

It was a pattern intelligence agencies and experts on terrorism had seen emerge in South America and the Middle East. "It's not at all unusual for insurgent groups to deal in narcotics to finance their operations," U.S. attorney-general Edwin Meese said in vowing a crackdown in 1985.

Regular funding for terrorism is hard to find. While Irish Republican sympathizers would donate to help the families of IRA members, they often refused to pay to support the violence or the hard men themselves. The Sikhs were no different. They were prepared to donate money to aid families in Punjab and legal fees but providing cash for weapons was a different issue. The Sikhs who were engaged directly in terrorism in Punjab relied heavily on robbing banks, immigration fraud, and drug smuggling for funding. It was not a new pattern.

Only when terrorists operating in Bolivia, Columbia, Peru, and other Central and South American countries began to benefit from the growth in the cocaine business did they became a serious threat. The PLO, perhaps the most successful terrorist movement in modern times and one that enjoys political support by the Indian government, has made millions of dollars by expanding and commercializing hashish cultivation in the Beka'a Valley. Almost 80 per cent of the valley is now producing a crop that the U.S. Drug Enforcement Agency has valued at more than $100 million a year at local prices.

Journalist James Adams has demonstrated convincingly that one terrorist organization after another — the Mafia, the Provisional IRA, the PLO — initially established to support a political cause has degenerated into criminality. Western prosecutors and police subscribed to the view that the extremist Sikh fundamentalist groups were no different.

Despite the complicity of many Sikh politicians in Punjab, the Indian government managed to make more drug seizures in 1986 than ever before. The country's police seized more than seventeen metric tonnes of hashish, nearly three tonnes of opium, and more than one hundred kilograms of heroin during the first eight months alone. This was partly because of the network of information-sharing established in response to the Sikh independence movement and the general crackdown on drug trafficking across the west. The United States, Canada, and Britain all shared smuggling information with India and the results were spectacular.

In Britain, police smashed one ring of fourteen Sikhs distributing heroin throughout Leicester, Bradford, and Birmingham. The owner of a spice shop in Queens, New York, accepted delivery of ten kilograms of heroin and about four thousand kilograms of hashish hidden in spices in 1985. Another Sikh connected to the smuggling ring was caught with twenty kilograms of heroin.

But even supporters of the Indian government were involved in smuggling drugs to fund their operations. British police caught a London publisher accepting high-grade heroin from an Indian diplomat. Ajit Singh Sat-Bhambra confessed to being a paid agent provocateur of the Indian government. The fifty-one-year-old was the owner of *Sandesh*, a campaigning anti-terrorist, anti-drug newspaper with a circulation of ten thousand. The profits from the sale of this contraband were to be used to finance his anti-Sikh-separatist campaign.

A month after Sat-Bhambra was arrested, his newspaper office was firebombed killing an editor. In court, Sat-Bhambra described his role as an Indian intelligence gatherer. "It is basically criminal and political information about the activities of the Khalistanis and some other people on drugs, illegal gold and so many other things that are happening," he explained. "I made two confidential reports passing information to the [Indian] High Commission — although they won't admit that I passed information or that they paid me. They paid up to last week even."

Sat-Bhambra told the court he received $3,000 a month from the Indian government. He claimed that his newspaper was firebombed because he was getting too close to a conspiracy against New Delhi. The Indian High Commission refused to discuss the case even though British customs officers caught a London-based envoy delivering a suitcase containing four-and-a-half kilograms of heroin, worth nearly $1 million.

Babu Lal Gupta claimed diplomatic immunity and fled to India. He would return to New Delhi and a job as a senior civil servant in the Indian upper house, the Raj Sabh. The Indians rebuffed British requests for his extradition. Sat-Bhambra was sentenced to nine years' imprisonment. "It gives me no pleasure to sentence a man like you," Judge Derek Holden said, "because you are clearly well-educated, intelligent and running a good newspaper — a man who must have a degree of courage in taking the stand which you have in relation to the Khalistan movement and I accept all that I have heard about the pressures that were on you. Heroin is a pernicious substance — it is horrifying, causes death and suffering and the commission of so many other crimes."

The Sat-Bhambra case and the other activities of Indian intelligence agents confused the issue of Sikh separatism for western democracies. They were sympathetic to Rajiv Gandhi's complaints about terrorism and the criminal activity of expatriate Sikh separatists. But they were also caught by the dictates of democracy. Justice not only must be done, it must be seen to be done.

India railed against the Sikhs for smuggling drugs and engaging in terrorism. The militant Sikhs responded that their acts of terrorism were no different than the slaying and torture of Sikhs by the Indian army. The Sikhs also pointed out that despite its posturing, the Indian government supported Tamil separatist groups who engaged in terrorism. It was New Delhi who helped the Tamils win concessions from the Sri Lankan government in 1987 that may ultimately win them some form of autonomy. The Sikhs claimed they were often victims of entrapment by Indian agents and that if they sometimes resorted to crime to fund their crusade for Khalistan the Indian government was similarly engaged in illegal acts to generate foreign exchange to fund its intelligence operations. As long as the Sikhs could protest that they were only fighting fire with fire, it was difficult for western police agencies to gain support among the moderate Sikh community.

Police on both sides of the Atlantic shook their heads. It was the same with the Italians, British Columbia prosecutor James Jardine said. Two generations ago, police couldn't break the Sicilian gangs who operated in North America. It took time for children to mature in North America and accept the values of western democracies and abandon the feudal perspective of the first immigrants.

"Not this generation, maybe not the one after," he said, "but certainly the next will be on our side. They will not see heroin as just another commodity to be smuggled like gold or silver. They will not see the end as justifying the means. Especially not the criminal means we're seeing now."

It was an expression of the standard conservative political perspective: no matter how repressive a tyrant may be, no subject may challenge duly constituted authority. Mrs. Gandhi may indeed have made a serious and even heinous mistake in ordering the attack on the Golden Temple. But to most people who live in a western democracy, that did not justify taking up arms against the government of India, or the killing of 329 people whose only crime was to book a flight on an Air-India jet. To western politicians, the attack on the temple was the desperate act of a government struggling, no matter how heavy-handedly, to contain an actual threat to its legitimacy and survival; the bombing of a passenger plane was simply the unprovoked murder of innocent people.

Most fundamentalist Sikhs disagreed with such reasoning. They believed Mrs. Gandhi was executing their relatives and engaged in a malicious program of genocide against their faith. During religious services they listened to sermons by priests such as Parmar that were littered with references to famous historic martyrdoms and included the 1984 casualties among them. In such sermons, the Sikhs were hailed for taking up arms against oppression. The attack on the Golden Temple was considered such a moral outrage that it justified any retaliation; the creation of Khalistan was imperative, an end that justified any means.

8. BRITAIN

For Indian prime minister Rajiv Gandhi's two-day visit to London in October 1985, marksmen were stationed on the rooftops and troops in armored carriers watched over the route he would follow into the city. At Heathrow airport, he and his wife, Sonia, stepped onto the red carpet and received a rare personal greeting from Prime Minister Margaret Thatcher who led them to a cavalcade of limousines. Mrs. Thatcher was determined to restore healthy links between the two countries and defuse the threatened protests against Gandhi.

All efforts were insufficient to put the Indian leader completely at ease, however. Gandhi continued his anti-terrorist diplomacy later at a dinner given by the British leader. He said he was pleased with the action taken against Sikh separatists in Canada and the United States and was looking for the same sort of response from the British. "We do not permit our territory to be misused for destabilizing other polities," he said, ignoring his own country's role in harboring and supporting Tamil separatist guerrillas. "We know you share this approach, as Britain, like India, has suffered much from terrorism."

During two hours of talks, Gandhi and Mrs. Thatcher discussed the problems of Sikh and other Indian terrorists operating out of England and she emphasized the British government's concern. No one disagreed: Terrorism is the bogeyman of the 1980s. The tough question was how to neutralize it as a political strategy without turning the country into a police state. The British government was already under the censure of human rights groups for its extensive use of wiretaps during 1984.

Mrs. Thatcher told him her security services had foiled two assassination bids against him. Three days before his arrival police had conducted a round-up of the usual suspects in a series of raids. They arrested and jailed fifteen Kashmiris and Sikhs under Britain's Prevention of Terrorism laws. Most of the men were later released.

Four of the Sikhs arrested, three businessmen and a tradesman, were charged after Gandhi departed with plotting to murder the Indian prime minister. Jarnail Singh Ranauna, Sukhvinder Singh Gill, Harminder Singh Rai, and Parmatma Singh Marwaha were prominent members of Leicester's 15,000-strong Sikh community. About 150 of their supporters held a noisy demonstration outside the court in the central English city.

The Sikh extremists claimed — as had their counterparts in Montreal and New York — that they were framed by undercover policemen and agents provocateurs. This time when they went hunting for an assassin they found policemen from Scotland Yard posing as Irish Republican Army gunmen. Three of the Sikhs said they continued to be involved in the plot only because they were terrified of the undercover detectives. The undercover policemen told the Sikhs they had murdered the Conservative party's Northern Ireland spokesman Airey Neave with a car bomb at the House of Commons in 1979. The forty-six-year-old Ranuana was "putty" in their hands, the court was told, after the policemen threatened to kill his family if he pulled out. He denied offering them the equivalent of about $90,000 for the killing.

"They did get him to do almost anything they wanted," said Lord Gifford, the defense lawyer. Ranuana admitted asking the two undercover men about "blowing away Gandhi", but said he wasn't serious. Like his co-religionists in Montreal who were convicted of trying to blow up a plane, he testified that he was only trying to recover $420,000 from a former business associate. There were, however, surreptitiously tape-recorded conversations that created a different picture.

Ranuana said their meeting at the Post House Hotel in Leicester was just "loose talk". On the tape, he called the $90,000 fee "peanuts" and offered another $15,000 if the assassins were successful. Ranuana told the policemen he would supply them with heroin if the money wasn't enough and went to London to arrange a safe house for them. At one point on the tapes, one of the undercover cops made it clear what was being discussed: "I want you to understand you are asking me to terminate a head of state. You are not talking about some simple crime, but the biggest form of criminal offense a man can get caught up in."

But Ranuana claimed he had just been playing along. Marwaha, a forty-four-year-old factory owner, told the court he thought it was a joke when Gill told him that the IRA imposters were willing to kill Gandhi. He said he went along in an attempt to stop the plot. But the man who was the secretary of the International Sikh Youth Federation showed the would-be killers a $130,000 bank receipt to prove he intended to pay for the assassination. Police said he was the real leader who supplied the gun and a sample of heroin. Marwaha was not only a former associate of Bhindranwale's, but he had close ties to the Canadian Sikh separatists. The Sikhs were also able to supply a copy of Gandhi's secret itinerary from a source within the Indian High Commission in London.

As had happened in North America, the trial was initially aborted at an early stage when the undercover policemen defied a court order to identify themselves. (In 1987, Parmar's Hamilton trial collapsed when police refused to identify their anonymous sources. In Montreal at the trial of the Babbars a few months earlier, the corroborating evidence and even the name of the missing police informant were deemed irrelevant by the trial judge.) Three of the British Sikhs were rearrested outside the courtroom following the ruling. The fourth, thirty-year-old Rai, was freed and demanded compensation for the six months he was kept in jail awaiting trial. Gill and Ranuana were sentenced to fourteen years and sixteen years in prison, respectively. Marwaha was acquitted.

Thatcher's administration was more worldly in its understanding of espionage and terrorism than either Canada or the United States, mainly because terrorism was a more immediate threat in the United Kingdom than it was in North America.

The British had learned through experience that a few individuals with several hundred dollars' worth of guns and grenades were capable of waging war against the most affluent democracies. Although there were only about three hundred activists in the IRA according to intelligence sources, prophylactic measures cost the British government millions of dollars.

More than three thousand officials from civilian agencies in Canada, Britain, and the United States had participated in the U.S. State Department's anti-terrorist assistance program. There were high-level talks between the governments, and intelligence information was being more freely shared among the western allies. The U.S. Special Operations Forces also began joint training programs with foreign military and counter-terrorist units such as the Special Air Service (SAS) of the United Kingdom, GSG-9 from West Germany, and Canada's recently created military SWAT team.

The United States was spending more than $4 billion for security and anti-terrorism programs over ten years for its three hundred overseas legations. Washington tightened laws against military training for foreign nationals. One estimate put U.S. spending on anti-terrorism research at between $20 million and $30 million. "It's been a real learning experience for the FBI," said one State Department analyst at the end of 1986. "Two years ago I don't think they even knew what a Sikh was."

The leaders of the world's most powerful democracies often spoke as if it didn't matter whether the gunman wore a black balaclava, a kaffiyeh, or a turban. Indeed the definition of terrorism created by the U.S. Central Intelligence Agency in 1980, and adopted by the American government, was sweeping: "The threat or use of violence for political purposes by individuals or groups, whether acting for or in opposition to established governmental authority, when such actions are intended to shock, stun, or intimidate a target group wider than the immediate victims. Terrorism has involved groups seeking to overthrow specific regimes, to rectify perceived national or group grievances, or to undermine international order as an end in itself."

But terrorism wasn't an ideology that could be rooted out by the modern acolytes of McCarthyism; it was the strategy of desperate people. The word "terrorism" littered the anti-partisan communiqués of the Third Reich, the handouts of the Red Army in Afghanistan, the propaganda of the South African military in Namibia, and was in everyday use during the decline of the British Empire. In the Middle East, Northern Ireland, Punjab, and elsewhere, terrorism was the weapon of a landless, economically depressed minority who felt aggrieved. Palestinians oppose the Israeli government just as Republican Irishmen oppose the British and the Sikhs oppose what they consider the Hindu Raj for their own social and economic benefit.

In many ways, terrorism represents an avenue of social mobility for Sikh youths. Sikhs are proud to belong to the Babbar Khalsa and the International Sikh Students Federation. Such membership confers status and glamor: they move from temple to temple as revered holy men and martyrs. The leaders of such groups receive international authority and independence from financial worries. Talwinder Singh Parmar, for example, had risen from unemployed laborer to high priest in less than a decade.

The fundamentalist Sikh leaders have successfully persuaded the faithful that they can win political control of their province through violence because there is no "peaceful alternative". The Indian government's callous clumsiness has served to validate that argument. Convinced they couldn't win the fight from a base within India, the separatists moved the struggle onto the global stage by following the blueprint of the IRA and the PLO.

In spite of their violent methods, since 1971 the IRA has managed to raise between $3 million and $5 million from U.S. sympathizers. The Sikhs raised that much in less than five years in the 1980s just to pay the legal fees for those accused of terrorism. As with the flow of funding to Northern Irish extremists, so the flow of funding to the Sikhs has increased dramatically with the perception that those who fight and die for the cause are martyrs. Those who are killed by the money given to the martyrs are not considered. The situations are so similar it is almost possible to simply substitute Hindu for Protestant and Catholic for Sikh in the equation; at one level the dispute is the product of economic bigotry hiding behind a religious mask. Protestant fury is grist for the IRA mill in the same way Hindu fury is grist for the Sikh separatists. In both cases the anger gives credibility to the extremists.

How can anyone consider the Sikhs oppressed, Gandhi asked, when they occupied the highest positions of power and were among the most affluent Indians? He branded the extremists as simple fanatics, a species the French philosopher Voltaire divided into two classes: the first does nothing but pray and die; the second wants to reign and massacre. Gandhi did not apologize to the Sikhs for the attack on the Golden Temple. He demanded the prosecution of no one in his party for the bloodbath that followed his mother's assassination, and he was adamant that never would he accede to the demand for a separatist Sikh state.

Authorities in India, Britain, Canada, and the United States focused on trying to dry the swamp of sympathizers the Sikh extremists relied on. The Sikh terrorists used sympathetic people living normal lives or on the fringes of the underground to pave the way for their attacks, appearing themselves only at the last minute to detonate the bombs or fire the shots. Then they melted back into their environment.

The open-door immigration policies of the 1960s and 1970s allowed thousands of the little-educated, fundamentalist, rural Punjabis into Canada, Britain, and the United States. The ethnic suburbs they inhabited in Vancouver, Toronto, London and New York have become the breeding grounds for separatists the same way the Catholic slums of Northern Ireland supply recruits for the Irish Republican Army, and the Palestinian refugee camps of the Middle East provide volunteers for the Palestine Liberation Organization.

Most of the people who were involved in Sikh militant groups were recruited from the ranks of the faithful who considered themselves no different from anyone else who has ever volunteered for a dangerous, patriotic duty. Within the Sikh community, they were not ostracized. Many, in fact, were priests. They considered themselves the bravest and the best of the faithful and anything but psychiatric cases. They operated in small squads, which are the building blocks of any military or paramilitary organization. But they also required continual indoctrination until their common anger erupted in an act that a healthy human nature would balk at, and none on his own would have been capable of committing.

Britain was the political capital-in-exile for the Sikh separatist movement. There were roughly 500,000 Sikhs in Britain, inhabiting industrial neighborhoods throughout the Midlands and concentrated in the London suburb of Southall, an exotic "Amritsar-on-Brent" known locally as "Little India".

Sikhs had become one of the most affluent of Britain's ethnic communities. More even than in Canada, the Sikhs permeated every strata of British society. There were Sikh magistrates, policemen, doctors, executives. The country's only immigrant judge was a Sikh. Thousands of pounds a week are collected in the country's 140 temples, and much of it fed the cause of Khalistan. Southall travel agents routinely and legally arranged for export permits for British-bought handguns being carried overseas by departing Sikhs. Dozens of Sikhs appeared at West Midlands gun clubs wanting instruction in everything from 9 mm Beretta pistols — the fifteen-shot automatic favored by Mel Gibson in the movie *Lethal Weapon* — to automatic rifles. The situation soured Anglo-Indian relations to the extent that New Delhi delayed a major order for helicopters from a major British aviation company.

What made the job of monitoring Sikhs difficult for law-enforcement agencies in western democracies was the Gandhi administration's refusal to differentiate between those who hurled insults and waved placards in legitimate dissent, and those who would kill. New Delhi was as quick to jail a journalist as to arrest a Sikh militant — sometimes quicker in the case of a reporter who was inside Punjab during Operation Bluestar. India's democracy is rough and flawed. The Sikhs have legitimate grievances about its legal system and the manner in which vast numbers of them have been treated. It can take up to ten years or longer for a case to come to trial because of the subcontinent's congested courts. Civil-rights groups and the mainstream Sikhs who opposed terrorism wanted those issues addressed before anyone was handed over to the Indians.

The British told Gandhi that they were doing all that could be done to curb Sikh militancy. They introduced visa controls on immigration as more than four thousand people a day were arriving from India, Bangladesh, and Pakistan. In the fall of 1986, Britain demanded that all visitors from these countries obtain a visa and submit to checks at British government offices in their own country. At least 250 more staff would be required and nearly $30 million would be spent to make the change.

But Gandhi wanted even tighter control on his enemies and those who would usurp his power. British foreign secretary Geoffrey Howe traveled to India in 1986 and stressed his determination to combat terrorism by naming a junior minister, Timothy Renton, to deal directly with India on the issue. "There is no safe haven in my country for those who act to destabilize others by violence or intimidation," he told an Indian press conference. "I hope the appointment will underline the determination we share with the Indian government to stamp out terrorism."

Renton's main job was to craft a new extradition treaty between the two countries that would meet civil libertarian challenges in British courts and India's desire to get its legal hands on self-proclaimed enemies of the state. Britain maintained that its existing extradition law was adequate. "We have no doctrinal objection," Howe said, "but it would be like trying to design a belt when you already have a pair of braces. We are prepared to strengthen the braces."

Extradition law has been a quagmire since the days of the French and American revolutions. The "political defense" was developed then as an escape hatch for those who were fugitives because they had fought for democracy. The courts made the loophole even bigger during the nineteenth century when it was fashionable to harbor revolutionaries. In this century, the repercussions are still being felt.

In the 1950s, the United States and other western allies refused to allow the extradition of hijackers who commandeered planes, trains, and ships to escape eastern-bloc countries. In 1959, a U.S. federal court even refused to extradite to Yugoslavia a man wanted for murdering 200,000 Croatians in Nazi concentration camps because it deemed the murders political.

When the west was hit by a plague of skyjackings in the late 1960s and early 1970s, however, there was immediate pressure for the new treaties that restricted the use of the political defense. [The birth date of the Modern Age of Terrorism is generally given as Sunday, September 6, 1970, when the Popular Front for the Liberation of Palestine hijacked four airplanes. Before that week ended three of the planes — one each belonging to Swissair, TWA and BOAC — were blown up at Dawson's Field, an old British air base near Amman, Jordan. Another plane, a PanAm 747 hijacked on its way to New York, was destroyed in Cairo.] In recent years, for instance, four separate cases have been heard by U.S. courts involving men accused of murdering or attempting to murder British authorities in Northern Ireland. None of the IRA terrorists was extradited because the U.S. courts found the crimes to be politically motivated. Britain and the United States signed a treaty in June 1985, closing that loophole. Canada and India several months later concluded a treaty that allows extradition for political offenses if they are serious crimes such as murder or hijacking. India wanted similar treatment from Britain.

After independence, India inherited the extradition treaties that existed among Commonwealth countries. The loosely worded political escape clauses in the pacts were never removed as the country saw no pressing need to redraft them until the advent of Sikh separatism. India's struggle to become a nation and its history after independence militated against such a reciprocal change. The Indian nationalists had fought the British. During the Second World War, they had undermined the Allies in Asia, and after the war they had voluntarily aligned themselves with the communist bloc. Rajiv Gandhi maintained his mother's international stance of non-alignment, which in practice meant anti-West and anti-Israel, two policies in direct opposition to the stands of Britain, Canada and the United States. His support of the PLO also made it hard for Western leaders to warm to the subcontinent.

Nevertheless, Rajiv Gandhi pressed Sir Geoffrey Howe on the matter by blaming the unrest in the Punjab on people living in Britain. Howe was emphatic that only those who had committed actual crimes be subject to extradition. "We cannot take action against people who have done nothing but express opinions."

He was under considerable political pressure at home not to bow to the request. British MPs were demanding the return of the drug-smuggling diplomat Babu Lal Gupta, and John Wheeler, chairman of the Home Affairs Select Committee, said the Indian government was conniving at covering up for Gupta.

At the same time, the Sikhs presented their political aspirations as being decidedly western and anti-Soviet. Amnesty International, the charitable organization that monitors human rights violations, also published a report backing many of the Sikh concerns and charging India with holding large numbers of political detainees. The London-based organization said many of those interned in Indian jails were being held without charges or trial. The human-rights group disputed the Indian government's account of Operation Bluestar. It estimated that 493 civilians were killed in the operation and said it had received reports that many of the Sikhs were killed by the Indian army after they were captured. Amnesty blamed several Congress (I) Party members for instigating the riots after Mrs. Gandhi was shot and said several policemen encouraged the killings.

The British were not prepared to throw the Sikhs to the Indian government just because Gandhi said he disliked their politics.

Instead of addressing the issues, the Indian government prevaricated or insisted that the British were hypocrites for protecting the two leading Sikh separatist figures, Jaswant Singh Thekedar and Jagjit Chauhan.

Thekedar was a leader of the Bhindranwale's Dal Khalsa party in India and operated out of an unprepossessing flat on the edge of

Southall. He is a small, black-bearded Sikh who dresses conventionally and lives on social security. He is wanted in India for murdering two policemen.

Thekedar, who is a close friend of Talwinder Singh Parmar, sat in his flat protesting his innocence in broken English. The charges that he cut the tail off a cow and pitched it inside a temple are made up, he said. The murder charges were instigated only after he fled to Britain and took up the Khalistan cause. He calls himself the Defense Minister of Khalistan and explains that under his party's organizational structure the movement is led by the traditional five-man council, or Panchat, the power hierarchy developed in the Punjab's villages. He is evasive on his early ties to the Congress (I) Party but claims he and the shadow Sikh separatist cabinet control a military force of ten thousand.

When questioned about extremism, he quotes Bhindranwale: "I have been called the leader of the extremists. Yes I am an extremist but of the sort that I described above. If you too are ready to become such extremists, raise your hands. What kind of extremists are you going to be? Be very clear about this. One who is [the] Guru's Sikh and will avenge the guru and the martyrs, one who will serve the Panth till the last breath, one who will obey the orders of the Panth, one who will serve under the saffron flag, one who will avenge the abuse and insult of women, one who will avenge the blood of the innocent, only such extremists should raise your hands."

He smiles, and hands over a pamphlet extolling the virtues of his kingdom-to-be: "The COUNTRY called KHALISTAN will be a sort of PARADISE ON EARTH. A Human will no longer be the Slave of another human in this promised land .... Everyone will earn equal emoluments and will enjoy an equal standard of living. There will be no hankering after egotistical offices like the PRESIDENTSHIP. The administrators and the EXECUTIVE who will be running the country will be guided by the spirit to serve with devotion, rather than the ambition to rule .... The Hindu imperialists and their henchmen are hell bent on disreputing and destroying the Ministry in EXILE. But we have high hopes, and our resolve is further strengthened by their antics."

Across town, in the slightly better neighborhood of Bayswater in west London, explosives experts dismantled a bomb on the litter-strewn street outside Dr. Jagjit Chauhan's home at the end of a run-down terrace. India has repeatedly but vainly sought the return of the retired, elderly physician because of his seditious activities but he continued to foment revolution.

A few days after the bomb incident, in November 1986, Chauhan sat on a green chesterfield by the coal fire in his silver Oriental slippers and tunic of primrose silk. Above him hung a painting of Sikh Maharaja Ranjit Singh astride a rearing roan stallion. Chauhan, whose right hand is a plastic prosthesis, was the central figure in the Khalistan movement. He was a doctor from the small village of Tanda where his wife of thirty-seven years still lives and where he has a small clinic. He entered politics in 1956 but was defeated. Although he won election to the Punjab legislature in 1962, he wasn't declared elected until four years later when the courts ruled his opponent, an incumbent minister, had illegally claimed victory. Chauhan became general secretary of the Akali Dal.

"I saw how the political maneuvering was being done by the center and how they were playing the chess game with the states," he said over afternoon tea. "Actually the states have no power . . . . The powers are so limited, so primitive, you can't imagine. Nobody can. Even to construct a bridge over a small stream you have to get the sanction of the center [Gandhi's Congress Party administration in New Delhi]. Even to put a forest somewhere you have to go to the center because they call it flood control. You can't do anything in the state without the interference and sanction of the central government. Things are so bad.

"That was the reason I thought something should be done. For the Sikhs the only solution is they must have their own independence. So must the other nations in India. Separate countries and then we could have a United States of South Asia."

He traveled to England, established his opposition in exile, and soon afterwards the Indian government revoked his passport because of his rhetoric. To listen to the Indian government, Chauhan is one of the terrorist masterminds behind the Sikh separatists. About a year after he left India, he called for Khalistan in an advertisement carried in *The New York Times*.

"This India," he says sounding professorial, "was created by British. It is British India, an artificial India. After conquering one nation after another, they put them together. This is how this British India was formed. So this transfer of power in 1947 was a very wrong act on the part of the British. It was in the interest of the British to have one strong center ruled by district administrators. So when they handed over this same machine to the Nehru family, since then the objective of the Nehru family has been just to make it a state controlled by this family. This has been the tendency. This is why I revolted.

"In 1970," he said sipping his sweetened tea, "I had left the government. I was the finance minister for two years and every year New Delhi changed the government. Because the center could do it simply through a telephone line order they could dissolve the assembly of a state. I could see what game the center was playing and I realized that the ultimate aim of Mrs. Gandhi was to form a government completely controlled by Delhi. She wanted to be a dictator. She wanted to be the strongest family in history. That was her pride. I had been meeting her and I could sense it."

Chauhan tried to return to Punjab politics in 1977 but was rejected by the Akali leadership. He met with Zail Singh and also with Sanjay Gandhi, but when he was rebuffed again, he returned to London. In the following years, he forged ties with Agha Shaki, Pakistan's foreign minister. He visited Pakistan often and became friendly not only with the military government but also with the rebel Afghan leaders. India's central government also monitored calls and letters between Chauhan and Sikh leaders in the Punjab. Whenever the high priests came to England to raise funds, Chauhan joined them. The Hindus in India labeled him a traitor.

"The declaration for Khalistan was actually made on May 15, 1980, when I was in Punjab. Only five people made that formal declaration at the same holy place at the Akal Takht," he said. "That's when we declared Khalistan. The government thought it was only a joke. They were not serious. On June 16, 1980, I came to London and again they revoked my passport.

"All my letters to my wife are censored and she is watched. One old lady. One of her kidneys has been removed. Her abdomen was opened and there were some problems so the doctors wanted to send her here to London, Reading. She was on the plane when the Indian police snatched her passport and her luggage. She's still in India."

Chauhan considered senators Sam Nunn, Jesse Helms, and Mark Hatfield his supporters, and he has met with Alexander Haig, the former secretary of state and candidate for the Republican presidential nomination. They are curious political bedfellows.

"Actually Sikhism is a revolutionary peasant movement — it is not a religious reformist movement," said Chauhan, who was a communist in his youth. "It was a revolutionary social-political movement, which took the form of the Sikh religion or the Sikh nation. Sikhism is a revolutionary movement, social-political, with a strong religious base."

Helms, a right-wing conservative, was a harsh critic of New Delhi and circumvented a State Department refusal to issue a visa to Chauhan in 1983 by inviting the Sikh renegade to testify before a congressional committee. "It was a very peaceful movement and very non-violent up to 1983 and then the government of India wanted to actually create an atmosphere where they could get the sympathies of the majority Hindu community of India because the elections were coming," Chauhan said. "So they managed all these violent incidents and it was all planned and maneuvered by the Indian intelligence agency. Especially RAW [the Research and Analysis Wing of the government's intelligence apparatus]."

After Operation Bluestar, Chauhan called on the BBC for Mrs. Gandhi's death, and led a demonstration against the Indian government through the streets of London. He prophesied a partnership between the British and the Sikhs to create Khalistan and found himself suddenly thrust into the limelight again.

"The Russians were definitely involved in Bluestar," he says, explaining why Britain and other western nations should be concerned about the Sikhs' fate. "They have been asking Mrs. Gandhi to create some problem with Pakistan so they could get some relief on the Afghanistan side. Mrs. Gandhi was always reluctant. So they wanted to get her involved in something serious. They misinformed and misadvised her. The tentacles of the KGB are very subtle. I think the West always goes when the fire is on. They never take preventive measures. They cared about Afghanistan only when the Russians moved in. They are very satisfied with their Indian policy because they see it only as trade. If the Americans can get more dollar trade with India they are satisfied. I talked to one State Department diplomat and he looked at me and said, 'We have very good trade with India. No problem for American interests. Our interest is safe.' The West always counts in terms of money and trade. That's it. So when the fire will be completely on, then they will rush with their engines and their fire extinguishers. But then it will be too late. This is what they did in Vietnam. This is what they did in Afghanistan."

Nearby, his press aide and adviser, a Kashmiri Brahman named Pyare Shivpurr, nodded in agreement. The former BBC broadcaster now works as an independent film producer. He met Chauhan while trying to raise money for a feature movie on the *Komagata Maru* incident. Although the project didn't take off, the friendship did.

"The movement is going to be more and more visible," Shivpurr predicted. "Up until now, and I say this as a criticism of the Sikhs as well as our south Asian society, the feudal element in our minds has not disappeared. India is supposed to be the world's largest, functioning democracy. Yet out of eight hundred million people, the only able person to lead the government was Mrs. Gandhi's son. I personally find that he's not capable. So over the period up until now it has been an inward movement, basically mobilizing grass roots emotions. Very necessary, very important but not enough. It will have to grow looking out.

"My contention is that out of all the fourteen million or so Sikhs, if each single one of them were to cast a vote that we want a Khalistan and that that particular ambition did not fit into a geopolitical equation acceptable to at least one superpower, there will be no Khalistan. On the other hand, if the idea of Khalistan, the very notion and its existence, fits into the equation of both superpowers it will be there." He snapped his fingers. "Whether the Sikhs want it or not, it will be forced on them.

"The situation today is that the Sikhs have to create that geopolitical equation which makes Khalistan, their sovereign state, a necessity in the geopolitical equation of the power game."

Shivpurr was trying to wean the Sikhs off their esoteric religious rhetoric and focus instead on their human-rights grievances.

"Why does one have to be a Sikh to see injustice? I'm a Hindu Brahman and my quarrel with Sikh gentlemen is that they feel it's their inheritance to see injustice and fight against it. I say absolute bullshit. Justice is a sense that is indivisible. It doesn't matter whether you are a Sikh, or a Jew, or whether you are a black or white or brown. I see the Khalistan movement as a vanguard movement for the liberation of peoples in south Asia. The India we know today exists by coercion. It's not one nation. And unless all the nationalities of that mass of south Asia find their free expression, there can be no basis for cooperation, there can only be basis for coercion and collision.

"I feel that in the past two years that the movement for Sikh sovereignty is beginning to talk to the West in a language the West can understand, which is the language of oppression and against it, the language of justice, the language of human rights, the language of creating that possibility where cooperation becomes necessary rather than coercion. For that particular dialogue with the West, I think the Sikhs went through the wilderness, through probably areas of ignorance, areas of darkness, areas of conjecture. They have tried to discover which way they are going. The process is continuing. A hell of a lot of Sikhs are still not clear as to what the hell do they want. I keep saying to them that unless they make up their minds, right or wrong, if you keep on prevaricating between two options you will never get anywhere. If you make up your mind that that is where you want to be, okay, you say for us it is good that we be slaves of Delhi. Okay fine. That is your position. It may be debatable. To certain other people it may be wrong. But nevertheless it is a very definite position and a debate or a dialogue can follow. But if you say that well either we will have our own autonomous province, or we might merge with Haryana, or we might even have our own separate nation, there is no possibility for a dialogue.

"I think in the last two years Sikhs all over the world, including Punjab, have come to realize that the sole option is sovereignty. Because that is the only armor that can protect their lives, their liberty, their property. It's a fight for survival and a fight for justice."

In the spring of 1987, between two hundred and three hundred Sikh separatists from around the globe met in London to discuss strategy. They echoed his sentiments. "The time has come for Sikhs to change tactics," Chauhan said in opening the meeting. "Instead of swords, stress should be laid on stronger weapons, like the pen. Sikhs must educate themselves to the reality of the situation and learn to use modern methods to deal with it."

But it was difficult to see the connection between a "fight for survival and justice" or "modern methods" and the cold-blooded murder of a sixty-year-old Sikh peasant in the Punjab who opposed extremism, or the machine-gunning of a busload of Hindus. The gaudy slogans and fine-sounding geopolitical theories were all well and good, but they appeared to be culled from the realm of political fantasy. Every day brought a new body count from the Punjab and both sides were blaming the other while maintaining their own innocence. The truth about the situation in the Punjab had been hidden from the world by press gag orders, travel restrictions, and widespread violence. The great mass of Sikhdom was hunkered down trying to survive as their ancestors did during similar periods of bloodshed and civil war.

9. THE FRONT LINE

Lahore, the city of Rudyard Kipling's Kim, remains as dusty and congested as it was in the days when the Mogul emperors held court in its massive red fort. The former capital of Sikh Maharaja Ranjit Singh is the first stop for any Sikh separatist intent on slipping unnoticed into India. Heroin is freely available in the back alleys as is an array of locally produced armaments: Kalashnikovs, rocket launchers, AK-47s, grenades, and machine guns.

In a white-washed room in the basement of the Lahore shrine that houses the relics of Ranjit Singh, seven Canadian Sikhs huddled in blankets, sipping sweet tea. The Indian government labels them terrorists. "We're freedom fighters," twenty-three-year-old Balbir Singh of Calgary disagreed proudly.

The shrine they inhabit is part of a complex built by the only Sikh Maharaja to ever rule Punjab. The saffron-colored flag flutters over the gilded fluted dome that has become the crossroads for Khalistan, the most forward and open check-in station for anyone who wants to get involved in the struggle for a Sikh homeland. There are almost no Sikhs living in Pakistan and all who visit usually come to this shrine first. Those who want to aid the cause by helping to smuggle guns across the border can make a connection here. They can also make a donation, pray, or encourage those engaged in the struggle. The Pakistan government does not intervene.

The Canadian Sikhs are officially under house arrest but come and go as they please. The unarmed, elderly Pakistanis who monitor their movements also occasionally run errands for them. Two or three of the Sikhs sometimes leave for days at a time.

The Canadians were awaiting trial on assault charges stemming from two incidents in Lahore in which Indian diplomats were beaten. Their passports were confiscated and their tickets home have long since expired. They have lived in the temple since May 1986, playing host to visiting Sikhs and spreading the gospel of Khalistan.

Their beds are the only furniture and the walls are covered with pictures of the butchered bodies and destruction of Operation Bluestar and the riots that followed Indira Gandhi's murder. The Indian army is to blame for it all, they are eager to point out. They say they are so angry over the Indian government's treatment of Sikhs that they would gladly kill Rajiv Gandhi or his supporters.

Separatist Sikh leaders from around the globe have visited them often. They come to Pakistan to preach and lecture about Khalistan to Sikhs who have crossed the border because they are fugitives from Indian security forces or because they are on a pilgrimage to the Sikh shrines that exist in Pakistan. Members of the Canadian Babbar Khalsa and the International Sikh Youth Federation and representatives of the London-based Council of Khalistan have traveled to Pakistan to spread their message.

In the town of Faisalabad, more than five hundred Sikhs, mainly teenagers and young men, were housed in a local jail for almost two years. They had crossed the border from India seeking refuge from the Indian army's anti-terrorist programs. When they began drifting home, many were captured. They told their Indian interrogators of the indoctrination process they had undergone.

"Pakistani officers would come and talk to us every day and tell us that we had to work against the government of India when we got back, that we had to create Khalistan," said one of the young

Sikhs. "We were told that we must make sure that we kill Hindus only so that there would be communal riots in Punjab. They said there must be complete havoc, a blood bath, because that was the only way we would get Khalistan."

Others told the same story.

The border is less than half an hour's drive from Lahore and it has not been a peaceful place since Sir Cyril Radcliffe drew the dividing line in 1947. The religious strife that marked Partition has become endemic. The tension was palpable at the end of 1986. The Indian army was on maneuvers in Punjab and in the early morning the sound of artillery rolled across the plain like the thunder of an advancing storm.

The Indo-Pak border is a porous 3,000-kilometer-long boundary. It cuts across the farmland of Punjab, the deserts of Rajasthan, and the swamps of Gujarat. Forty years after it was drawn, the division in the north, in the Himalayan province of Jammu and Kashmir, remains disputed. At night the only activity was the armed patrols. A Pakistani soldier pulled a blanket tightly around his shoulders to ward off the chill and adjusted his gun. In the darkness, he says, both sides shoot anything or anyone that moves near the dividing line.

The Indians have sealed the Punjab to foreigners unless they have obtained special permission from New Delhi. Three days a month, the northwestern, overland corridor into the subcontinent is opened to foreigners as long as they are inside a vehicle. At the crossing at Wagah, a collection of baked brick and mud huts on the highway between Lahore and Amritsar, those who are cleared for entry are herded into a convoy. Armored troop carriers take up positions at the front and back. Then, during the night, the escorted column is spirited several hundred kilometers across Punjab and out the other side — non-stop.

Those foreigners given permission to stay in Punjab enter a world of fear, violence, and constant scrutiny.

For the fourth time in less than a kilometer, during the short drive to Amritsar from the border, an Indian soldier stuck his carbine through the taxi-cab window and demanded to see the passenger's documents. Over the last few days more than thirty people had been murdered, the telephone lines for five districts were severed, and the soldiers patroling the Punjab were armed with special powers of detention, interrogation, search and orders to "shoot to kill". The grim-faced troops rummaged through the baggage efficiently, examined the papers, and shook their heads: Why would anyone come here?

In the border districts such as Gurdaspur, there are newly built temples named after Satwant Singh, one of Indira Gandhi's assassins, and other Sikhs killed by government troops in "terrorist encounters". Throughout the region such martyrs are revered; young Sikhs are weaned on tales of their heroic exploits to defend the faith. A survey of the village around Dera Baba Nanak, a border town in the district, indicated that several hundred young men had fled after the attack on the Golden Temple.

In Mand, a 500-square-kilometer tract of bogs, islands, and wild terrain at the confluence of the Beas and Sutlej rivers, several hours by jeep south of Amritsar, police patrols are regularly ambushed. They have adopted a "shoot-first" policy and, as a result, many of the Sikhs who tried to return to India surreptitiously were shot. In 1984, only eighteen were killed, but in 1986, India's Border Patrol Force killed more than three hundred. The dead Sikhs were usually teenagers, or men in their early twenties.

Aboard trains traveling through the Punjab porters shuffle from car to car, drawing light-tight shutters and locking windows before the engine pulls out of the station. At the near-deserted Amritsar International Hotel, the restaurant has long since been closed for lack of business and the doorman won't venture beyond the marquee's light to hail a cab. "Even members of the legislative assembly can't move about among the people without bullet-proof vests and armed guards," says Dalbir Singh, a businessman who heads the Khalsa Diwan, the largest Sikh society in Amritsar.

A few weeks before, twenty-two people were gunned down in a single incident by terrorists in the northeast slice of the state near the town of Hoshiarpur. Some died where they sat on the bus. Others died while trying to flee across a sugarcane field.

Iqbal Singh, a Sikh passenger on the bus, was spared although his son was killed. "I told him that my son wanted to be clean-shaven," said the slight man whose own beard is streaked with gray. " 'What kind of Sikh is he?' [the terrorist] growled and immediately put a bullet through my son's temple and walked on."

By the spring of 1987, six people a day on average were being gunned down — most of them opponents of fundamentalist Sikhs demanding Khalistan.

Soldiers ringed the Golden Temple in Amritsar. They stood every eight meters or so, carbines chained to their belts and resting easily on their shoulders. The Gandhi administration had won the battle for the Golden Temple, but the war for Khalistan dragged on. Reassuring political speeches delivered from behind bullet-proof glass lacked conviction, while the least sophisticated Sikh separatist thug argued with passionate intensity about the destruction of his religion and the genocide perpetrated by New Delhi.

The terrorist strategy has worked. Hindus are moving out of Punjab and Sikhs elsewhere are moving back. The Sikh majority is growing, there has been a marked return to a fundamentalist interpretation of the Sikh scriptures and there is widespread hatred of the central government in New Delhi.

In the disputed city of Chandigarh, where the streets have no names, Surjit Singh Barnala lives at number forty-six in sector two, an affluent residential neighborhood. The city was built after independence by a Swiss architect and about 100,000 people, most of them Hindus, live there.

Barnala's home has been transformed into a bunker. The entrance to the courtyard is protected by sand-bagged machine-gun towers, and coils of razor-edged barbed wire are looped over the tops of the walls. Troops lounge at their posts in the fierce sun watching a kite hawk circle overhead in a widening gyre. Inside, behind heavy curtains, the white-bearded leader of the Akali Dal government says he feels deserted. Barnala was excommunicated by the priests of the Golden Temple for failing to follow the dictates of the extremists. The sixty-three-year-old politician was bitter.

"Militancy is no answer," Barnala said. "You can't have a peaceful state through militancy. It will only put the state government on the wrong course. . . . I placed a lot of faith on some of these people. They ditched me at a crucial moment. They betrayed me."

The Sikh fundamentalist leaders backed by a cadre of committed extremists were running the state. There were twenty thousand *granthis*, or scripture readers, in the province's thirteen thousand villages and most followed the dictates emanating from the Akal Takht. It is solidly in the hands of the militants. Barnala faced daily personal threats. He traveled surrounded by ten commandoes bearing assault rifles and never far from his side was his son-in-law with a small, gleaming pistol shoved into his waistband.

The central government's policies played into the hands of the fundamentalists. Draconian laws stipulate that anyone accused of terrorism is guilty until proven innocent. They supercede the existing legal provision for a three-month deadline on laying charges. They allow suspected terrorists to be detained for up to one year without charge, and up to two years with the approval of special courts that meet in closed session and can accept evidence from anonymous witnesses. The average Sikh feels trapped: the security forces view him as a potential terrorist, the fanatics as a potential collaborator. He is a suspect in his own country because of his faith.

The situation deteriorated at such a rapid rate, that Punjab's governor, Siddhartha Shankar Ray, dismissed Barnala's elected administration in the spring of 1987. The sixty-year-old lawyer had been trained at London's Inner Temple. In a letter to Indian president Zail Singh explaining the suspension of the elected administration, Ray bluntly admitted New Delhi had lost the battle for the hearts and minds of Punjabi Sikhs.

"I told you of the gravity and seriousness of the situation existing in the Punjab and the tremendous terror and fear that prevailed everywhere, in some detail," Ray wrote:

However, ever since the new fundamentalist movement commenced with its, originally seven-point, and later thirteen-point program, the situation began getting out of hand to such an extent that from the middle of April 1987, there was not only a parallel authority working in the state by the fundamentalists and/or the extremists in the temple and the gurdwaras as opposed to the Punjab Government secretariat at Chandigarh, but terror stalked the land and fear abided in almost every heart with the inevitable result that migration and the consequent communal tension and bitterness commences again. . . .

"Lawlessness, lootings, snatchings, bank robberies, burning of shops, kiosks, the brutal maiming or murdering of innocents, et cetera commenced with renewed vigor, making not only many of the fundamental rights guaranteed under the constitution illusory but also even the main right under it — the right to life — non-existent. What made matters worse was the deep involvement of some of the ministers in the present cabinet and their relations with the terrorists/extremists and the unwarranted attempted interference with police activities . . . Corruption has also become rampant. . . . There is total chaos and anarchy. Nothing is safe.

Ray is convinced the violence will continue until at least the twenty-first century. "Tell me, is it possible to haul up all the terrorists in just a week's time or even a month?" Ray asked rhetorically. "It is simply not possible. It is difficult tracing them and the local villagers, I am sorry to say, have sympathies for the terrorists, whom they shelter every now and then."

Police arrested more than nine hundred Sikhs in the days following the Punjab government's dismissal. The state was on the brink of civil war. Daubed on walls across northern India were Sikh separatist slogans or quotations from their holy book: "The armies of the guru will rule Delhi, and only those will survive who seek the protection of the Khalsa."

Around the world, the measures fanned the revolutionary fire of the fundamentalist Sikhs. They formed a central committee to coordinate the expatriate separatist activity and to direct the main terrorist groups: the Bhindranwale Tiger Force, the Khalistan Commando Force, the Khalistan Liberation Force, the Babbar Khalsa and the militant wing of the All-India Students Federation. Each was represented on the new five-member Panthic committee that would become the Sikh separatist high command.

In Canada, Talwinder Singh Parmar, free after nearly a year in prison and cleared of the charges that had been brought against him, went from temple to temple, in Toronto, Hamilton, London, Montreal, and Vancouver preaching his message to thousands of saffron-turbaned Sikhs eager to serve in the holy war. "The only way is to take our own land and live in our own country," he said. "Give me Sikh unity for six months, just six months, and I will deliver Khalistan." The dark-eyed heir of Bhindranwale raised his fist and in Punjabi spoke the words of the Sikh prayer: "Raj Karega Khalsa — the Khalsa shall rule."

Parmar smiled broadly and easily and he handed out press releases explaining that all true Sikhs supported Khalistan. He shook hands and talked of having baptised ten thousand during his trip to India in 1978. Although many of the temple leaders and others were older, they deferred to him when he spoke. His stature among the Sikh expatriate community was unchallenged in public. His lawyer, David Gibbons, says Parmar was in regular contact with Barnala in the dying days of his regime.

"When I am preaching and baptising, I always tell people not to break any laws here, that they should live within the law here," said Parmar. From his days as an angry young man in the mold of Bhindranwale, Parmar was trying to become a more diplomatic spokesman for his cause — a Sikh Yasir Arafat. "We wanted to keep the fight over there [in India]," he said. "Like some people said, this is Canada, the fight doesn't belong here. But they [the Indian government] brought it over here, they harass everybody."

Parmar said he believed he was making progress in his crusade. "Many people have learned," he said. "People on my say so will take holidays, they will go where I tell them, they are willing to do anything . . . I am the mailman for my guru. I deliver his messages."

The fundamentalist Sikhs had shown they were capable of striking at the Indian government anywhere in the world. The separatists had proven themselves capable of orchestrating global operations requiring phony documents, careful timing, and lots of money. The fanatics who supported them have destroyed an airliner, sabotaged railways, bombed buildings, and killed thousands of Hindus as well as their fellow Sikhs. They are prepared to build their heaven on earth by unleashing the forces of hell. They are committed, well-organized, and without scruples: the end will justify the means; the creation of Khalistan will wash the blood from their hands.

"It doesn't matter whether Canadians like Sikhs," Parmar said.

"In Punjab, they [the central government in New Delhi] have killed the Sikh's mom, or killed his daughter, so they have no choice. Sikhs are fighting now. We had no choice. We had to fight. We fight for our defense. The [Indian] government forced the Sikhs to do that. The people who are fighting have no homes, they are running for their lives, their families have been killed, their houses burned. They don't want to live like that, but they have no choice. What can they do? What would Christian do if the [Italian] army invaded the Vatican?"

In New York, in the spring of 1987, six batteries bound together were found under the passenger seat in an Air-India jet. They were meant to look like a bomb, and the fear of another disaster shuddered sickeningly through the minds of North American police. Fortunately, this time there were no explosives. But until the Indian government solves the problem in Punjab, the lawmen believed it was only a question of time before another jet went down. After all, those who destroyed Air-India flight 182 and sent a bag bomb to Japan from Vancouver B.C. were still fugitives.

Such fears spurred an unprecedented security operation in Vancouver for the 1987 Commonwealth leaders summit meeting. More than four thousand police were deployed and an estimated $20 million spent to make the city safe for politicians such as Rajiv Gandhi. He was considered the most likely target of terrorists at the conference. Despite all of the precautions, the Canadian security officials remained jittery: the embattled Indian prime minister was venturing into a city where thousands of people had publicly vowed to kill him.

The Canadian Security and Intelligence Service visited the homes of dozens of Sikhs, demanding assurances that they would remain peaceful. Many were placed under surveillance.

Gandhi called them "terrorists", they called him a "dictator conducting a genocide". One side talked of the geopolitical equation that would create Khalistan; the other spoke of the need to maintain the political integrity of a country that had not existed until 1947. Some called themselves "God's elect", and others cursed them as the "ungodly". But the debate diverted attention from the reality: men were hunting men around the globe, waging a hideous war with all kinds of victims. There was only one difference that really mattered: the Sikh fanatics could identify their target.

British police arrested four Sikhs in the days before the Commonwealth Conference and seized several electronic detonators they said were bound for North America. In Canada, the RCMP and the CSIS say they had reason to believe that their surveillance and security precautions had prevented or discouraged three possible attacks on Gandhi by different Sikh separatists living in Sudbury, Montreal and Vancouver. A week after the conference ended, a sophisticated shrapnel bomb — a propane cylinder stuffed with gunpowder and wired to a circuit board and three batteries — was found in a bus-terminal locker in downtown Vancouver. Police said it could have killed or maimed dozens of people if it had exploded in a crowd. All it needed was a detonator, they said.

The embattled Indian prime minister existed as a prisoner of his own security forces. The only city in the world believed safe enough for his children was Moscow. Like his mother, Gandhi believed that everyone was to blame for his troubles except himself. He, too, broke promises to the Sikhs, and oppressed their political aspirations. Similar action by his mother led directly to her assassination and the bloodiest terrorist strike in modern times. Rajiv Gandhi was headed down the same path.

GLOSSARY

Adi: First.

Akal: "Timeless," God.

Akali: A worshiper of the Timeless God. Used by the Sikhs who did not recognize the authority of Maharaja Ranjit Singh. Since 1920s, the Akali Dal has been a Sikh political party. It began as a movement dedicated to the recovery of Sikh shrines and regards itself as the faith's political voice.

Akal Takht: Literally the throne of the Timeless One. A shrine in the Golden Temple that is one of the four seats of Sikh spiritual authority. The others are at Anandpur Sahib, Patna Sahib and Nander. Its main feature before it was destroyed in the Indian army assault ordered by Indira Gandhi was a throne three times higher than the Mogul throne balcony in the Red Fort at Delhi. It is a symbol of Sikh sovereignty.

Akhand Path: The continuous reading of the Granth that usually takes forty-eight hours and is a way of marking special occasions of joy or sorrow.

Amrit: Nectar; the water of immortality; sanctified water usually mixed with sugar.

Bangla Sahib Gurdwara: The New Delhi temple in which the assassination plot was hatched.

Baisakhi: The first month of the Indian calendar year. It coincides with the spring harvest festival.

Dharm Yudh: A holy war.

Diwali: The major Hindu festival of light that falls at the beginning of the month of Kartic (October-November).

Granth: Book.

Granthi: Professional reader of Sikh scriptures and often the manager of a gurdwara.

Gurdwara: A Sikh temple; literally, home of the guru.

Gurmukhi: "From the mouth of the guru," the thirty-five-letter script used for writing Punjabi.

Guru: Gu = darkness, ru = light; one who delivers a person from ignorance.

Harimandir: The seat of God shrine in the Golden Temple complex at Amritsar.

Kachha: Short pants or soldier's breeches worn by Sikhs so they are ready to defend themselves; one of the Five Ks.

Kanga: A comb to be worn by the Sikhs as a symbol of neatness; one of the Five Ks.

Kara: The steel bracelet worn on the right wrist of Sikhs; one of the Five Ks.

Kesh: A Sikh's unshorn hair and beard; one of the Five Ks.

Keshadhari: One who keeps his hair uncut.

Khalsa: The pure ones. The brotherhood of initiated Sikhs. The Dal Khalsa was the name of Ranjit Singh's army and, later, Sant Jarnail Bhindranwale's political party.

Khatri: The mercantile caste of the Sikh gurus that was particularly important in the Punjab.

Kirpan: The sword or dagger worn by Sikhs; one of the Five Ks.

Kirtan: The singing of devotional songs.

Kshatriya: The warrior division of the classical fourfold caste hierarchy.

Kurta: The blue skirt-like uniform of the Nihang warrior sect.

Langar: The community kitchen maintained in all Sikh temples and open to all.

Lok Sabha: The lower house of the Indian Parliament called the Assembly of the People.

Nihang: A warrior sect that grew out of Ranjit Singh's front-line troops who are also known as temple guardians.

Nirankar: The "Formless One," God.

Nirankari: Worshiper of the Formless God.

Panth: Literally, the path, or system of religious belief and practice. Spelt with a capital "P" it designates the Sikh community.

Purdah: Literally, curtain, but normally used to indicate the segregation of women.

Sahajdharis: Literally, slow adopters. Those Sikhs who have not been initiated into the Khalsa and who do not wear the Five Ks.

Shiromani Gurdwara Parbandhak Committee: The Sikhs' central shrine management committee that is responsible to the Indian government for Sikh affairs in the Punjab.

Shudra: Fourth section of the classical Hindu caste hierarchy.

SELECTED BIBLIOGRAPHY

Adams, James. *The Financing of Terror: How the groups that are terrorizing the world get the money to do it.* New York: Simon and Schuster, 1986.

Akbar, M.J. *India: The Seige Within.* Harmondsworth: Penguin Books Ltd., 1985.

Bains, Hardial. *The Call of the Martyrs: On the Crisis in India and the Present Situation in the Punjab.* Toronto: Marx, Engels, Lenin, Stalin Institute, 1985.

Bajaj, Rajeev K. "Dead Men Tell No Tales." *Surya India,* Vol. 8, no. 12 (September, 1984), pp. 8-15.

Barrier, N. Gerald. *Banned: Controversial Literature and Political Control in British India (1907-1947).* Columbia: University of Missouri Press, 1974.

Cave-Brown, Rev. J. *The Punjab and Delhi in 1857.* 2 vols. New Delhi: Punjab National Press, 1970 (reprint of 1861 edition).

Chopra, V.D., et al. *Agony of Punjab.* New Delhi: Patriot Publishers, 1984.

Choudhary, Darshan Lal. *Violence in the Freedom Movement of Punjab.* New Delhi: B.R. Publishing Corp., 1986.

Citizens for Democracy. *Oppression in Punjab.* Columbus, Ohio: Sikh Religious and Educational Trust, 1986.

Cole, W. Owen, and Sambhi, Piara Singh. *The Sikhs: Their Religious Beliefs and Practices.* New Delhi: Vikas Publishing House Pvt. Ltd., 1978.

Collins, Larry, and Lapierre, Dominique. *Freedom at Midnight.* New York: Avon Books, 1976.

Committee on Human Rights. *The Turning Point: India's Future Direction?.* New York: Privately published, 1985.

Derivative Assassination: Who Killed Indira Gandhi? By the Editors of Executive Intelligence Review. New York: New Benjamin Franklin House, 1985.

Dharam, S. S. *Internal and External Threats to Sikhism.* Arlington Heights, Ill.: Gurmat Publishers, 1986.

————.*The Only Option for Sikhs.* Privately published monograph.

Draper, Alfred. *The Amritsar Massacre: Twilight of the Raj.* London: Buchan & Enright, Publishers, Ltd., 1985.

Fallaci, Oriana. *Interview With History.* New York: Houghton Mifflin Co., 1977.

Gill, Surjan Singh. *Case for Republic of Khalistan.* Vancouver: Babar Khalsa, 1982.

Government of India. *White Paper on Punjab Agitation.* New Delhi, June 10, 1984.

Gupte, Pranay. *Vengeance: India after the Assassination of Indira Gandhi.* New York: W.W. Norton & Company, 1985.

Hardgrave, Robert L., Jr., and Kochanek, Stanley A. *India: Government and Politics in a Developing Nation.* New York: Harcourt Brace Jovanovich, Inc., 1986.

Hibbert, Christopher. *The Great Mutiny India 1857.* Harmondsworth: Penguin Books Ltd., 1980.

Jiwa, Salim. *The Death of Air India Flight 182.* London: W. H. Allen & Co., 1986.

Johnston, Hugh. *The Voyage of the Komagata Maru: The Sikh Challenge to Canada's Colour Bar.* Delhi: Oxford University Press, 1979.

Joshi, Chand. *Bhindranwale: Myth and Reality.* New Delhi: Vikas Publishing House Pvt. Ltd., 1984.

Juergensmeyer, Mark, et al. *Sikh Studies: Comparative Perspectives on a Changing Tradition.* Berkeley: Graduate Theological Union, 1979.

Kapur, Rajiv A. *Sikh Separatism: The Politics of Faith.* London: Allen & Unwin, 1986.

Kaur, Amarjit, et al. *The Punjab Story.* New Delhi: Roli Books International, 1984.

Kaur, Jitinder. *The Politics of Sikhs.* New Delhi: National Book Organisation, 1986.

Kishwar, Madhu. "Gangster Rule: The Massacre of Sikhs." *Manushi,* No. 25, Vol. 5, no. 1, (November-December 1984), pp. 10-37.

Laqueur, Walter. *The Age of Terrorism.* Boston: Little, Brown and Company, 1987.

Mason, Philip. *A Matter of Honour: An Account of the Indian Army, Its Officers and Men.* Harmondsworth: Penguin Books Ltd., 1976.

McLeod, W.H. *Early Sikh Tradition: A Study of the Janam-sakhis.* Oxford: Clarendon Press, 1980.

_____. *Textual Sources for the Study of Sikhism.* Manchester: Manchester University Press, 1984.

_____. *The Evolution of the Sikh Community: Five Essays.* Oxford: Clarendon Press, 1976.

Meda, Ved. "Letter from New Delhi." *The New Yorker,* September 23, 1985, pp. 61 – 70.

Moravia, Alberto. "The Terrorist Aesthetic: Of artists, stockbrokers, and other Jacobins." *Harper's* magazine, June 1987, pp. 37-44.

Narang, A.S. *Punjab Accord and Elections Retrospect and Prospect: A study in Development Democracy and Distortion.* New Delhi: Gitanjali Publishing House, 1986.

Nayar, Kuldip, and Singh, Khushwant. *Tragedy of Punjab: Operation Bluestar & After.* New Delhi: Vision Books, 1984.

Netanyahu, Benjamin, ed. *Terrorism: How the West Can Win.* New York: Avon, 1986.

Oakley, Robert. "International Terrorism." *Foreign Affairs: America and the World,* Vol. 65, no. 3 (1986), pp. 611-29.

Security Intelligence Review Committee. *Annual Report 1985–86.* Ottawa: Minister of Supply and Services Canada, 1986.

Shourie, Arun, et al. *The Assassination and After.* New Delhi: Roli Books International, 1985.

Singh, Kushwant. *A History of the Sikhs.* 2 vols. Princeton: Princeton University Press, 1984.

———.*The Sikhs Today.* Hyderabad: Orient Longman Ltd., 1985.

Singh, Patwant, and Malik, Harji. *Punjab: The Fatal Miscalculation, Perspectives on unprincipled politics.* New Delhi: Privately published, 1985.

Sofaer, Abraham D. "Terrorism and the Law."*Foreign Affairs,* Vol. 64, no. 5 (Summer 1986), pp. 901-22.

Spear, Percival. *A History of India, Volume 2.* Harmondsworth: Penguin Books Ltd., 1978.

Thapar, Romila. *A History of India, Volume 1.* Harmondsworth: Penguin Books Ltd., 1966.

Tully, Mark, and Jacob, Satish. *Amritsar: Mrs. Gandhi's Last Battle.* London: Jonathan Cape Ltd., 1985.

Weisman, Steven R. "The Rajiv Generation." *The New York Times Magazine,* April 20, 1986, pp. 18-69.

Wilkinson, Paul. *Terrorism and the Liberal State.* London: The Macmillan Press Ltd., 1977.

INDEX

A

Adams, James, 201
Adams, Jeannie, 137-8
Adi Granth, 27, 32, 38
Air-India disaster, 1, 137, 139-41, 151-2, 154; suspects, 153, 154-8
Akal Takht, 28, 32, 43, 82, 185, 230
Akali Dal, 11, 12, 14, 46; attack on Golden Temple, 77-8, 82; Bindranwale's challenge to power of, 59-62, 65, 67-9; demanded Punjabi state, 47, 50-2; disruption caused by, 69, 75; formation of, 44; grievances, 55-6, 65, 68; political strength of, 54, 55, 58-9, 64; state of emergency, 57-8
Akbar, 27
Akhand Kirtani Jatha, 62, 125
All-India Sikh Students Federation, 66, 76
All-World Sikh Convention, 65
Amnesty International, 216
Amritsar, 24, 50, 228; attack on Golden Temple, 15, 17-18, 76-82; massacre at Jallianwala Bagh, 41-3; temples built at, 27-8, 34
Anandpur Sahib Resolution, 56, 58, 65

Asian Games, 13, 14, 70
assassination: of Indira Gandhi, 5-10, 15-21, 88-9, 114, 147; of Sidhu, 197-200
Atwal, Jasbir Singh, 199
Atwal, Jaspal Singh, 197, 199
Aulakh, Dr. Gurmit Singh, 149
Aurora, Jagit Singh, 69

B

Babbar Akalis, 44, 75, 126
Babbar Khalsa, 75, 126-7, 130, 136, 141, 151, 152, 165, 171, 191, 211
Badal, Prakash Singh, 58, 62, 63, 68, 72, 75, 77
Bagri, Ajaib Singh, 130, 155, 175
Bahadur, Tegh, 29
Bains, Didar Singh, 115, 185-6, 188
Bajpai, K. Shankar, 80, 184
Bajwa, Sukhinder, 186-7, 189
Barnala, Surjit Singh, 229
Barrette-Joncas, Madam Justice Claire, 173

Beatty, Perrin, 170-1
Besso, Paul, 152, 153, 200
Bhagat, H.K.L., 85
Bhakna, Sohan Singh, 96
Bhinder, P.S., 63, 72, 77
Bhindra, Inderjit Singh, 167-8
Bindranwale, Sant Jarnail Singh, 58-
  60; arrested, 66-7; attack on Golden
  Temple, 77-9; blamed for extremist
  violence, 74, 75-6; demonstrations
  in New Delhi, 68; death of, 79, 112;
  Dosanjh's meeting with, 119-20;
  followers, 62, 63, 69-70; on
  extremism, 217; Parmar's views on,
  127; prophesy, 184; rise of Sikh
  fundamentalism, 59-61; supported
  by Congress Party, 59-64, 70;
  vision to purify Sikhs, 73
Bhullar, Major-General Jaswant Singh,
  70, 115, 145, 187-8
Billy Joe, 171-3
Birk, Gurpartap Singh, 114, 145-50,
  151, 186
bombings. See Air-India disaster;
  Narita Airport explosion
Brar, G.S., 189
Brar, Jarnail Singh. See Bhindranwale,
  Sant Jarnail Singh
Brar, Joginder Singh, 59
Brar, Lakhbir Singh, 192, 196
Britain: clashes between Sikh
  separatists and Indian government
  supporters, 196; extradition law,
  214, 215-16; illegal drugs, 200,
  202- 4; immigration policy, 214;
  Rajiv Gandhi's visit to, 207-8; Sikh
  community in, 213; Sikh reaction to
  events in India, 80, 91, 114;
  terrorism in, 210
British Columbia: criminal activities of
  separatists, 200; Sikh immigrants,
  94-8, 105; Sikhs endorsed
  Khalistan, 181
British rule: diplomatic relations with
  Ranjit Singh, 34; East India
  Company, 35, 36; Jallianwala Bagh

massacre, 41-3; Sikh community
  under, 36-7, 39-40
Burton, Dan, 182

C

Camper, Frank, 144-6, 150
Canada: Sikh reaction to events in
  India, 80, 91, 113-15; used as base
  for Sikh separatism, 106, 111-12
Canadian government: airport
  security, 138-9, 141; dealing with
  Sikh terrorism, 143, 150-3, 163,
  164; extradition law, 215; Gandhi
  praised, 207; growing business with
  India, 166; illegal drugs, 200, 202;
  immigration policy, 93-100, 103-4,
  212; intelligence-sharing pact, 170;
  refugee policy, 191-2, 196;
  surveillance of separatist Sikhs,
  134-7, 170
Canadian Security and Intelligence
  Service (CSIS), 124, 134-5, 137,
  141, 150, 162, 168, 170; campaign
  to get terrorists, 171, 174, 176;
  immigration cases, 168-9;
  Commonwealth Conference in
  Vancouver, 233-4; Sidhu's
  assassination, 197, 198-200; trial of
  Reyat and Parmar, 161-3
Central Shrine Management
  Committee. See Shiromani
  Gurdwara Prabandak Committee
Chadha, Avininder, 176
Chandigarh, 50, 54, 55, 56, 229
Chauhan, Dr. Jagjit Singh, 129, 216,
  218-21, 223
Chellaney, Brahma, 80-1
Congress Party, 46, 53; after
  independence, 47, 52; in Punjab, 54,
  56-7, 61, 63; instigated riots after
  assassination, 83-8, 216; linked to
  Sikh extremists, 70-1; Rajiv
  Gandhi's election, 91
Cripps, Sir Stafford, 47
Crosbie, John, 198

D

Dal Khalsa, 61, 62, 67, 73, 106
Dam Dami Taksal, 59
Das, Dyal, 38
Dayal, Har, 40, 95
Dayal, Lieutenant-General Ranjit
  Singh, 77
Devi, Bimal, 17
Dhalawi, Beant, 104-5
Dhaliwal, Annand Singh, 145-7
Dhawan, Rajender Kumar, 19-20
Dhillon, Ganga Singh, 125, 188
Dhillon, Gurdial Singh, 106
Dhillon, Kashmir Singh, 171-3
Dhillon, Rampal Singh, 175
Dhillon, Dr. S.S., 189
Dhindsa, Amarjit Singh, 198, 199
Doman, Herb, 100, 102-3
Dornan, Robert, 182
Dosanjh, Raminder, 116-17
Dosanjh, Ujjal, 116-21
Doyle, Cuimin, 154
Duncan, Gerald, 137
Dyer, Brigadier General
  Reginald, 41-2

E

East India Company, 35, 36
Erickson, Arthur, 107
extradition law, 214-15

F

Fairclough, Ellen, 99
Federal Bureau of Investigation, 143,
  144, 146-8, 171, 190
Finn, Ted, 163
First World War, 40, 98

G

Gandhi, Indira, 73, 86; assassination
  of, 5-10, 15-21, 88-9, 114, 147;
attack on Golden Temple, 15, 18,
  24, 76-80, 82, 205; Congress Party
  in Punjab, 56-7; dealing with Sikhs
  after return to power, 63-5, 67-8,
  127; Dosanjh's meeting with, 120;
  followed Zail Singh's advice, 11, 12,
  56, 59, 63-5, 68; out of power, 58;
  Sikh demands, 53-5, 65, 68-9; Sikh
  opponents of, 10- 15, 112; state of
  emergency, 57-8; successor to
  Shastri, 53; violence after
  assassination, 83-8, 216; vision of
  India, 21
Gandhi, Mahatma, 41, 50, 86
Gandhi, Rajiv, 12, 13, 16, 20, 58, 68,
  69, 76, 86, 165; appealed to stamp
  out Sikh terrorism, 91, 136, 207;
  Commonwealth Conference in
  Vancouver, 233-4; dealing with Sikh
  terrorists, 211, 213-14; distrusted
  Zail Singh, 19, 83; eager to attract
  western capital, 166; election
  campaign, 88, 90; non-alignment,
  215; Sikh extremists living in
  Britain, 216; transfer of power to,
  8-10, 19; visit to Britain, 207-8;
  visit to U.S., 134
Gandhi, Sanjay, 11, 12, 58-9, 219
Gandhi, Sonia, 7, 20, 90, 207
Germany: Parmar's imprisonment,
  124, 130; Sikh community in, 40,
  43, 98-9
Ghadr movement, 40, 41, 43, 96, 98-9
Gibbons, David Walter, 159-62, 171,
  175-7, 179, 195, 199, 232
Gifford, Lord, 208
Gill, Joginder, 135
Gill, Nachhattar, 197
Gill, Satinderpal Singh, 192
Gill, Sukhdial Singh, 197, 199
Gill, Sukhvinder Singh, 208, 209
Gill, Surjan Singh, 125, 128-9, 134,
  155
Girard, Jacques, 139
Gladstone, W.B., 42
Globe and Mail, 154

Golden Temple attack, 15-18, 24, 76-82, 153, 216, 220, 229; effect on Sikh community, 18, 20, 112, 183, 185, 187; Grewal's videotape, 183-5, 186; North American reaction to, 103, 111-14, 205
Grewal, Gurmit, 183, 189
Grewal, Manohar Singh, 183-6, 187
Green, Mendel, 195
Gumman, Harpal Singh, 168-9
Gupta, Babu Lal, 203, 216
gurdwaras, 37, 39, 44, 95
gurmukhi, 26-7, 51, 95
Gyani, Bhagwan Singh, 96

H
Haig, Alexander, 220
Hargobind, 28-9, 30, 31
Harimandir, 27-8, 34, 80
Haryana, 51, 53, 55
Hatfield, Mark, 220
Helms, Jesse, 182, 220
Henderson, Corporal Doug, 155-7
Hinduism, 26-7
Hindus: economic benefits of converting to Sikhism, 37; growing strife between Sikhs and, 64-75; in Punjab, 54, 62, 229; Indian independence, 45, 47-8; reaction to assassination, 9, 83-6; shared temples with Sikhs, 37, 39; signs of Sikhs to distinguish from, 31
Holden, Judge Derek, 203
Howe, Sir Geoffrey, 214, 216

I
Indian government: actions assessed by western democracies, 204-5; at independence, 45-9; attack on Golden Temple, 76-82; attempted extradition of Parmar, 123, 124, 128; Babbar Khalsa, 126-7; Bhindranwale's arrest, 67-8; Britain's extradition law, 214-16; Canadian Sikhs protested against, 106; compensation for refugees, 86-7; control of industrial licenses, 55; disinformation campaign, 80-1, 153-4; eager to attract western capital, 166; global operations of extremists, 143, 232; illegal activities against, in North America, 115-16; illegal drugs, 200-2; instigated violence after assassination, 83-8; policies played into hands of fundamentalists, 230; promised Sikh state, 53-4; relations with Britain; 213; role in Sikh violence, 163; sealed Punjab, 227-9; state of emergency, 57-8; surveillance on external groups, 167-8; Tamil separatists, 204; treatment of Sikh separatists, 190, 211; water policy, 56
India Mahila Association, 118
Indian National Army, 46-7
India-Pakistan War, 53
International Sikh Youth Federation (ISYF), 148, 151, 152, 155, 165, 169, 189, 191, 195, 199, 211
Irish Republican Army (IRA), 202, 210, 211-12, 215
Islam, 26-7. See also Moguls; Muslims

J
Jallianwala Bagh massacre, 41-3
Janata Party, 58, 60
Jardine, James, 204
Jats, 25, 36, 37, 53, 56, 91
Jehangir, 28
Johal, Hardial Singh, 130-2, 137, 155

K
Kahlon, Tejinder Singh, 90, 174-7, 178

Kaur, Amarjit, 62, 69, 126
Kaur, Gurdip, 85
Kaur, Rajinder, 126, 128
Kaur, Surindar, 127
Keller, Stephen, 177
Kemp, Jack, 182
keshadaris, 31, 32, 33, 36-7, 110
Khalistan, 15, 47, 91, 115, 219-20;
  Gill opened consulate, 128-9;
  financed by overseas treasuries,
  191; role of Pakistan in creation of,
  225-7; supporters in North
  America, 115-16, 181. *See also*
  separatist movement
Khalsa, Dr. Arjinderpal Singh, 189
Khalsa Sikhs, 30, 33, 35-9, 44;
  Bhindranwale's impact, 60, 64, 66,
  68; expatriate, 114
Khela, Santokh Singh, 172-3
Khun, Satnam Singh Khun, 130
Khurana, Sarbjit, 114-15
King, William Lyon Mackenzie, 95
Kipling, Rudyard, 42
Kirpal, Justice B.N., 141
Komagata Maru, 97-8, 193
Ku Klux Klan, 105
Kumar, Sajjan, 85
Kunstler, William, 149-50

L
Lahore, 33, 46, 225
Lal, Bhajan, 66, 68, 69, 147
Lal, Bri Mohan, 167
Lally, Lal Singh, 145-7
Laurier, Sir Wilfrid, 97
Le Corbusier, 50
Lewis, Dana, 113-14
Lipinski, William, 182
Longowal, Harchand Singh, 58, 65,
  67-8, 70, 75-7, 127; Dosanjh's
  meeting with, 120; Johal
  campaigned for, 132

Lowe, Larry, 135-6, 160, 161, 162

M
Maia, Roy, 152, 200
Maken, Lalit, 85
Mal, Arjun, 27-8
Malik, Raminder Singh, 129-30, 133,
  163
Malik, Surinder, 113, 166
Mann, Simranjit Singh, 63, 71, 81, 89-
  90
Marwaha, Parmatma Singh, 208, 209-
  10
McAdams, Margaret Lynne, 135, 160,
  161
McBride, Sir Richard, 97
McCarthy, Grace and Ray, 194
McDonald Royal Commission, 161
McLeod, Hew, 178
Meese, Edwin, 201
Metzer, Robert, 161
Miele, Frank, 171-3
Miller, George, 182
Moguls, 27-9, 30, 32, 34
Morning Post, 42
Mulroney, Brian, 136, 140
Muslim League, 45, 47
Muslims: in Punjab, 25, 37, 39; Indian
  independence, 45, 47, 48

N
Nanak Das Bedi, 23-7, 30, 47
Narain, Lala Jagat, 65-6, 127
Narendra, Captain H.S., 139
Narita Airport explosion, 1, 138, 151
National Council of Khalistan, 67, 73
Nehru, Arun, 8, 9
Nehru, Jawaharlal, 11, 49-53, 58, 86
New York Times, 141, 219
Nihangs, 32
Nirankaris, 38, 60, 73, 75, 126
Norris, Thomas, 146
North America: illegal activities of

Sikhs, 116, 119; lifestyle of Sikhs, 111, 117-18, 165; perception of Sikhs, 165; Sikh immigrants returned from, 39-40; Sikh reaction to events in India, 80, 91, 110-14
Nunn, Sam, 220

O

O'Brien, Joanne, 177
O'Dwyer, Sir Michael, 41, 42-3
Operation Bluestar. *See* Golden Temple attack
Oppal, Justice Wallace, 100-3, 108, 109
Osborne, Lord William Godolphin, 34
Osler, Justice John, 107

P

Pakistan, 47, 56; role in separatist movement, 91, 181-2, 190, 219, 225-7
Palestine Liberation Organization (PLO), 202, 212, 216
Paquette, Dean, 176-7
Parhar, Malkit Singh, 193-5
Parmar, Talwinder Singh, 2, 91, 123-6, 128, 133, 151, 164, 188, 195, 211; blamed for bombings, 141, 153, 154-5, 179; charges dropped, 162, 179, 181; circle of separatist agitators, 128-32; CSIS followed, 124, 134-6, 174, 175; fund raising, 133-4; leader of Babbar Khalsa, 75, 126-7; leadership of, 179, 232; went underground, 127-8; trial in Duncan, B.C., 159-63; trial in Hamilton, 176, 178-9
Partition, 47-8, 227
Perrault, Ray, 194
Peterson, Dwayne E., 193
Pumma, G.S., 189
Punjab: after independence, 50-1; Barnala's government dismissed, 229-31; British control of, 35-7, 39-40; growing strife between Sikhs and Hindus in, 64-6, 70-5; in 15th century, 24-5; opium and heroin production, 200-1; Partition, 47-8, 227; President's rule imposed on, 73; prosperity of, 54; recession, 55, 62; sealed to foreigners, 227-8; Sikhs demanded control of temples, 43-5; under Ranjit Singh, 33-4; violence in, 226-31
Punjabi languages 26-7, 51-2, 67

R

racism: in Canada, 93-5, 99, 103, 105
Rai, Gobin. *See* Singh, Gobind
Rai, Harminder Singh, 208, 209
Ranauna, Jarnail Singh, 208-10
Ray, Ashwini, 83
Ray, Siddharta Shankar, 230-1
Reagan, Ronald, 148, 182
Renton, Timothy, 214
Reyat, Inderjit Singh, 135-7, 139, 191; Gibbons defended, 159-63; RCMP interrogation, 155-8
Robertson, Flight Lieutenant Neil, 140
Rockwell, Corporal Glen, 155-6
Ross Street Temple, 107, 112, 137
Royal Canadian Mounted Police (RCMP), 106, 136, 138, 141, 150, 152, 164, 170-1, 234; McDonald Royal Commission, 161; Reyat's interrogation, 155-8; Sidhu's assassination, 198-200

S

sahajdharis, 31, 35, 110
Samra, Kuldip Singh, 107
Santiago, Dominic, 193, 195
Sarich, Anthony, 199
Sarswati, Swami Dayanand, 38-9
Sat-Bhamba, Ajit Singh, 203

Second World War, 45-7
separatist movement, 47, 50-1; as seen by western democracies, 204-5; Canada used as base for, 106, 111-12; central committee formed, 231; educated spokesmen for, in U.S., 113-15; global terrorist network, 143, 232; illegal activities in North America, 116, 191; illegal drugs used to finance, 200-4; in Britain, 213; in U.S., 181-3; international support for, 190-1; Khalistan consulate, 128-9; need to change tactics, 223; recruitment for, 212-13; similar to IRA, 211-12; violence in Punjab, 226-31; within expatriate community, 190, 231; youth attracted to, 211. *See also* Khalistan

Sharma, Jagdish, 113, 164-5
Shastri, Lal Bahadur, 53, 58, 86
Shiromani Gurdwara Prabandhak Committee (SGPC), 14, 44-5, 52, 56
Sidhu, Joginder Singh, 108-11
Sidhu, Kulwant Singh, 168
Sidhu's assassination, 196-200
Sikh Council of North America, 90
Sikh Gurdwaras Act, 44-5
Sikhism: beliefs of, 15, 31, 37; founder of, 23-6; militarization of, 18, 28, 29-32, 60-1; Punjabi language, 26-7, 51; under Moguls, 27-9, 30, 32
Sikhistan. *See* Khalistan
Sikhs: Amritsar massacre, 41-3; assassination plot, 16-19, 88-9; attack on Golden Temple, 15, 17-18, 24, 76-82; Canadian immigration policy, 93-100, 103-4; consulates discredited, 167-8; demanded control of temples, 43-5; effect of central government's policies, 230; First World War, 40, 98; growing strife between Hindus and, 64-75; illegal immigrants, 191-6; Indian independence, 47-8;

lifestyle in North America, 111, 117-18, 165; McLeod's view of, in India and abroad, 178; opponents of Indira Gandhi, 10-15, 112; political refugees, 105, 119, 168-9, 191-2, 195-6; Rajiv Gandhi's view of, 212; reaction to attack on Golden Temple, 79-82, 111-14; reaction to Birk's arrest, 148-9; rise of fundamentalism under Bhindranwale, 59-61, 72, 110; Second World War, 45-7; secular, in British Columbia, 100-3, 116-21; threatened to disrupt Asian Games, 69; treatment in court, 173, 177; under British rule, 36-7, 39-40; under Nehru, 50; violence after assassination, 83-8. *See also* Khalsa Sikhs; Khalistan; Nirankaris; separatist movement
Singh, Amerjit, 189-90
Singh, Amrik, 60, 66, 68, 76
Singh, Autar, 189
Singh, Baba Deep, 59
Singh, Balbir, 16, 89, 177, 225
Singh, Balraj, 144
Singh, Balwant, 201
Singh, Beant, 5-6, 16-17, 18-19, 20, 89, 134
Singh, Buta, 68, 90
Singh, Dalbir, 228
Singh, Dalip, 35-6
Singh, Darbara, 66, 68, 70, 72, 73; policy of confrontation, 65, 67, 72
Singh, Fateh, 53, 65
Singh, Gajender, 106, 132-3
Singh, Giani Zail, 8-9, 11, 12, 20, 115, 219; attack on Golden Temple, 79, 81-2; Dhillon's ties with, 188; policy of appeasement, 65, 67, 68; political career, 19, 43, 55-7, 59, 83, 91; supported Bhindranwale, 63, 64, 66, 69, 70, 71
Singh, Gobind, 15, 18, 29-32, 34, 37, 55, 59
Singh, Gurbachan, 59, 60, 64

Singh, Gurdev, 63
Singh, Gurdit, 97
Singh, Gurinder, 167
Singh, Harsiman, 70
Singh, Jasbir, 124, 169, 192
Singh, Jwala, 96
Singh, Kartar, 60
Singh, Kehar, 89
Singh, L., 137-8, 151
Singh, M., 136-9, 151
Singh, Mohinder, 133
Singh, Naunihal, 188
Singh, Ranjit, 33-5, 37, 47, 225
Singh, Sabha, 39
Singh, Santockh, 96
Singh, Santokh, 67, 68
Singh, Satwant, 5-6, 17, 19, 88-9, 228
Singh, Shahbeg, 70, 76, 168
Singh, Sukhdev, 75
Singh, Tara, 46, 50-3
Singh, Udham, 43, 57
Singh, Zail. See Singh, Giani Zail
Shivpurr, Pyare, 221-3
60 Minutes, 75
Smedley, Agnes, 99
Sodhi, Sodhi Singh, 130
Soviet Russia: Ghadrites shifted allegiance to, 99
States Reorganization Commission, 51
Sukerchakia, Ranjit Singh. See Singh, Ranjit

T
Tamil separatist groups, 204
Taylor, James, 199
terrorism, 210-12, 215

Thatcher, Margaret, 207-8, 210
Thekedar, Jaswant Singh, 216-17
Thiara, Sadhu Singh, 175-6, 178
Times (India), 72
Times (London), 81
Tohra, Gurcharan Singh, 58, 62, 77
Trudeau, Pierre, 127
Tytler, Jagdish, 85

U
Uboke, Major Singh, 201
United States: anti-terrorist assistance program, 210; educated Sikh spokesmen in, 183-5; extradition law, 215; Gandhi praised, 207; illegal drugs, 201, 202; illegal immigrants to, 192-5; immigration policies, 95-6, 212; Rajiv Gandhi's visit to, 134, 136; Sikh reaction to events in India, 80, 91, 114; Sikh separatists, 181-3; terrorists arrested in, 142-50
U.S. Central Intelligence Agency: terrorism, 210-11
U.S. Secret Service, 146, 150
Ustinov, Peter, 6-7

V
Vancouver Daily Province, 94

W
Wheeler, John, 216
Wickie, Joseph, 160-1
World Sikh Organization, 114-15, 168, 169, 191